THE COMPLETE IDIOT'S GUIDE® TO

Divining the Future

by Laura Scott and Mary Kay Linge

ALPHA

A member of Penguin Group (USA) Inc.

For Great Granny

International Standard Book Number: 1-59257-088-7
Library of Congress Catalog Card Number: 2003108339

05 04 03   8 7 6 5 4 3 2 1

Interpretation of the printing code: The rightmost number of the first series of numbers is the year of the book's printing; the rightmost number of the second series of numbers is the number of the book's printing. For example, a printing code of 03-1 shows that the first printing occurred in 2003.

Printed in the United States of America

Note: This publication contains the opinions and ideas of its authors. It is intended to provide helpful and informative material on the subject matter covered. It is sold with the understanding that the authors, book producer, and publisher are not engaged in rendering professional services in the book. If the reader requires personal assistance or advice, a competent professional should be consulted.

The authors, book producer, and publisher specifically disclaim any responsibility for any liability, loss, or risk, personal or otherwise, which is incurred as a consequence, directly or indirectly, of the use and application of any of the contents of this book.

Most Alpha books are available at special quantity discounts for bulk purchases for sales promotions, premiums, fund-raising, or educational use. Special books, or book excerpts, can also be created to fit specific needs.

For details, write: Special Markets, Alpha Books, 800 E. 96th Street, Indianapolis, IN 46240.

Publisher: *Marie Butler-Knight*
Product Manager: *Phil Kitchel*
Senior Managing Editor: *Jennifer Chisholm*
Senior Acquisitions Editor: *Randy Ladenheim-Gil*
Book Producer: *Lee Ann Chearney/Amaranth*
Development Editor: *Lynn Northrup*
Copy Editor: *Molly Schaller*
Illustrator: *Chris Eliopoulos*
Cover/Book Designer: *Trina Wurst*
Indexer: *Angie Bess*
Layout/Proofreading: *Mary Hunt, Ayanna Lacey, Donna Martin*

Contents at a Glance

Contents

Foreword

Take the best books ever written about the intuitive arts, squeeze them into one articulately written volume, and what you get is this vast reference guide about discovering and understanding your future. *The Complete Idiot's Guide to Divining the Future* is an encyclopedic undertaking created to explain the multitude of divination tools available to you: from Astrology to angel cards, biofeedback to breath work, journaling to joyous movement, meditation to medicine wheels, palmistry to past life regression, runes to Reiki, Tarot to Tibetan bowls, and numerous other methods and exercises that will both fascinate and educate you.

Holistic, spiritual, and intuitive arts experts agree: Everything from our bodies to our thoughts is made up of energy—the life-force energy. And it is this life-force energy that holds the key to personal transformation. Once you learn the secrets to understanding and affecting this energy, you will not only be better able to predict your future, you will also be able to direct it. That is what this book teaches you: how to understand the power and potential of your body, mind, and spirit to manifest the future you desire!

By the time you finish reading *The Complete Idiot's Guide to Divining the Future*, you will be armed with an arsenal of tools to help you know your life's purpose, direct your energies toward that purpose, and express yourself in accomplishment of that purpose in a way only *you* can do. The result of this *soul work* is a life journey—*your* journey. Your path may not always be easy, but it will prove infinitely rewarding.

Your life-force energy is the reason you have been led to this book. It is certainly no accident that this book has found its way to you. At this time in your life, your energy is vibrating at a frequency that has requested this information from the Universe. You are ready to increase your knowledge and understanding in this area, so the Universe has sent you a most gifted teacher.

Laura Scott is one of the most extraordinary human beings I know. I first met Laura during my research on spirit communication. After booking a reading with her, I was instantly blown away by her ability to *channel* spiritual elders and masters from The Other Side. She was the first person I ever met with the ability to obtain insights about my life purpose and life themes from the Akashic records (something you will learn about in this book).

Then, as I got to know Laura better, I discovered that she is also a remarkable teacher of spiritual principles. I have learned that she did not learn all this wisdom from books. It is as if she plugged into some mystical computer and downloaded the secrets of the Universe into her brain. I feel extremely lucky to have attracted this gifted teacher into my life.

I have personally implemented the tools Laura taught me to increase my income, attract inspiring people into my life, increase my opportunities for joy and fulfillment, and obtain an inner peace I once never thought possible. Using the same principles you will learn here in this book, I was able to direct my life-force energy toward my desired future, and I am constantly expanding my vision of that future as I increasingly realize the power I have to direct it.

The principles Laura teaches in *The Complete Idiot's Guide to Divining the Future* have changed my life and they can change yours, too. If you do the necessary work, you will soon effect change in every area of your life—physically, mentally, and spiritually—simply by implementing the proper tools. Whether you are seeking health, prosperity, or joy, this book holds the secrets you need to create the future you desire. Don't take it for granted. Remember, this book is a gift that you have attracted to yourself. Learn its wisdom, explore your power, and navigate your way toward the life of your dreams.

Warmly,
Bob Olson

Bob Olson is an author and the editor of OfSpirit.com Magazine at www.ofspirit.com. He writes and lectures on the subjects of spirit communication, life after death, and the spiritual principles of success and overcoming life's obstacles.

Introduction

Intuition is something we all have access to, a sense that everyone has within. Whether you use it or not is another story.

This is a book for anyone who's been startled by a premonition, awakened by a dream, or guided by a "vibe." It's for anyone who's dabbled in the Tarot, checked a daily horoscope, consulted the *I Ching*, or interpreted runes. All these experiences, and many more besides, are doorways into the intuitive arts.

We hope you will read along with us (we do recommend chronologically!) and build your intuitive skills for divining the future as we progress. We can't guarantee the number of "light bulb moments" these chapters will hold for you, but chances are great that there will indeed be some. You may gain a new appreciation of the links between your physical body, your mind, and your spirit. You may learn how to interpret and use your dreams. You may begin to practice meditation, or spot synchronicity, or acquire insight on your destiny and life path. Whatever it is you take away from this book, you'll have some powerful cornerstones for a solid foundation in the intuitive arts by practicing the divining methods we explore in this book.

About This Book

There are six parts to this book:

Part 1, "The Quest to See What Lies Ahead," covers all you need to know to get started: why people throughout history feel the need to look into the future, the many divining methods and techniques we've developed for this purpose, and how you can begin to look within and listen for your own intuitive sense.

Part 2, "The Fourth Dimension," explores the big concepts: time, space, and the nature of the Universe itself. From Eastern medicine to Western scientific studies, we'll look at energy from every angle.

Part 3, "Reading the Body," looks at physical energy, the energy of the body. We'll talk about energy medicine such as Reiki and acupuncture, energy analysis such as aura reading, and energy redirection through yoga and affirmations. It's a whole new way to understand the Body Beautiful and see your future within it!

Part 4, "Reading the Mind," is pure emotion. From meditation to visualization to dreams, harnessing the energy of the mind in all its incarnations is what these four chapters are all about. Use your mind to see the future more clearly.

Part 5, "Reading the Spirit," is about the spirit's energy—the very heart of your intuition. We'll talk about your soul's journey, your guides and other helpers on The Other Side, and how to bring all your energies together in harmony as you look toward the future.

Part 6, "Endless Possibilities: You Choose!" brings it all together: energy, tools, and intuitive skills. Here, we'll look ahead and consider how to use intuition and free will to shape your future.

You'll also find three appendixes, including a list of other books that will be helpful to you as you continue to explore the intuitive arts, a chakra chart to show you where to find your body's all-important energy centers, and information on Laura's own divination tool, the Ancient Stardust Directional Cards.

Extras

Each chapter contains boxes with interesting and useful information:

Divine Inspiration

Here you'll find tips and information on integrating the intuitive arts into your daily routine.

Resonances

This box contains true stories and real-life examples of intuition in action.

Future Focus

Here's where you'll find definitions of the terms we use in the intuitive arts.

Take Heed

Check these boxes for cautionary tales and words to the wise—because like anything else in life, divination has its pitfalls.

Acknowledgments

Laura extends her utmost gratitude to Sema, Fr. Garamone, and The Committee (and all the other Exquisite Helpers: H., R., G., B.N., C.T.F.) for their continual support, guidance, and sense of humor. Without you, none of this is possible. She thanks her faithful friends, companions, and teachers Xavier, Tyler, Camry, and Rizon for reminding her to keep some balance, and to "quit banging on the clicking keys and go outside, *now.*" She extends love to her family of human friends Joyce, Jen, Ziggy, Judy, Ev, and Buzz for their wonderful support, encouragement, and presence in her life. Special appreciation goes out to MAJ, my wonderful earthly mentor and touchstone through the years who helped me (more than they know) to make sense of it all; and Leilumtong, for inventing the Hendrix point and being willing to use it on me whenever I get too caught up in the illusion of life. Bob Olson, who through a series of Divinely Ordered events (what other kind is there?), appeared on a refreshing breeze in the middle of one summer and launched us both into exciting new adventures to fill a lifetime. You have done a wonderful service to the world through OfSpirit.com and BestPsychicMediums.com, and your integrity, honesty, and earnestness make me proud to call you a friend. Special thanks go to Mary Kay, for your willingness (and lest I forget, your stellar organization and memory skills!), and to Lee Ann, for an exciting journey of learning. Thank you to everyone else who knew long before I did that it was time to emerge and "get to work!" To my clients around the globe, and all the wonderful "seekers" reading this book, I am honored to be a part of your path, and I thank you for teaching me every day. And lastly, a grateful nod of understanding, respect, and awe to The Universe for the events of a decade past—so intricately woven together—a Divine Catalyst for discovering my place on "the path" and putting everything in motion.

Mary Kay sends virtual roses to her "guinea pigs," especially Tom, Ann, Regina, Kate, and Tim, for their time and interest. Thank you, Barbara, for your stories and your inspiration. Thanks to Maggie, Peter, and Tess for being so very understanding (most of the time). You, too, Tom—and make the most of those synchronicities, okay? Thanks to Goggie for a lifetime of lessons. And thank you, Lee Ann, for your trust, and Laura, for being so patient with me on my learning curve!

Trademarks

All terms mentioned in this book that are known to be or are suspected of being trademarks or service marks have been appropriately capitalized. Alpha Books and Penguin Group (USA) Inc. cannot attest to the accuracy of this information. Use of a term in this book should not be regarded as affecting the validity of any trademark or service mark.

Part 1

The Quest to See What Lies Ahead

In this part, we'll talk about the basics: the who, what, where, when, and how of divination and the intuitive arts. We'll help you start to look within and listen to your inner voice—the voice of your spirit, of intuition itself.

Why Do We Want to Know the Future?

In This Chapter

- Patterns and predictability
- Access to the intuitive arts
- Exploring the bigger picture
- Using what you learn to understand and shape your life

Why do you want to know the future? To help you make a life-altering decision—such as changing careers or moving to another part of the country? To find out if your life is "on track"? To help you choose a life mate, or to determine when's the best time to start a family? To understand what that recurring dream means? Or perhaps you've already had one or two "psychic moments" and you want to learn how to access your intuition more often.

Perfect! You've come to the right place. Most of us are curious about the future. We all want to know what lies ahead, what's up for us around the next corner, so we can figure out how to make it work to our advantage. Whether we will be happy or healthy or rich or find the mate/house/job of our dreams … or all of this and more. You have questions, and you want answers. You might feel that your life moves ahead of its own volition and is just taking you along for the ride, and you want to more consciously direct your path. Or maybe you feel your life is great in some areas but could use improvement in others.

You might have already explored a few of the many ways to look into the future. Perhaps you've had astrology, Tarot, or palmistry readings, or you've dabbled in some of the intuitive arts yourself. Maybe you haven't yet explored these or any of the many other tools and methods for divining the future, but you're eager to do so and aren't quite sure where to start.

Whatever your reasons for wanting to know more about what the future might have in store, this is the book for you! In the chapters ahead, we'll explore more than two dozen methods for divination, giving you lots of examples and exercises that let you try the tools and find answers to the questions you have about *your* life and future. In between all these wonderful techniques, you'll find answers to the most basic questions about universal energy and how it works. And in the process, don't be surprised if you come to understand more about who you are and what you want your life to be—because in the end, that's what the future is all about!

Knowledge Is Comfort

In Laura's everyday work as a professional psychic, she hears from people around the world, and they all have one thing in common: They are curious! They want to know. They want to understand. The simple things, the really big things, the past, the present, the future things—*and* all the stuff in between. The human mind is endlessly curious. We like to know how and why things work. We take comfort in this knowing, because it implies predictability. Predictability means we can adapt and prepare—and even plan ahead. In patterns of predictability we find reassurance not only that there *is* a future, but also that *we have a place in it!*

In addition to the human curiosity that's part of our very nature (even Eve couldn't resist that apple!), we also live in a time when we know more about our place in the future than generations before us ever dreamed possible. Technology has given us almost unimaginable accessibility and predictability. Computer models project the outcomes of elections (well, almost), along with the paths of hurricanes, the risks of health conditions, and the fluctuations of the stock market. Live in Boston and want to know what the weather will be like in San Francisco when your flight lands there in seven hours door to door? With a few keystrokes you'll know just what clothes to pack!

We know now that there are far more choices in all dimensions of life than humankind has known in all of its existence. And because we *can* know, we feel we have the *right* to know. When we don't know, we feel disconnected and anxious. We want options and control in our daily lives, as well as in our life paths. We want to know not only what the patterns of the present are, but also how to use our knowledge of them to influence the shape of the future. We want to know so we can be better prepared.

The Purpose of Our Existence

At the end of the movie *Forrest Gump*, Forrest ponders human existence from two opposing viewpoints, those of the two most important people in his life. "I don't know if Momma was right or if it's Lieutenant Dan," he muses. "I don't know if we each have a destiny or if we're all just floating around, accidental-like, on a breeze. But I think maybe it's both. Maybe both are happening at the same time."

Most of us, like Forrest, view our lives as a combination of *destiny* and *free will*. We believe there is a reason for our existence, a reason that we are here. Different belief systems express this in various ways, but many share the understanding that the soul exists along a continuum. Its travels through this physical life—either in a single lifetime or in many lifetimes—are essential for its evolutionary progress. In other words, our souls are here on Earth to *learn*.

Future Focus

Destiny is your life's theme: the lessons your soul has chosen to work on. **Free will** is your ability to shape and direct your thoughts and actions to influence the events of your life.

As recently as 150 years ago, open talk of past lives would have landed you in trouble with the law for blasphemy or heresy. You might even have been branded as a witch or sorcerer. Today, people—and many faiths—see this idea as a foundation for provocative discussions about the soul's eternal existence. Celebrities like Shirley MacLaine have written best-sellers on this very topic; Hollywood studios regularly employ storylines involving souls, spirits, universal energy, and time portals—and not just in the land of sci-fi.

Why Are We Here?

The short answer is simple: We are here on Earth to learn. (We'll explore the long answer in later chapters, especially in Part 6.) Along with being naturally curious, part of our very humanness is our ability and our desire for our lives to have meaning in a scope that is larger than we are. We want to know that our choices matter. We want to know that our actions affect the path of our journey. We want to know that we make a difference.

Destiny and free will are the two parameters that shape and guide your journey. Destiny is the theme of your life, the reason your soul is on this particular path. Your destiny defines the lessons your soul needs to learn in this life. Your free will is the plot of your life, the events and circumstances that happen in your life, your life story. Free will influences how your soul learns the lessons of this life. It is your ability to consider options, make choices and decisions, and take actions that direct the course of your life's path. *Everyone* has his or her own free will: the young, the old, and the in between. What you do with your free will is entirely up to you (just ask the parent of any three-year-old!).

Who Are We?

Well, as Laura tells her clients, it's really pretty straightforward. We are spiritual beings on a physical journey. Eventually the physical form will fail, and the spirit will live on, elsewhere. See, that's not so complicated.

Or is it? There is also an ongoing interplay of larger forces and directed forces in your life that ends up shaping your life and who you are. You might have a very specific question: "Should I buy this house?" "Should I marry this person?" But what you really want to know is whether this is the right decision *for you*. When you ask the question and open yourself to the answers, you end up knowing more about yourself.

Many people let external events alone shape and define who they are. They might choose to be hardened by life's experiences, or to be broadened by it. Part of the reason they may want to know the future is to better know who they are. Or if you flip the concept around, you can use your self-knowledge to make the decisions that will shape your future.

The divining methods of the intuitive arts tap into the potential that exists for your future. They give you insight and understanding from which you can make choices and decisions.

Where Are We Going?

With the unprecedented accessibility and predictability that today's technology offers us, we may feel a sense of entitlement and impatience. Think about it. Never before have we seen so many seekers exercising their "right to know," using mammoth online databases to search, discover, explore, and uncover. Never before have we been so impatient when it comes to waiting our turn in line, in traffic, on the phone, or through those dreaded commercials. It's an interesting dichotomy. On the one hand, technology affords us limitless possibilities; on the other hand, we bang our heads against limitations every day. Somehow, even with all this accessibility, we have become awfully impatient. And the truest essence of divination is learning to strike a balance between both.

We often hear talk about the need to "take a leap of faith" when it comes to events and circumstances in our lives. Yet perhaps it would be more appropriate to talk about living a life of faith, of living each moment with as much confidence in our spirit connections and purpose as in our physical abilities. We are living in a time of change. We feel that we are on the edge of *something*, but we don't know what. This can be unsettling or sometimes frightening, and further intensifies our desires (and demands) to know what the future holds.

Interestingly, we are also living in a renaissance of discovery. Consider all that is happening in science and medicine, for example. One of the greatest discoveries of human history has been the unraveling of the human genome, which is providing unimaginable knowledge and insight about how the human body functions. Future generations might well know of today's diseases and ailments in the same way that present generations know of the plague and polio—by reading about them in history books.

We are approaching our collective future in ways that previous generations lacked the resources to do. We are on the verge of being able to do things that have never before happened in the history of humankind. We have the opportunity to take the best from all directions and to use it to create synergy for ourselves.

Questions of divining are becoming matters of knowing. *And there lies the key to your own future, as well as to the future of all humankind.* Although many of the methods of divination are ancient, we now have the ability to apply them in new ways to integrate body, mind, and spirit. Our Western world is opening up, learning to integrate Eastern ideas and otherworldly approaches. When it comes to divination, each of us now has the ability to explore our questions using whatever method resonates with us. What historically was a choice dictated by region and accessibility is no longer so limited. Today's divination enthusiasts are free to reach for traditions from all over the globe. There is no "right" or "wrong" when it comes to selecting an avenue for divination. You can try one or two or three or four—or more—so you can make an enlightened decision and choose your own course.

Resonances

A client once came to Laura indignantly demanding to know where he had buried his treasure in a former life. Because he thought he'd been smart enough to know he would be returning to the earth plane, he was sure that he'd have had the foresight to leave a stash for his future comfort. Laura gently explained that the treasure he had left himself was not material, but rather spiritual: the knowledge that life was a continuum, and the knowledge to know better than to be caught up in materialistic pursuits. Although he really wanted precise mapping coordinates, he thanked Laura sincerely for reminding him to think bigger instead of smaller.

Empowerment and Free Will

Most of us approach the idea of divining the future from the context of *what* we want to know. But an equally important context is *why* we want to know. What will you do with the information you receive? How will you use the information to make choices and decisions? You want to make the right decision about what you're doing, and you want to make the choice that is right for your future.

It's easy to look at much of what happens in our lives and say, "I can't change that!" Maybe so. If your company downsizes or goes out of business, that is certainly a circumstance outside your ability to control. It's fate, you might tell yourself. So what's next?

Your next job! Now is the perfect time to reconsider your desires and your options. How you choose to find your next job is as important as what that job is. Your choices shape who you are and what your future can be. Why did you have your last job? Did you like it? Were you secretly relieved when you were laid off? What do you want in your next job?

The many tools of the intuitive arts can help you to better understand your needs and interests—not just about your job or your career, but also about your life in a bigger perspective. As you make decisions, you learn more about what's right for you and for your future. You can't always control the outside world or the circumstances of your life. But you *can* make informed decisions that channel those circumstances in ways that shape the future you desire.

Maybe it's just one aspect of your life that needs more attention from you. Many people do well in their professional lives while their personal lives are in disarray. Maybe you can pick the "dark horse" stocks that post runaway earnings but can't choose a date. Or perhaps your love life is in orbit but your job status is continually on the rocks. What you want is to bring balance and security into your life. Divining methods can help deliver all that.

The Peace of Understanding

The intuitive arts give you insights and understanding about a picture of your existence that is larger than your everyday life. This is knowledge that can put order to the chaos that seems to mark your daily existence. There are larger forces at play, beyond the minutia of your day-to-day experience. Understanding this will bring you comfort.

A numerology reading might reveal that your life path number is 5—that is, that your lifetime is about learning the lessons of change. If this is your personal year 5 as well—a year of transition and change—then it's no wonder that, as much as you enjoy the travel your job requires, you are thinking seriously about making some changes. Maybe you'll return to school to take those classes in real estate law that have been on your mind.

It relieves stress to make sense out of the chaos that is your daily life. If your horoscope says, "Be careful not to fly off the handle today," you can choose to increase your awareness and better cover your hot buttons. Open the *I Ching*. What sign appears? What is its message? How can you use this message for your life today? Turn over a Tarot card, or an angel card, or an animal totem card. What is the message? How is that relevant in your life?

There is a sense of peace and comfort that comes about when you realize, hey, I'm on the right track! Or when you begin to understand why something is happening to you, or your life is unfolding in a certain way even though you want desperately for it to take a different direction. And there's security in knowing that there are forces larger than yourself at work in the Universe.

Awareness: Blessing or Curse?

As much as we want to know what the future holds, most of us are quick to acknowledge that we want to know the good things that await us—and not so much the challenging things. It's much more exciting to think that you could win the lottery than to learn that you're about to experience a career change (otherwise known as "losing your job"). Is it a curse for health intuition to tell you that you have something growing in your body, or a blessing because you can do something about it?

Remember, the future is dynamic. Whatever information you receive about what it holds exists in the form of potential. You must make the decisions and take the actions that help manifest that potential in the circumstances and situations of your life. And again, it's what you do with the information that makes the difference. Divining the future is not a "get out of jail free" card that lets you dodge the tough stuff (or pass Go, or collect $200). Instead, it offers insight you can use to determine how to respond and react.

Why Tools?

If you've got a picture to hang, you pull out your hammer and your level. And if you plan to do some cleaning, you wouldn't start without your mop or broom. Sure, you could use the heel of a shoe to slam that nail into the wall; you could go through a stack of dinner napkins to scrub that floor. But the right tools go a long way toward getting the job done quickly and well.

The same is true if you're looking for inspiration and insight on your life. Divining methods are the supports that can help you enhance or tap into your own intuitive ability.

Throughout history, people have used a mind-boggling array of methods and objects to contemplate and interpret the future. Today, we can draw on this wealth of tradition and experience in ways that our ancestors could never have imagined. A trip to your local bookstore or a basic Internet search will turn up hundreds of choices in the subject, from Tarot decks to rune stones to *I Ching* sets and more. It's a far cry from the days when the village shaman was your only source of information and guidance!

Divine Inspiration

Some metaphysical and general bookstores are customer-friendly enough to set out samples of various divination cards and other tools, letting you get a feel for their artwork and imagery before you buy. Unfortunately, many others keep such items tucked away in a locked case or behind the counter, tightly shrink-wrapped and safe from shoppers' eyes. Sometimes you just have to take a leap of faith and choose according to the packaging. But because it's *so important to find tools that resonate with you,* you may want to seek out a shop that will give you a good look at many different types.

With so many options available, it's easy to get overwhelmed. We hope that this book will give you a taste of many different methods, helping you steer yourself toward the right ones for you. But personal experience will be your best guide. Everybody connects with divining methods differently, so look carefully at the bookstore's sample cards before you purchase a Tarot deck; ask a friend if you can give her rune set a test drive. And don't be discouraged if a method "doesn't work." It's not that you've done something wrong; it might be that the one you're using simply fails to resonate for you. (Is that a hammer in your hand when you're trying to clean the floor? Are you driving a backhoe when all you need is a little handheld trowel?) Be empowered to look within yourself to find the divining path that will suit you best.

How They Work

Have you ever found yourself daydreaming, mentally "drifting off," while washing dishes or mowing the lawn? As your body performs a routine task, your mind is free to roam. The use of a divining method performs the same function in divination. The casting of coins, the shuffling of a deck, the numerological calculation focuses your mind, body, and spirit on the task at hand, rather than on the answer you want to create.

Some people believe that divining methods tap the human mind's subconscious power, allowing us to answer our own questions and solve our own problems. Others theorize that tools link us to archetypal truths—ideas and themes that are present, and repeat themselves, in all human cultures. Many believe that tools help you tap into Universal Power and knowledge. Perhaps "synchronicity" is just another word for the unseen guides, angels, and loved ones on The Other Side who intervene on our behalf. There is no such thing as coincidence.

Laura feels that divining methods provide an avenue of access, a "way in," to the eternal intelligence of The Other Side, the life beyond our life on Earth. Tools shift us into a position of neutrality that opens us to truths and messages that might otherwise be beyond the reach of our consciousness.

Whatever their ultimate source, messages do "come through" with the use of tools, and they have for centuries.

Choosing the Right Tool

Are you an analytical person, comfortable with numbers and symbols? Then astrology is a tool that could play to your natural strengths. Are you a visual learner, someone who needs to picture a face before you can remember a name? Divination cards like medicine cards or the Tarot, which connect imagery with meaning, could really resonate for you. Are you especially sensitive to touch, someone who can tell the difference between corduroy and velvet with your eyes closed? You might search out the tactile tools, like rune stones, or have your palm inked for a palmistry reading. Or perhaps you've always been fascinated by people's handwriting, and want to learn more about what graphology's strokes and loops are telling you.

The methods of divination are many and varied. There's the perfect match out there for every kind of person. When you choose one, it's important to know yourself, to have a sense of what makes you comfortable and relaxed. Remember, the idea is to quiet your "thinking" mind—in whatever way works for you—and then to leave yourself open and receptive to what may come.

We use about two dozen divination methods in this book. Be ready to sample several methods so you can choose the perfect one to fit your personal needs.

Take Heed _____

Even if you can do your own oil changes, sometimes you need a mechanic. It's the same way with the esoteric arts, and that's why there are professional intuitive practitioners. When it comes to choosing a pro, technology is your best friend. The telephone and computer have opened the whole world to us. Laura marvels at this every day, as she advises people from New England to Greece to Australia and everywhere in between. With so many options out there, don't settle for a practitioner who's anything less than a good match for you. Check references, ask questions, and learn how and why they do this work.

A Tool Is Only as Good as Its Practitioner

All the more reason, then, to make sure you try them out, so you can see how a divining method may fit or complement you.

It is possible to use divination methods irresponsibly, and often that happens when we turn to them in desperation rather than strength. Go slowly at first. Once you've chosen a divining tool, it can take a lifetime to master all its nuances. In the meantime, you are free to soak up all the divination messages and lessons it has to teach you. With practice, it is possible that you can become your own expert astrologer or seer!

People often ask Laura, "How can I do what you do?" The truth is that everyone is born with intuition, but as we leave childhood behind, the veil between the worlds slips down again for most of us. With practice, anyone can rediscover and strengthen her or his own intuitive powers. That said, few people are able to develop their intuition to levels that match those of professionals. Just as anyone can love music, not everyone is wired to play or perform it; with practice, you might manage a round of "Row, Row, Row Your Boat" for your own appreciative family. Others are natural musicians, able to perform at concert caliber.

What matters is your *intention*. Is your goal enlightenment or power? How are you going to put this information to use? Are you searching for guidance, or trying to assert control?

Hits and Misses

"What's the weather like today?" How you answer this everyday question depends very much on what you need to know.

◆ A glance out the window will tell you if it's rainy, sunny, or snowing right now.

◆ Short sleeves or long? The newspaper forecast will give you a general idea of the expected temperature.

◆ Should you carry that bulky umbrella? Better check the Weather Channel for the updated chance-of-showers stats.

◆ Is it safe to go sailing? Then you'll need to heed your marine radio's advice.

Same day, same weather—totally different information. None of these predictions will be necessarily wrong, but any one of them could be wrong for *you*. It all depends on what you need.

Divination methods are the same way. For example, your newspaper horoscope is like a glance out the window. It gives you a general idea of the astrological conditions that may affect you, but not much more than that. (And if you look at more than one paper on any given day, you're sure to find disagreement!) Your own natal birth chart, the astrological horoscope wheel based on your particular date, time, and place of birth, will be a much more specific guide to the "weather patterns" in your life—but it gives more information than some people need.

Even when looking at a particular birth chart or a certain spread of cards, different practitioners will offer different interpretations of the same information. It's up to you to grasp the meanings and messages that are important to you. You might consult several astrologers and go with the reading that rings most true, or listen for the overall messages from them, however differently described. You might pull three card spreads and look for the common threads they share. (More often than not, they will share a lot!) That doesn't necessarily mean that some of the readings were "wrong." Perhaps they simply carry meanings that aren't yet clear.

There's a very important difference between weather forecasts and divinatory messages, though. We can't affect the weather. We *can* change our destiny. No matter what the cards or the stars say, you can always exert free will in any situation. The tools can reveal the forces at work around you, but you are in the driver's seat when it comes to your future.

Divine Inspiration _____

Laura has often seen someone pull one or two angel cards from the deck, then decide that they would like a "better" or "more resonating" message. So they return the cards to the deck, stir them up well, and then reselect. Imagine their surprise to find that they have "somehow" selected the very same cards! We might not like the messages we get—but they might be the ones we need to hear.

Viewing the Future in Our Modern Times

Technology has brought us full circle to a renewed desire to understand who we are and why we are here. This opens new directions of thinking. Once there were few aids for insight and understanding and few who knew how to use them. Now there is an abundance of methods that make access to them infinitely easier.

The newest of these is technology itself—particularly the Internet, the world's most complex network of computer systems, which connects us with information and with each other in ways we've only just begun to explore. We have at our fingertips the information that we need to better understand and make decisions about our personal lives so that we can grow and improve as individuals. As important, we now have the ability to see and understand how our individual actions affect our communities and the world at large, so that we can make decisions that support humanity's best destiny.

The Least You Need to Know

♦ Destiny defines your soul's themes and the lessons that come with them in this life; free will influences how your soul learns them.

♦ Today's technology makes the intuitive arts accessible and available to anyone.

♦ Information is power; the more of it you have, the better able you are to make the choices and decisions that will take you where you need to go in your life.

♦ Combining the traditions of divination with modern technology gives us an unprecedented ability to consider options and choices as they relate to our futures.

2

Divination's Past, Present, and Future

In This Chapter

- ◆ Nature's links to Divination
- ◆ Appeasing the gods and goddesses was a full-time job
- ◆ Many divination tools are steeped in history
- ◆ Sci-fi: the shape of things to come?

Divination is hardly new! From people of power like shamans, to places of power like Camelot—and to a lingering stigma of disrespect, as was seen at Salem—divination has always been either embraced or opposed as an important supplement to people's daily lives. Today, divination and intuition are coming to the fore once again.

Culture has acknowledged Higher Energy all through history, and peoples throughout the world have acknowledged that Something or Someone bigger than ourselves surrounds us all and influences everything.

Observing Nature's Patterns

Our earliest observations of predictability came in noticing that there were many patterns in nature. By watching the environment around them, ancient cultures saw that there were times for certain events and circumstances. There was a time for hunting or harvesting, another time for procreation. There was a time to plant and nurture, a time to gather and store, a time to expend resources and a time to conserve. Their very survival hinged on the earliest patterns of predictability they could glean from nature.

Divine Inspiration

Before recognition of the earth's patterns and nature's cycles, people felt powerless and confused. Many cultures developed rituals in an attempt to appease the "angry gods." Their seasonal offerings and regular sacrifices were made to "control" future harvests, epidemics, conflicts, and other events. Today, not much has changed. We still tend to think that things happen *to* us when really they're happening *for* us. When we recognize events and circumstances as learning opportunities, then we can expand our understanding and truly grow.

Nature still has a powerful effect on each of us today. Those who live closer to the equator seem to have a harder time keeping warm when they travel to colder climates because their bodies are acclimated to warmer temperatures. For those in higher latitudes, lack of light in the winter has been directly linked to seasonal affective disorder (aptly known as SAD). Recent research shows that just a few minutes of fresh air and natural scenery each day can help ease depression and increase mental wellness. For all the benefits of technology, it seems there's nothing like nature to soothe and balance the spirit—a fact that science is only just beginning to quantify.

Design, Connections, and Planning

Eventually humankind recognized that the design of existence was much grander than just the sequence of the seasons alone. The cycles of the earth followed the cycles of the heavens. People observed that at regular intervals of time, both changed. In these patterns there was predictability and an increased understanding and awareness of life in the context of past, present, and future. And in these patterns was the beginning of planning, of understanding that there are connections between current and anticipated events. By noting specific plant and animal behavior, humans began to take note and prepare for coming storms, drought, and "bad winters." There was no weather channel to turn to so they used what they had: nature. Divination at this point was germane to survival. Those who didn't pay attention to the changing sky and the exposed undersides of leaves were left vulnerable and at risk to incoming storms.

People learned that they could use their knowledge of such connections to make their lives better, and increase their chances for survival. Remember, getting caught in the weather even a century ago meant exposing oneself to illnesses and germs that couldn't be treated with the ways and means we have available today. Seeing these connections meant they could determine the best times to plant and to harvest, when to hoard water and when to stock up on firewood, when to rest and when to work. From these observations came the various calendar systems followed by many different cultures—the earliest tools of divination—and a way to structure and perceive time that we still use in our lives today. Through the centuries other divining methods have come into use, tools that look at the patterns and connections in our lives to present possibilities of future events. As humans have evolved, so have our methods for seeing into the future.

Gods and Goddesses

Whatever the God of your understanding, history is rife with a wide array of Gods and Goddesses that have long been seen as worthy of worship and divination. From Zeus to Quetzalcoatl and from Kwan Yin to Morgan le Fay to Ganesha, people the world over have associated deities with nature's cycles and with humanity's pursuits.

It's easy to see how the sky itself played an important role in religion and divination. Our ancestors knew that the sun provided not only a source of light, but also the heat needed for plants and animals to grow and survive. The fact that things fall *down* (rain, hail, snow, and even meteor showers) convinced them that something "up there" had to be more powerful and omnipotent than anything "down here." Something celestial must be keeping the energies of life flowing!

To placate the "angry gods" they thought were sending them punishments from on high, people would give valuable things as sacrifice. The idea of human unworthiness in the face of divine power is thousands of years old. In some places, farmers created altars and left large portions of their crops out to wither in the elements to ensure the success of future harvests. (One way of trying to affect the future!) In other areas, rituals of dance, prayer, chanting, and singing would be offered to the gods, or perhaps objects of beauty (such as ceremonial weapons, bowls, or tools). In some societies, sacrifice rituals went beyond inanimate objects. Animals might be sacrificed, or their blood might be ritually shed; even humans might be sacrificed to the gods.

The imagery of powerful giant versus mere human (as in the fable of Jack and the beanstalk, or the biblical tradition of David and Goliath) can be found in many cultures and folklores, an echo of the powerlessness humans felt in the face of forces bigger and larger than themselves (like nature!). In Connecticut, for example, there's a mountain range called "Sleeping Giant" which, when seen from a distance, clearly resembles a man lying face-down on the ground—much like the way the giant fell down to earth when Jack cut that beanstalk. Its history is steeped in Native American lore. In northwestern New Mexico near Four Corners lies El Huerfano Mesa, sacred to the Navajos. Suspended from the heavens by sunbeams, this mesa is revered by Navajos even today as the home of Changing Woman.

But let's be honest: Without the benefit of the Weather Channel or our radio forecasts, any one of us could imagine a Greek Zeus or an African Oya if we were caught out in a vicious lightning storm, whipped by wind and pelted with sheets of rain. Although we have indisputably evolved, we still naturally drift into "why me?" mode when we have a raging, record-breaking winter, or when a massive hurricane surges up the coast and destroys our property. It's hard to see the bigger picture when you feel singled out and overwhelmed. And that's exactly where today's accessibility to divination can come in. The techniques of divination can help you get that all-important perspective.

Modern Access to the Tools of Divination

Astrology, Tarot, and other divining methods were part of the technology of earlier times, and the people who used them were considered the visionaries of their time. They were the village mystics, tribal healers, seers, holy men, and astrologers: skilled intuitives who often had status and respect in their own social structure. Through both prophecy and their basic divining traditions, they accumulated a substantial amount and range of information and knowledge, and it became their roles to counsel, comfort, and heal. Local people turned to them for help, advice, and insight.

For centuries the *intuitive arts* remained the exclusive domain of these visionaries, those who were said to have a direct line to interpreting the will of the gods or of God—because they were the only ones who had Divine access.

Today, technology gives each one of us broad access to vast amounts of information, including dozens of intuitive arts that anyone, of any culture, can use to gain insight and understanding. Books, television, computers, and telecommunication have been available for a relatively short time in the scope of human existence, but they have changed the way we view and access information regarding the future. And where once these subjects were talked of in back alleys and secret meetings, now the local supersize bookstore has entire sections devoted to the intuitive arts. Online book-stores allow readers to search entire databases for books and tools and order them all from the comfort of our own homes. Cable TV networks regularly feature shows devoted to this increasingly accepted and fascinating field that, as we know, has existed for centuries!

Just like the traveling fortune-tellers and gypsies of the past (and who can still be found in some places), today's technology and interest in "knowing" has opened the door to a new breed of charlatan that seriously undermines the credibility of legiti-mate and reputable intuitive practitioners—900 numbers and "psychic" hotlines.

Sadly, many of these hotlines are crass, money-making enterprises. It's impossible for you to know if the voice on the other end of that line (or the person on that other computer screen) is a legitimate intuitive. The people who work for these services are often just ordinary folks like yourself who are paid to have calls forwarded into their homes at all hours of the day or night. You are charged by the minute, so staffers are trained to keep you on the line for as long as possible (and after the first few minutes, the rate often jumps significantly). They are taught to listen for clues from you, and then develop rapport and trust by mirroring back whatever you want to hear. How psychic do you have to be to know that someone calling in at 3 A.M. is lonely, depressed, confused, having a hard time, and in need of some basic TLC?

Sure, some 900 numbers might have legitimate intuitives working for them. But as you have no way of safely or accurately verifying that, we encourage you to consider different avenues before you forge ahead! When it comes to genuine, legitimate div-ination, 900 numbers are not the sustenance of tomorrow.

Today there are fewer and fewer limitations on who can have access to divining methods and to the body of knowledge they can make available. *Divining tools* such as Tarot cards, angel cards, runes, crystals, and astrological charts are available in stores everywhere. Books like the one you're reading right now give instruction and understanding about the tech-niques, their uses, and the information they can provide. The Internet and our modern telecommunications system enable experts around the world to share their knowledge and expertise with anyone who is interested.

Future Focus

The **intuitive arts** are approaches and methods for gaining insight and understand-ing, collectively. "Divination" comes from the Latin word for heavenly; **divining tools** are spe-cific aids for accessing the intu-itive arts.

> **CAUTION**
>
> **Take Heed** _____
>
> Laura cautions her clients against using 900 numbers and "psychic" hotlines. It might be tempting to contact such easily accessible forms of help—after all, who else can you call at 3 A.M.? But the voice on the other end of the line might not be an intuitive professional at all, but simply an employee trained to lend a sympathetic ear and accept your credit card payment!

Although certainly you can (and at times should) consult with intuitive arts professionals who can help you interpret the information you receive to make sense within the context of your own life, you can learn to use the tools of the intuitive arts to understand yourself and your life path—past, present, and future. Today's technology affords us the opportunity to enlighten ourselves in ways never before possible. From online horoscopes and Tarot readings to the inspirational message of the day, technology gives us more of what we crave: knowledge and options.

But no matter how technologically adept we may become, the "old ways" still carry special resonance. Let's take a look at the roots of some of the most popular and widely used divination methods.

Astrology

The first science was astrology. Ancient peoples around the world, from Sumer to China to Egypt to the Americas, contemplated the heavens and their connection to human affairs. Pythagoras, Isaac Newton, and the "Three Wise Men" all studied astrology. In the 1600s, though, the discipline diverged into two streams. Astronomy, the study of the physical characteristics of the stars and planets, gained in influence with the invention of the telescope. Astrology became discredited in scientific circles. But it never lost its hold on the popular imagination. After all, almost every daily newspaper today runs an astrology column—but do any of them do the same for astronomy?

Mercury

Venus

Jupiter

Neptune

Pluto

Astrology and astronomy link the gods and the planets.

Numerology

The idea that the Universe as a whole, and everything in it, obeys mathematical laws is credited to Pythagoras, the Greek thinker and astrologer (connections, connections …) who worked in the sixth century B.C.E. Numbers have carried mystical meanings in every society, and these meanings can be seen in the Bible, the Mayan calendar, the Chinese system of feng shui, and many other traditions. The numerology system we use today was influenced by all these sources and developed in the early years of the twentieth century.

Tarot

The oldest existing Tarot decks date from the 1300s, though its roots are much older. Most decks today base their art and imagery on the Waite deck, developed at the turn of the twentieth century and influenced by the then-new thinking on archetypes and dreams.

Runes

Rune stones feel like a direct connection with the Stone Age, and in a way they are. Ancient peoples around the world would "roll the bones" in divination rituals, and rune stones are a modern (and much less creepy) adaptation of this tradition. Although we know the names of the ancient rune symbols, their original meanings are less clear; they, too, are a modern adaptation. Still, there's something very primal, some kind of tactile connection with the earth, that comes of handling and using the runes. Some people find even more resonance in runes they've made themselves from found rocks or bits of wood, or sculpted out of clay.

Palmistry

Our hands have always been seen as unique marks of selfhood. Witness ancient cave art, which was frequently "signed" by a print of the artist's hand. Aristotle wrote about palmistry in 350 B.C.E., and it's discussed in the Bible, too. But the art has had a bit of a carnival-sideshow stigma attached to it for all too long. In the twentieth century, as more people have come to accept the idea that our bodies and minds are connected and affect each other, palmistry has come into its own.

Science, Sci-Fi, or Futurism?

Who knows what the future will be? We can look back at the work of Leonardo da Vinci, a true visionary, whose exquisitely rendered sketches of flying machines could never be realized in his own time, fifteenth-century Italy. It took 500 years for technology to catch up with Leonardo's incredible imagination. Are artists and dreamers today envisioning our own far-off future?

Laura regularly "sees" future inventions—and she keeps a record of these visions for proof! In the very early 1990s she predicted that traditional telephone and communications technology would soon become more portable and comfortable to accommodate our rapidly changing lifestyles. Multitaskers (like herself) would need to have their hands free while they worked and used the phone. (Remember, cordless phones and pagers were just emerging then. The phones were heavy, clumsy, and unreliable; pagers only worked one way.) Fast forward to today: Not only are cordless phones *everywhere*, they're also extremely light and portable—and each one can accommodate that all-important hands-free headset. Now we don't just have pagers—we have text messaging! Laura also predicted the mainstream acceptance and wide availability of a handy little device called the caller ID.

> **Resonances**
>
> What's next? Well, how about a gray hair pill? Laura predicted it in 1998, and late in 2002 scientists found that restoration of hair color was an unforeseen side effect of a cancer treatment drug they were researching. Later, perhaps, will be dental procedures done by suction that simultaneously remove and insert a tooth all in the same procedure.

Remember watching TV in the early 1970s? (Okay, maybe not—we're dating ourselves here.) Could you ever have imagined, while sitting on the shag rug in your living room, that one day your television would be a flat plasma screen hanging on the wall like a picture, and that it would operate off a central *remote control*? Well ... *someone* did!

But when it comes to the subject of futuristic imaginings, nothing beats the work of Gene Roddenberry, the creator of *Star Trek*. Our first experience with the Starship *Enterprise* ("going boldly where no one has gone before!") came decades ago. And, bless it, for all its hokiness, we were hooked. We'd never seen laser beams before, or even automatic electronic doors, for that matter. And the reality is, in the '60s these things didn't exist! The automatic-door effect was created by prop men, working off-camera to quickly and smoothly open and close those doors. (Okay, sometimes they didn't do it so smoothly.) But that's the charm of watching those reruns today! The new *Star Trek* series like *The Next Generation*, *Voyager*, *Deep Space Nine*, and *Enterprise* have adapted all that technology and more.

In Roddenberry's imagined future, the role of divination is given more than a passing glance. On the series *Star Trek: The Next Generation*, the character of Deana Troy is an empath—someone with the ability to sense and feel what is going on in the minds and hearts of others. This gift is so well-regarded that Troy is a high-ranking officer who reports directly to the venerable Captain Picard, offering her vibes to counsel him on how to deal with other species, cultures, and events. In her spare time, she supports the crew as the ship's counselor.

Vulcans (they of the pointy ears, the people that Lenard Nimoy made so famous) have reappeared throughout the evolution of the *Star Trek* family. They always approach the "mysterious" with their innate powers of sheer logic. But the Vulcans also possess a power that defies all logic: the power to "mind meld" with anyone and literally gain access to their every thought, feeling, experience, and emotion. They use this ability as a tool for—you guessed it—a logical sort of divination: "based on x, I predict an outcome of y"!

And let's not forget that wonderful replicator, a device that assists our favorite travelers with everything from tea ("Earl Grey, hot"), to clothing, to that vase in your quarters that was accidentally broken. But as any devout "Trekkie" knows, even a device like a replicator has its limits and proper uses!

There's a lot we can learn from the *Star Trek* shows of today … concepts like service, unity, "the greater good," and, of course, honoring the prime directive: Under no circumstance should a more advanced culture's information or technology interfere with the natural evolutionary process of a less advanced one, if its people are not ready to handle the responsibility that comes with such knowledge.

From Imagination to Reality

Some of today's best technology has come from our own real-life space program, NASA, which has given us a whole lot more than Tang! Things like Velcro, tires that will never wear out, sleep technology (memory foam now used in pillows and mattresses), space blankets (thin as a slice of paper, yet able to retain the body's heat), microwave ovens, and more have been developed from NASA's "space-age" research. Today, sending a ship into space—an undertaking we once viewed with such solemnity, sacredness, and importance—is now so routine that we only take notice when it results in trouble or tragedy. Not only is space flight becoming ordinary, we now have a permanent space station with astronauts from around the globe in residence!

Several years ago Laura had the awesome privilege of seeing the space shuttle a split second after its launch in Florida. It streamed into the early morning skyline of South Carolina, appearing distinctly on the clear horizon and streaking upwards at an incredible speed. Meanwhile, thousands of folks obliviously sped along in their cars, intent on their morning commutes to work. In less than a minute the shuttle was gone from our atmosphere and into the beyond. Laura is still amazed at the incongruity of that moment, and at how easy it is for us to become so complacent about our awesome technology.

Today's inventions are wonderful things that we regularly incorporate into our daily lives and quickly get accustomed to (until the power goes out and we are left, literally, stumbling around with "nothing to do"). They were created because someone, somewhere, had a wonderful idea and the amazing audacity to say, "I think that can be done differently." Inventors refuse to accept the world's limits as an unchanging, unchangeable status quo. By striding to the future in this open state of mind, they're able to take all of us into the uncharted territory of the land of limitlessness—a concept we'll be exploring together in *future* chapters. Let's go!

The Least You Need to Know

- ◆ Nature is the source of the earliest forms of divination.

- ◆ Historically, divination is part of the religious rituals of many cultures.

- ◆ The technologies of today began with an idea someone had years ago—and acted on.

- ◆ Our present and our future hold many parallels with the creative imaginings of Gene Roddenberry.

The Gift of Intuition

In This Chapter

- ◆ Intuitive gifts are a matter of degree
- ◆ Flexing your intuitive muscles
- ◆ A quiz evaluates how intuitive you are
- ◆ Grounding yourself
- ◆ Keeping a journal of your experiences
- ◆ What can—and cannot—be seen

Mystics, visionaries, psychics, seers … throughout our history and around the world, humankind has called upon the special talents of the intuitively gifted to look into the future for us. Many astrologers believe that now that we are moving in the Age of Aquarius, intuitive knowledge will become an increasingly important method of knowing and understanding the world around us. Aquarius is ruled by the planet Uranus, and the Age of Aquarius will be marked by innovation, quick knowledge, and spiritual exploration and growth. The Information Revolution of our current time, made possible by electricity, computers, and the Internet, confirms that a renaissance in the transmission of information—almost at intuitive speed—is here. We suggest that this renaissance of intuitive communication means we are seeing the changes that will be the hallmark of this new Age of Aquarius and its revolutionary affect on humankind. This is a time of forging global union, experiencing mystic crystal revelations, and liberating the mind.

Although all of us have some level of intuition, not everyone has the ability to access and hone his or her intuition the way a true professional psychic intuitive can. Even though this is true, we do encourage you to dabble, sample, and practice developing your own innate, intuitive abilities. That's why you are reading this book! By exploring your own intuitive nature you will find yourself resonating to the Aquarian energy of the heavens in this time when the bridge between science and intuition seems nearly ready to navigate with sure footing. In the words of Albert Einstein, "The most beautiful thing we can experience is the mysterious. It is the source of all true art and science."

As you discover and use divination tools and personal rituals far more frequently in your everyday life, you might find it comforting to also check in on a yearly basis with a professional intuitive for more in-depth insights and information.

What Do the Pros Know That You Don't?

Plenty! Although everyone is intuitive to some degree, professionals in the intuitive arts are highly skilled individuals whose natural gifts have been honed and sharpened over many years of disciplined practice. Most professionals operate on a much higher intuitive level than the average person, if only because the professional is using intuitive ability full-time.

Divine Inspiration

Astronomers and astrologers from the time of the ancients to the present day have debated the specific timing of the transition from the Age of Pisces, the zodiac sign of flow and water, to the dawning of the Age of Aquarius, the sign of the water bearer. Most believed the Age of Aquarius would start somewhere between the years A.D. 1997 and 2000—proponents of this view included Nostradamus, Edgar Cayce, and psychologist Carl Jung, known for his interest in the intuitive arts.

Have you ever watched a foreign film without subtitles in a language you don't know? It can be an unnerving experience. There's only so much you can infer from images without understanding the language; it's very possible that you'll misinterpret even these images if you're not familiar with the social customs, dialects, and nuances of the filmmaker's culture. Think of a skilled intuitive professional as your interpreter of the "language" of divinatory messages. That's why you may want to seek out someone with experience in the intuitive arts who can be an integral part of the process for you. A professional can validate your own reactions to your intuitive experiences, as well as elaborate on them—giving you context, guidance, and deeper understanding.

Take Heed _____

Before consulting with any intuitive professional, always ask questions, check credentials, and get references—and trust that inner voice that tells you if this is the right person, and the right advice, for you.

Like other professional psychics, when Laura works, she will often tell a client that although she can see, hear, relay, sense, feel, and describe things in great detail, if something does not resonate with the client, then that piece of information should just be left behind. Always listen for the pieces that make sense and connect with *you*—whether as examples of evidence or as information that resonates with what you know and feel in the issues surrounding your situation. Laura uses this idea particularly when inviting clients to do post-session "homework." When advising clients to meditate, for example, Laura may recommend three or four possible meditation exercises to choose from. But she'll also remind each person that these are just suggestions or ideas. In practice, each individual should do whatever form of meditation feels natural or right.

So whatever a professional intuitive may tell you, you're still responsible for making your own choices and assessments. This is why learning and sampling several forms of divination tools is such a great idea. Soon you'll begin to get comfortable tuning in with yourself and understanding what it means to resonate with an idea or a message—that is, to be intuitively sure of something, right down to your bones.

You can start by taking the simple quiz a little later in this chapter to see where your own strengths may already be waiting within you.

Practice Makes Perfect (Well ... Almost)

So if professional psychics and seers are like skilled language translators, does that mean only they can guide you through the world of the intuitive arts? No, of course not. If you were planning a short trip to a foreign country, you wouldn't hire a translator to come along with you; you'd learn a few words and phrases on your own, or maybe take a crash language class. It's the same way with divination. A professional can be an invaluable guide and adviser, but there's a great deal you can learn on your own, if you're motivated enough to do so and if your mind is open.

Resonances

When Laura taught intuition development classes, she'd use a physical fitness analogy, enthusiastically calling each session a "psychic workout" that would stretch her students' "intuitive muscles." That is, until the day she opened a class with her regular spiel ... and an insistent student demanded to know exactly where the "intuitive muscles" could be found in the human body. The answer: *everywhere!*

And one more thing: To divine what's in your future, you need to practice. Your intuitive "muscles" need to be in good shape.

Professionals in the intuitive arts, like professionals in most respected fields, usually start out with a natural talent—a gift, we might say. Most of them are naturally sensitive to energies that the rest of us can't ordinarily sense. But few would agree that the talent they were born with is all they use. The psychically gifted continue to stretch their intuition, to keep their energies flowing. They may have specific rituals—daily breathing exercises, grounding visualizations, filters, meditation, journaling, yoga, a healthy diet, and balanced living—that help support them as they do their work. Just as professional athletes spend time in regular preparation, training, stretching, eating right, and getting proper rest, skilled practitioners in the intuitive arts are wise to do the same—and so are *you*. Without proper respect of the body, intuitives can lose the long-term stamina that's necessary to do this sacred work.

One of the most important seers of modern times was Edgar Cayce, who worked during the first half of the twentieth century. Cayce was a deep trance channel whose extensive readings and professional ethics are very well documented. He would go into a trancelike state that looked very much like sleep, which is how he came to be known as the Sleeping Prophet. In this meditative state he could access information on The Other Side and would speak at length of what he saw. His secretary, son, and other observers would fastidiously write down every word he spoke. Cayce could also prescribe holistic medical remedies to cure certain ailments and health conditions. His channeled medical remedies are still used by holistic practitioners around the world today.

There was a rare sense of sacredness to Cayce's work; he was a common man transformed by his honorable calling. Some would even say he became ultimately consumed by it, as Cayce proved so driven to help the many who sought his advice that he refused to pace himself and disregarded the warnings of his spirit guides and earthly assistants to honor the physical needs of his own body. He worked himself to exhaustion, so much so that some believe he died decades before his time. Edgar Cayce's story is a reminder of how important it is to pace yourself as you explore and unfold in the intuitive arts. Take it slow! And always reserve time to renew and restore yourself after any intense energy work.

Do You Have the Gift? A Self-Quiz

So what about *you?* First, it will help to know how naturally intuitive you are—or how willing you are to acknowledge your own gifts.

Please answer yes or no to the following questions. Record your answers in the appropriate columns of the answer section that follows.

1. Have you ever heard a voice saying your name or telling you to do something when no one else is physically near you?

2. Have you ever been able to tell when a faraway loved one is in pain or distress?

3. Have you ever seen the outcome of an upcoming event in a dream or while meditating?

4. Have you ever thought of someone you hadn't seen in years, and then bumped into them that same week?

5. Have you ever heard the voice of a familiar but unseen person giving you a word of encouragement in a stressful situation?

6. Have you ever sensed (through smell, taste, or touch, or just through intuition) that a person was ill before they told you, or before illness was diagnosed?

7. Have you ever seen a pictorial image, detailed or not, of a current or future state or situation?

8. Have you ever been talking with someone who is dear to you—a spouse, a sibling, or your best friend—and found yourself finishing their sentences or mentioning a specific thing they were thinking of before they could say it out loud?

9. Have you ever heard or understood inaudible words of protest or pleasure from an animal, particularly a pet?

10. Have you ever felt someone's depression behind their smile, or known that they were in emotional knots though they said they were fine?

11. Have you ever held an object belonging to someone else, such as car keys, and felt that person's energy or presence?

12. Have you ever spontaneously stopped to pick something up on your way home, only to find that your family had been trying to reach you and ask you to run that very errand?

13. Have you ever heard a voice—not your own—speak a word of warning when you were in danger?

14. Have you ever taken on someone else's physical symptom, like a headache or stomach pain?

15. Have you ever encountered a perfect stranger and "known" about their health— almost as if you could see into the person?

16. Have you ever thought of a friend or loved one, and received a call or message from them before you had a chance to get in touch with them yourself?

Answers

Column 1	Column 2	Column 3	Column 4
1. _____	2. _____	3. _____	4. _____
5. _____	6. _____	7. _____	8. _____
9. _____	10. _____	11. _____	12. _____
13. _____	14. _____	15. _____	16. _____

If you answered yes to any question in Column 1, you've experienced the gift of *clairaudience,* the psychic sense of inner hearing. It's something like hearing a voice inside your head when no outside human source can be seen. Sometimes the voice is familiar; many people have heard a word from a deceased loved one, or a faraway living person, giving praise or reassurance, or just calling the listener's name. Sometimes the voice is one you've never heard with your physical ears. That forceful "*Wait!*" that stopped you from stepping off the curb in front of an oncoming truck—was that your guardian angel's voice? Your spirit guide's? Or perhaps the voice seemed to belong to an animal, especially one that you know and love. Whatever the details, clairaudient experiences are powerfully moving ones.

Resonances

Several years ago, when Laura was just beginning to discover her own calling as a professional psychic, she heard her then-ill cat Xavier say quite indignantly, "*Put me down!*" as she carried him up a steep hill on the way home from their walk. His voice sounded as loud as if he had shouted inside her head. Shocked, Laura immediately dropped the cat. Xavier gave her a disgusted look and then "said," quite sternly, "*That was embarrassing.*" His mouth never moved, and he uttered no sound, but Xavier had distinctly spoken inside Laura's mind. It marked the beginning of a new kind of communication between Laura and Xavier—one they regularly continue to this day.

If you answered yes to any question in Column 2, you've encountered *clairsentience,* the gift of inner knowing, or intuition to the tenth degree! This is something that many professional psychics and mediums can feel all of the time. These messages often come through our physical senses, particularly the senses of smell, taste, and touch, as well as through an overall sense of a person, place, or thing. Indeed, clairsentient messages can give us a sense of "knowing," as a whole. The experience of clairsentience often involves several of the senses working simultaneously. For example, celebrity Sharon Osbourne's oldest daughter Aimee had a feeling her mom may be ill because she noticed that her mother's body scent had changed from sweet to foul, and it was coupled with a strong feeling that Sharon was seriously ill, possibly with cancer. She urged her mother to see a doctor. Just days later, Sharon confirmed a diagnosis of colon cancer.

Clairsentient messages might be hard for the beginner to interpret, because they can have metaphorical rather than literal meanings. You might be gripped with the feeling that your best friend is drowning, to the point of gasping for your own breath—but she may not be destined for a tragic and watery grave. Is she, perhaps, flailing about in a bad marriage or a dead-end job? Over time, you will learn how to interpret the messages you receive.

If you answered yes to any question in Column 3, you've experienced *clairvoyance*, or inner vision. A clairvoyant message can come in a precognitive dream, through a meditative vision, or just as a powerful intuition. Whatever it means, a clairvoyant message is entirely separate from logical thought.

We know someone, Emily, whose psychically gifted friend Linda insisted, after hearing the itinerary of Emily's vacation flight plans, that she not board the departing plane, *under any circumstances*. Linda felt so strongly about this that she accompanied Emily to the airport, insisted on her friend flying standby on an earlier flight, and waited patiently until she actually *saw* Emily physically board a different flight than the one she originally booked. (This all happened several years ago, *before* the security restrictions of post–September 11 travel.)

Later, the two explored Emily's astrological chart with transits for the place and time of the original flight Linda had the bad feeling about, and they discovered many serious challenges indicated there for Emily. The chart showed the potential for chronic health problems, which could have meant anything from a car accident on the way to the airport, catching a serious virus from another plane passenger, or any number of scenarios that could set in motion a chain of lasting events compromising Emily's health. At the time of this writing Emily is doing just fine, and is happy she didn't board that seemingly ill-fated plane! And to this day, any time she makes flight reservations Emily calls Linda to check in with her intuition before buying plane tickets!

Another example: If you have a strong feeling that your father *must* go in for a blood pressure screening—so strong that you not only tell him about it, but you schedule the appointment yourself and drive him there, too—you've been spurred by clairvoyance. But if you take all these same actions because you know it's been three years since he's had a checkup and heart disease runs in your family, that's just being a good son or daughter.

Future Focus

Clairaudience, clairsentience, clairvoyance, and **telepathy** are all methods of receiving intuitive messages. These methods vary from individual to individual. Identifying how *you* receive messages is one of the first steps toward developing your ability to divine the future.

If you answered yes to any question in Column 4, then you have experienced *telepathy*. Sometimes known as "thought transference," telepathy refers to a kind of mental link between two people. Telepathic ties are often strongest between people who are already emotionally close. Think of the many stories of twins who always know when their sibling is hurt or in pain; think of the bond between a mother and her child. (Did Mom really have "eyes in the back of her head" that could see you getting into trouble, or was it telepathy at work?) But telepathy isn't limited to relatives or even close friends. Sensitive people can telepathically link to anyone, friend or stranger, at any distance.

Finally, one last bonus question: Can you access your clairaudience, clairsentience, clairvoyance, or telepathy at will, or does it come and go inexplicably or randomly?

All of us have intuitive gifts of one kind or another, but few of us can use those gifts whenever we choose to. Usually they arrive without warning or reason, and leave just as unexpectedly. Professionals in the intuitive arts are among those people who can naturally access their intuitive gifts, often on command. (Or is that on demand?)

But if that's not you, don't despair. Even one episode of clairaudience, clairsentience, telepathy, or clairvoyance at any point in your life is an indicator that you have intuitive gifts waiting to be developed. And if these events have *never* happened to you, don't worry. Perhaps some practice with divination tools will help you open up to your inner eyes and ears in new ways.

Getting Grounded: The Nitty Gritty

Before you try any of the exercises in this book, and later on before you begin a session with any divination tool, remember: You are the most important part of the process, and you'll only get out of it what you put in. Any exploration of divination tools would be remiss if we didn't stress the importance of *grounding*.

The ways to ground yourself, and the rituals you can create to do so, are infinite. But they are an absolute requirement for anyone (be it skilled professional or novice reader) seeking to explore further. Think of grounding as your psychic seatbelt. So buckle up! It's the law! Remember how the term grounding is used when considering electricity: to ground is to make a conducting connection between the earth and a conducting body. When you are properly grounded intuitively, you are conducting energy in a safe and stable way.

Future Focus

Grounding describes all the ways in which you can center yourself, remain anchored throughout your intuitive explorations, and protect yourself from opening up too quickly.

You'll find grounding exercises throughout this book. The amount of time and effort you spend on grounding yourself is up to you. Some people like to begin a session with an initial lengthy meditation, and then use symbolic reminders to quickly reaffirm their grounded state. For others, the grounding ritual can be as simple as a short and heartfelt prayer.

Grounding Visualization

This is a wonderful way to start a session using any intuitive tool or technique. It's also great on its own as an all-natural stress reducer!

1. Be seated with your feet flat on the floor, your arms and legs uncrossed.

2. Close your eyes.

3. Take three deep, cleansing breaths, filling the belly first, then the lungs.

4. Say aloud: "I am totally and completely surrounded by the powerful white Light of the God of my understanding, or spiritual power. I ask that any information that comes through today be of this Light, and that it be of the Highest and Best."

5. Follow with a few more deep breaths and then begin to work with your divination tool. You will feel calmer, more poised, and, yes, safer in the entire process when you remember to ground yourself.

The Pen Is Mightier ...: Keeping a Journal

It's a good idea for you to make a habit of journaling your experiences as you go forward. Your journal can be a powerful way of documenting and validating your own growing divining skills. Sometimes the message that makes no sense to you today turns out tomorrow to be something profound. And if you aren't keeping track, how will you prove to yourself or others that you really *did* know something before it ever happened?

Each journal entry should include your clinical notes as well as your feelings about and interpretations of your reading or experience. By "clinical notes," we mean that you must record your reading's *actual results*—the cards you drew, the images you saw, the dream you had, and so on.

Divine Inspiration

Often we find that the reading is right, but the conclusions we initially drew about it are not. Keeping clinical notes in your divining journal can help you go back and understand a reading's true messages, as well as learn the language of your own imagery.

Your journal can become almost like a trusted friend or confidant, always at your side on your journey. It can take time to feel that way, though, especially if you aren't accustomed to putting your thoughts and feelings on paper. Remember: You're writing for yourself and no one else. Spelling, handwriting, grammar—forget them! Just write, uncritically and regularly.

It is preferable *not* to use modern computer technology when journaling. First of all, there are already so many electronic energy interferences in our lives today, we are never without sound and stimuli. And even though you could use your laptop in bed, by the pool, or on a nature trail, there is something important and organic (and more in step with the natural energetic laws of the Universe) in making yourself available to sit and physically write something without simultaneously editing it—an inherent feature of computer use.

Because so many people use computers in their work settings, an "old-fashioned" journal provides a natural form of spiritual release. A paper journal is organic because it is as it is ... there's no spell check, no "do-overs," no cutting and pasting, and no additional steps such as printing out pages. If you put your coffee down on your open journal page, you get a ring mark that is part of the experience of that day. Computers, for all their wizardry, sterilize what is an organic process—and ultimately, intuition itself *is* natural and organic.

Your journal is a great place to review and consider the results of your divination samplings and readings. But did you know that it can be a divination tool in its own right? You can also use your journal to do a simple daily listening exercise—very much like the process that some people call "automatic writing." Also known as free writing, this is a technique of stilling conscious thought so that you can write down whatever intuitive messages may come to you. Try it now in the space provided.

Sit in a calm, relaxing place, with a pen or pencil in hand. Close your eyes and take a few deep breaths. You are preparing to quiet your busy mind for a few minutes and allow your "inner ears" to hear.

Now ask the question—of the angels, your spirit guides, your own body, or the God of your understanding—"What is it I need to know for today?"

Write down the answers that come into your mind. Don't analyze, and don't think. Give your mind the simple job of just writing! Only stop when you feel ready.

Now review what you've written. Don't worry if it's just one word, or even a mono-syllable; that's a common start for beginners. Sit with the words for a moment and take them into your heart. It's easy for your analytical side to jump in and contradict the message.

If your word was simply "Rest," your mind might respond "Rest?! You just woke up, for heaven's sake! What do you need rest for?" Instead, try to hear the greater wisdom of your body and your soul. This exercise creates a powerful connection to them both.

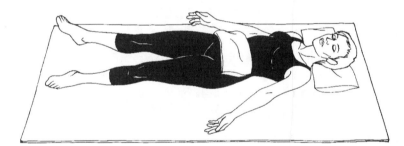

Yoga's shavasana, *or corpse pose, is an excellent tool for relaxation, as well as for grounding and renewal for energy work. Use a pillow on your abdomen to help you reinforce breathing from your diaphragm.*

Forecasting Your Future: Looking Deeper

As long as we humans have had a concept of time, we have contemplated the future, and we've used divination tools to help us do so. Today, people use divination for comfort and validation in the here and now, and also to tune into the future and get a peek at what's to come. We choose our words carefully here: We can only get a peek at the future. Remember that each of us has our own free will. You, and everyone around you, make the daily choices that make the future what it is. We can under-stand influences and undercurrents ahead of time, but it's our actions and inactions that help shape the future.

What Can Be Seen ... and How

Because of the force of free will, the future is always in a state of movement and change. Nuances in intention will influence what you can see and how you can see it. The fact that you have your own free will means that you are in control of your own future—each of us is—because *we make our own decisions*.

With tools, you can peek at the direction in which your future is going and, knowing yourself, can interpret these answers. Along with tools, dreams, meditation, and other ways of looking within can give you ideas about the future.

What It Is Not Possible to Know ... and Why

In short, anything can be seen—with one important limitation: *If something is meant for you to know, you will know it.* What can be seen is whatever's meant for you to see. Filters are in place (and we'll explore them in depth in Chapter 9). If you can't see an aspect of your future, it's because you're not meant to see it just yet.

It's frustrating to want to look ahead and to be unable to see the future. You may need to think or meditate on the question a bit longer. What might be standing in the way of your understanding?

The future is a little like creating a loaf of bread from dough: You can't tell its final shape while the dough is still rising! There's a process that has to happen before that bread can be baked.

Along with free will (our own and that of others), there's a bigger picture at work beyond your immediate surroundings. Your life is a great journey, and the whole of that journey can't always be seen on any given day. If you can be at peace as you take each step, if you can see each step as its own blessing, you're that much closer to the deeper understanding that you seek.

The Least You Need to Know

- To divine what's in your future, keep your intuitive "muscles" in good shape.
- Before you start working with any divining tool, take time to get grounded and centered.
- Journaling can help you stay centered over time, and a journal can be a divination tool in its own right.
- If you're meant to know something about the future, you'll know it.

Chapter 4

Your Personal Quest: What Do *You* Want to Know?

In This Chapter

- ◆ Your life is a journey
- ◆ Your soul's mission
- ◆ Your free will chooses the path to carry you to your destiny
- ◆ Mind power to manifest your goals
- ◆ Divination tools to map your life's journey
- ◆ The power within

Intuitives are special people, no doubt about it. But you don't have to have The Gift to draw on their divining techniques. There are many ways you can look within and find answers—especially if your questions have to do with your own life. Your journey, your relationships, your career, your health, even your soul's mission are all ripe for intuitive exploration. In this chapter, we'll look into the tools and terms you'll need to begin to answer the questions about your life that brought you here to us, and to this book. The truth is, we are *all* special, with unique gifts and purposes.

Each of us has the ability to touch the divine potential our life force embodies. In the words of Oprah Winfrey, "If I know nothing else for sure, I know that the big miracles we're waiting on are happening right in front of us, at every moment, with every breath. Open your eyes and heart and you'll begin to see them." We couldn't agree more.

Using the Intuitive Arts to Chart the Course of Your Life

"What's my life about?" is one of those Big Questions you might ponder from time to time, or *all* the time. But if you're like most of us, you never do figure out the answer. You get caught up in the daily routine, or you get distracted by the surprises that the world can throw you. Who has time for Big Questions, when there are so many little decisions to deal with every day?

If you let the intuitive arts give you a little boost, you might find some intriguing clues to divining your answers. Divination methods and tools, as we've seen, are great for focusing the power of mind, body, and spirit on an issue, a day's events, or the shape of a coming year. The tools are just as helpful in exploring the bigger questions of a lifetime:

- What is my destiny?
- What is my mission?
- Why am I here?

Imagine you're a sailor about to set off on an around-the-world expedition. The mystical journey of life has often been portrayed by writers and artists through the metaphor of navigation. You'll have to do a lot of work to chart your course before you can cast off: Everything from weather patterns to water depths to tide schedules must be researched and understood. And then, even with the best of preparation, a good sailor must always be prepared to deal with the unforeseen … the sudden storm, a waterspout, a pirate or two, a white whale, an albatross.

Life is like that, too. You make a plan, you pack your gear, and you head off, hoping to reach your final destination one day, but understanding that you might need to take shelter in a temporary port until problems or difficulties pass by. Sometimes these layovers will lengthen your journey, but ultimately, you *will* get where you're going—if you're willing to stay focused and persevere. You might even discover wonderful things on a detour!

You can use the intuitive arts to help you chart your own course to navigate life's ups and downs and, in the process, work toward a profound understanding of yourself as you divine your place in the Universe.

Life-and Soul-Mission Readings

Whether we know it or not, each of us has a theme that runs through our lives, a background motif that repeats, pops up, weaves itself into our very fibers. Your theme is your personal *soul work*. This is part of the essential you, something you carry with you from your birth into this life to your departure from it. And it's usually not very specific; your soul work is not going to be something such as "become a pediatric physician." No, usually your life theme is much more esoteric. The choices you may make within that context are nearly limitless.

Future Focus

Your **soul work** is what you, as an individual, are here on the earth plane to experience and do.

The things that "ring true" in your life, the moments that make you feel most real and alive, resonate and relate to your theme. These experiences might or might not relate to your paid work, to what you do for a living. (If they do, then congratulations!) But that doesn't really matter—because unlike a stranger at a cocktail party, the Universe doesn't define you by your job title. There are limitless ways you might choose to express your life's theme. But one way or another, your theme *will be expressed*.

For example, a humanitarian soul theme might express itself in the work of a missionary, or a doctor, or a parent, or even a neighbor who is always there for you, ready to help out in a jam. A performance theme could be seen in the life of a professional dancer, or a community theater actor, or an uncle who lives to tell jokes at the Thanksgiving table.

Resonances

When it comes to seeing prevailing patterns and themes in people's lives, Laura is one of only a handful of professionals who can access the Akashic Records (the cosmic record of all of a soul's travels, incarnations, and actions, past, present, and future), define soul themes, and offer related past-life information. Often, souls will incarnate several times to work on aspects of the same theme, so that they might "perfect" how they experience it.

Every individual has many paths to choose from and has to contend with larger forces beyond themselves. Divination tools can help you grasp *your* mission, *your* theme. With these tools, you can get an outside perspective on your earthly journey, removed from the here-and-now concerns that ordinarily cloud your vision. You can lift your attention off your shoelaces and raise your eyes to see the landscape around you.

And once you understand your life's theme (your soul work), you can decide, consciously, how to live out your time in this life.

Your Personal Pulse: A Journal Quiz

Another way to gain understanding of your soul journey is to meditate or write in your journal with this question in mind. You can use the thoughts and the spaces below to begin your own self-exploration process in the area of intuition and its role in your life, but you can use the same process to consider any set of questions. Remember to write your thoughts just as they come to you, without any self-criticism.

First, take a moment to ground yourself: Find a quiet, comfortable place to sit, free from distractions. Have a pen or pencil handy, and take several deep, cleansing breaths. Clear your mind. Close your eyes. Sit quietly until you are in tune with your body's rhythms, until you become aware of your heart beating and feel the force of the blood pumping through all the parts of your body. As you breathe slowly and deeply, feel that pulse slow and steady as you find your center. Become one with your pulse. Open your eyes. Meditate on each question in turn, writing out your initial, intuitive reactions in your journal.

What do you want to know about the future? _____

_____

What do you want to learn from reading this book? _____

_____

Which of the intuitive arts are you most drawn to and what about each art interests you most? _____

_____

In what areas of your life do you wish you could peek ahead and see information?

_____

_____

How would you use the information you divine about the future? _____

_____

What do you believe are your intuitive gifts? _____

_____

Would you like to develop your own intuitive gifts in order to help others divine the future? _____

_____

After you complete this journaling exercise, return to seated meditation and focus once more on the rhythm of your pulse. Has it quickened? Remained steady? Does your pulse flow like a river, gently rising and falling? Or, does it push, surging hard and insistent? Take a few more slow, deep breaths and commune one more time with your pulse. In Chinese medicine, physicians study the pulse to gain clues about their patients' physical and emotional well-being. In Part 3, you'll learn more ways to tune into your body's intuitive messages.

Destiny and Free Will Readings

"What's my destiny?" is another one of those Big Questions we all hunger to answer. If your life is a journey, then your destiny is the *destination*—the place you're bound for. Divination tools are great for identifying your destiny, because it's something that simply *is*.

"How will I fulfill my destiny?" is the follow-up Big Question, and that one is not so easy to answer. That's because the path you take to reach your destiny is constantly in flux. You choose it yourself, through your own free will.

Divine Inspiration

There are countless ways you can get to where you're going on your life's journey. If you're in Los Angeles and your destination is Chicago, you can catch the 3 o'clock train or the morning flight to O'Hare; you can get in a car and drive cross-country, on an interstate or a back road, through the desert or over the mountains or up the coast; you could even hike, if you don't care how long it takes. Chicago might be your destiny, but your route is subject only to your choice: your free will.

Free will is an incredible gift, and an incredible power. With it, your life is in your hands, your future at your disposal. Free will gives you dominion over yourself.

Divination methods can give you a peek at your destiny. But you may not understand what you see! The ever-changing landscape of your life, subject as it is to free will, can make it hard to discern your destiny, that bigger picture. But it is there. Open your mind and your heart, let intuition be your guide, and clarity will come.

When your destiny seems clear to you, you can see the swirl of events around you for what it is: all part of the journey, main roads and signposts and detours that you can follow or leave behind. Now, divination tools can help you focus your free will on the path you want to take. You have the map; the route is entirely up to *you*.

Wishing, Clarifying, and Creating: A Self-Exploration

Okay, we hear you saying, but how am I supposed to make this destiny thing happen? Wishing doesn't make it so.

Or does it?

Future Focus _____

Manifesting is the art of defining, exploring, visualizing, and preparing to receive the future outcomes you desire.

Actually, wishing *can* make things happen. Your mind has the inherent power to reach any goal. Wishing, or more properly, *manifesting*, is the art of clarification that calls to you that which you want. We're not talking about vague wish-upon-a-star notions here. We're talking about a purposeful naming of goals that metaphysicians have been using for decades to help people create the lives they want.

Barbara Sher's classic book, *Wishcraft* (see Appendix B), is a brilliant exploration of the power of free will and manifesting. Half the battle, she says, is understanding what it is you really want to wish for. When you define it, explore it, and visualize it, you've set yourself up to receive it.

This manifesting exercise is derived from Barbara Sher's ideas. Be willing to do the work of wishing, and watch as free will unfolds before your eyes.

1. Define your goal in as much detail as you can muster. Be clear in your wish. Do you want to move into a better house, find romance, get a piano? It doesn't matter what the wish is. Pick one thing, and make it your own.

   _____

   _____

   _____

2. Write down your goal on paper (you can use the following lines). Pay attention to what you want, *not what you don't*—be positive! Write down all the qualities and specifications you imagined in step 1. Be as specific as you can.

   _____

   _____

   _____

3. Visualize your goal. Meditate on the words you have written. Say them out loud to help your wish find its way to you.

4. Wait. Now, this can be the hard part. The time factor can vary, though people are often overwhelmed by the speed with which wishes can come true! While you're waiting, you may want to return to your written wish every now and then, to visualize and meditate again. Be patient, and be ready to accept the gift of your goal when it comes.

Clarity is critical when you're making wishes. Laura once had a friend who felt desperate for a new love in her life. Laura recommended a manifesting exercise like the one previously outlined (the one that you're about to try), and the friend duly wrote down all the qualities she wanted in a partner: He had to be cute, affectionate, playful, and trustworthy.

A few weeks later, the friend came to Laura and complained that the manifesting exercise had totally failed. She hadn't met any new men at all. But on the other hand, she said happily, "I got a puppy! He's so cute, and we have so much fun playing together, and he just *adores* me, and … wait a minute!"

No, she hadn't actually specified that her new love had to be *human!*

> **Take Heed**
>
> When you try manifesting exercises, it's important that you only manifest one thing at a time. Your ideal job, for example, with all its particular specifications, is more than enough to work on without also trying to manifest housing, romance, a new car, and a dozen other things all at once!

Readings to Map Your Personal Quest

One of the wonderful qualities of divination tools is that you can use them for any purpose, to ask any question. As we've seen earlier in this chapter, tools can help you answer your life's Big Questions: Why am I here? What is my purpose?

But tools aren't only useful for such rarefied purposes. They can also help you in your everyday life as you make choices, negotiate emotions, deal with others, and embark on new relationships. They can give you guidance and direction if you're having a hard time making a decision. They can also give you validation and confirmation of decisions you've already made.

What matters is not your tool, but your intention. If you're centered and focused, if your question is clear and your mind is uncluttered, you can get results through whatever tool you're most comfortable using.

Daily Life

Many people set aside time each day for regular meditation or prayer. You can easily incorporate a divination tool into such a routine, at whatever time of day you feel most receptive and open to guidance. (If you read your daily horoscope or faithfully follow the weather forecasts, you're already doing something like this!)

A daily reading can be a very calming exercise, helping you prepare for the day ahead or make sense of your recent experiences. A review of your biorhythm cycle, for example, can give you perspective on your daily moods or physical health. A glance at the astrological influences of the day, such as what sign the moon appears in, or whether a planet is in retrograde, or seemingly backward, motion will point out the push and pull of planetary influences in your everyday life. A simple three-card Tarot or rune spread can reveal an issue that needs attention, or advise you on how you might react to an ongoing problem. Use of divination tools such as these on a daily basis can become a reflexive habit and a way to set sail with confidence to meet the challenges and joys of your day.

Angel Cards: Spread for the Day

For this exercise, you'll use a deck of angel cards. Typically, angel decks contain a single word and a charmingly simple illustration on each card showing an angel in a related action. Create your own angel deck. Or there are also many wonderful and inventive angel card decks available at metaphysical stores that may resonate for you to explore.

Place the angel cards into a bowl or bag. Relax yourself, take a few deep breaths, and get centered. Quiet your mind and ask either out loud or in your thoughts, "Angels, what is it I need to know for today?"

Without looking at the cards, reach into their bowl or bag and select the card or cards that "feel" right to you. You may reach for just one and find that more than one emerges, as if stuck together. You may find that in addition to the card in your hand, another card "falls out" of the bowl as well. Or you may go among the cards two or three times until you feel you are done.

The first card that you select is your *power card*. Any subsequent cards will support, build on, and enhance this main message. Take a moment to reflect on the power card's message or messages. How does it resonate with you, validate you, or draw you into action? Now look at the other cards you selected (or that selected themselves!), and reflect on their messages in turn. You may want to jot down some notes in the following boxes as part of your reflection.

Power card: _____

Illustration: _____

My interpretation: _____

_____

Second card: _____

Illustration: _____

My interpretation: _____

_____

Third card: _____

Illustration: _____

My interpretation: _____

_____

Fourth card: _____

Illustration: _____

My interpretation: _____

_____

You can "ask the angels" for divination help whenever the spirit moves you. Because the cards are so simple, light, happy, positive, and supportive, they're appropriate for any time of day and any situation. Their inspired cartoons leave room for the nuances of individual interpretation, yet they are also completely universal.

Here's an angel spread that Laura did for herself one wintry morning.

Power card: *Adventure*

Illustration: *An angel walking with a staff and a large, fully equipped backpack.*

Laura's interpretation: *Considering a foot of snow had just fallen, I smile at this. Considering I'm in the second month of a home renovation, and "packed up" because of it, I smile again. I can use this card to reframe the appearance of chaos in my life into a concept of "adventure." Further, because I see my "soul work" as one big adventure and had just been repeating this idea to some friends, my smile widens. I'm also in the adventurous process of writing my first book! I make a note to see whatever else comes up today—yet another adventure.*

Second card: *Power*

Illustration: *Angel with outstretched arms, wearing a crown and regal robes, holding a scepter in one hand and a cross in the other.*

Laura's interpretation: *I smile again. Without seeing my adventure(s) for what it is, I am unempowered, feeling instead victimized, overwhelmed, and put upon. With power, I see instead opportunity, and I can keep my "trials" in perspective. Power says to me, "Steady on course!" I must know in my heart how much power there is in the adventure.*

Third card: *Simplicity*

Illustration: *A simple angel, with hands clasped in prayer.*

Laura's interpretation: *Keep it simple. Don't get tangled up in emotion or energy.*

Fourth card: *Healing*

Illustration: *One angel bandages another, smaller angel. She is adjusting the smaller angel's head bandage for her, because she has her arm in a sling.*

Laura's interpretation: *Among the various adventures in my life at present, an undercurrent of healing runs through them all. I know that one of the benefits of adventures is that they can inspire healing. I also take this card as a reminder to be kind to myself and to take care of my health through it all.*

Surprise! When Laura moved the bowl off to the side, there underneath it lay another card.

Surprise card: *Purpose*

Illustration: *An angel uses a pickax to make her way up a mountain. There are several mountains in the background, and the sun is shining brightly.*

Laura's interpretation: *Because this card serendipitously found itself underneath the bowl of cards, I take this as a big reminder to keep myself conscious of the purpose behind everything. Despite appearances, everything in my life is working for good, and there are reasons behind everything that happens, beyond what I can consciously know. I will keep climbing; I will stick to my purpose and to the work at hand. I will honor the special synergy this surprise card represents.*

For an interesting variation on this exercise, you can substitute Tarot cards for the angel cards and move from a daily reading to a karmic reading. Remove all the Major Arcana, or destiny cards, from the Tarot deck. Shuffle the cards, cut the deck into four piles and turn the top card of each pile. Study the images closely to divine insights into the larger karmic forces that influence your soul work.

Career and Prosperity Goals

Of course you might wish to consult your favorite divination tool on issues of jobs and finance. In fact, one of the most popular questions any professional in the intuitive arts encounters is "How can I win the lottery?" But all too few people ask the more important question: "If I did win the lottery, would it help or hinder me in my life's journey?" We already know that there are some powerful Universal Laws at work governing what can be seen and what cannot. So if divining the future *could* help you win the lottery, would you use it to take a permanent detour from your life work? Let's be honest, most of us probably would. We know one hard-working book producer who would head straight for Mexico's sunny beaches in a heartbeat and never look back! What would happen to all those books that need to manifest? And that's exactly why there are some things that you just aren't supposed to know. So for most of us, those lottery numbers remain obscured from view. Remember, *you will only see what you are meant to know right now*.

When it comes to divining the future, it's also possible that you won't always get a straight answer. After all, the God of your understanding has limitless ways of communicating and assisting you. Sometimes the answers to our most complicated questions seem too simple and easy to be "true." This is why it's important to practice, get comfortable, and learn what divining tools are best suited to you. You can decide to use more than one tool to ask the same question and see what comes up. Look for patterns in the answers, and see what resonates with you.

If you don't understand the information that your tool is trying to reveal to you, remember to use your journal and record everything regardless. Journaling is an important component for tracking your tool's data, your initial interpretations, and even your follow-up notes and later insights. You could also try asking the question in another way! Sometimes a simple rephrasing can "loosen up" further information and understanding.

For some people, divining tools are best used as guides to their own inner thoughts, showing the way to the answer that already lies within the heart. For example, if you're having trouble with a particular co-worker, and you want to ease the relationship, you might pick up your favorite tool and ask, "What do I need to know so I can deal with this person more effectively?" The answer may give you a peek at the energies at work around your colleague, or it might give you some insight into conflicts within yourself that are impacting the relationship with the other person. Whatever the result, just focusing your intuitive power on the problem can have a powerful impact on resolving it.

Relationships

Another question professional intuitive arts practitioners often hear is "Will I find my soul mate?"

Ah, love. Everybody wants it. But why does romance seem to fall into one person's lap, while another can search and search and never find "the one?"

Well, it could be in the way you frame the question. The concept of a single "soul mate"—that there's one other person in the world with whom each of us is "meant to be"—simply defies logic. With so many billions of people on this Earth, what are the chances that anyone would *ever* run into their one perfect match?

No, the romantic reality isn't quite a fairytale. In actuality, there are many, many people out there with whom you are compatible in terms of personality, values, and interests. Meeting those people isn't really the problem. *Making a romance work*—now, that's a problem.

Here's where the intuitive arts can really help. A question like "What do I need to know to make a relationship with this person better?" can open up worlds of understanding. And an openness to intuition can give you tremendous insight into the issues within you that might be getting in the way of true love. The more tuned in you are to the energies of others, the better you can choose and deepen your relationships, your friendships, and your family life. When it comes to romance, remember that no one needs another person to be "complete." Look for a partner who is a good complement to you, and learn to be whole all on your own.

Divine Inspiration

The Universe is a vast place, and soul mates come in all shapes and sizes ... and not just the shape of a particular romantic partner. A soul mate can be found in that unbreakable bond with a sibling, the childhood playmate who remains a loyal friend for life, the elderly aunt who has a special connection with you, the co-worker you just met but feel as if you've known forever. Is your search for one romantic soul mate drawing your attention away from the soul mates already in your life?

Try this if you are having a discord with another person—not necessarily a romantic partner—and need some assistance seeing the situation from a different perspective.

Get your journal out, or use the following space provided, and be prepared to write. Ground yourself using one of the exercises from Chapter 4. Now, with your eyes closed, begin by asking the question, aloud or silently: "What is it I need to know about [name]?"

Keep your eyes closed as you relax further, taking nice deep breaths. When you feel ready, open your eyes and begin to write down the first things that pop into your head, or the messages you "hear." Remember to remain detached from your emotions and stay in the state of neutrality as you write.

_____

_____

Ask another question, aloud or silently: "Is there something that I can do to help [him or her]?"

_____

_____

And a final question: "What is it that I need to do?"

_____

_____

When you are finished, give thanks to the Source of your understanding for whatever information you have received. Now take a few more deep breaths and reread what you have written. Reflect on the words, ideas, or concepts you have recorded. Has a solution suggested itself?

Health and Wellness

If you're plagued by health problems, major or minor, or if you're interested in leading a healthier life, several intuitive tools might be especially helpful. An aura reading could call your attention to areas of discomfort or disease that you could then soothe with meditation or visualization. Bodywork techniques, such as reiki, can redirect your inner energy flow in more positive directions. These kinds of tools will require the help of a certified or licensed professional.

> **Take Heed**
>
> Divination tools can be very helpful in supporting you through a health crisis, or in avoiding one altogether. But always remember to use the tools *in conjunction with* proper testing and medical treatment, not as a replacement for them!

Yoga is a technique you can learn on your own, and it has both physical and psychic benefits. We'll explore yoga in more depth later in this book, especially in Chapter 12, along with Louise Hay's ideas on health, manifesting, and affirming. Hay believes that our own negative thought patterns can erupt into what we know as illness. If you change your thoughts, through affirmations and visualization, you can eliminate your symptoms. Your mind is so powerful, and the body-mind connection so intimate, that the results can be amazing.

Here's one yoga pose that you can try right now. Stand in yoga's mountain pose, lifting your heart while dropping your shoulders and reaching down through your fingertips. Breathe fully and deeply from your abdomen. As you breathe, repeat in your mind as a mantra this affirmation from Vietnamese Buddhist monk Thich Nhat Hanh: *Breathing in I calm my body. Breathing out I smile.* When you are ready bring your palms together into prayer.

Yoga's prayerful mountain pose calms and centers the body, grounding one's mind, body, and soul with a mountain's majesty and power.

Divining tools can reveal any conflicts and hidden patterns within you that may be impacting your physical health. And as always, the better you understand yourself and the energies around you, the better you can heal and grow.

Seeking Knowledge, Finding Answers

As we explored in Chapter 4, it's important to know when you need help from an intuitive arts professional, and when you can just "go it alone." Some people like to consult a professional once a year or so, just to "check in." Others call for help when a situation seems to warrant it, or when an outside point of view would be especially helpful. And then there are those who seem almost addicted to professional readings—as if they can't trust their own intuitive power.

> **CAUTION**
>
> **Take Heed** _____
>
> If you are experiencing unremitting depression or have a problem in your life that you feel unable to cope with or to solve, you should enlist the aid of a therapist or psychological counselor to help you in your quest back to the positive fulfillment of your soul work.

Help from the Pros

If you have naturally curly hair, you know that you can't just go to any stylist and get the haircut you want. And the person your straight-haired friends swear by may not be the right one for you. You may have to endure a few bad hair days before you find a professional who can understand and meet your individual needs. Finding a professional in the intuitive arts is much the same. No two are alike, and a friend's recommendation may or may not be helpful in your case. It's okay if the first professional you consult—or the second or the fifth, if need be—just doesn't feel like the right match for you. Be willing to use your own intuition in your search for an intuitive practitioner.

Most important, never give your power away. A professional acting ethically will never make you feel dependent on her or him. Your practitioner should empower you and inspire you to know yourself better. She or he should never attempt to run your life, control your finances, or restrict your contacts with others.

Look Within!

If you learn nothing else as you journey with us through the ideas and tools of divination, we hope you'll come away with a new or renewed trust in yourself and in your own intuitive strengths. You *do* have the ability to tune in to your inner self and to understand and direct your course with divine intent and purpose. You can learn techniques to ground yourself, calm your mind, and listen to all your intuition has to say. And you can use tools to refine those messages and gain greater perspective. Professional practitioners are important, and they can play a part in your journey. But the journey is yours alone.

The Least You Need to Know

- ◆ Each of us has a theme that runs through our life and informs our soul work.
- ◆ Destiny is the end result of our life's journey, but free will is the route we choose to get there.
- ◆ You can use the power of manifesting to accomplish your goals.
- ◆ Whatever divination tool you choose can help you solve problems, make decisions, and validate past choices.
- ◆ The power to direct your life's course lies within you.

Part 2

The Fourth Dimension

Ready for the Big Picture? We're talking *BIG* in this part—as big as the Universe itself. We'll answer the skeptics, test a few divining methods, and even rearrange the furniture feng shui style (and beyond) in our quest to understand the energies that flow through us all and through our surroundings.

Chapter 5

Does Anybody Really Know What Time It Is?

In This Chapter

- Time is only one dimension in a Universe of many
- The finite and the infinite
- Understanding the space-time continuum
- Science, philosophy, and time
- Your future, in time

> There is no difference in the Lord's sight between one day and a thousand years; to him the two are the same. (2 Peter 3:8)

Religious systems of the world's many cultures throughout the centuries—ancient to modern—have recognized an essential truth: Time, which means so much to us in our world and our experience, means another thing entirely to God (or the pantheon of gods and goddesses, or the Universe, depending on what faith is practiced).

Time on my hands, time on my side, or no time to breathe, we've all been up against it. Singers write songs about it, poets wax upon it, athletes chase it, children lament it. We humans are deeply invested in time, perhaps now in the age of technology and multitasking—the Age of Aquarius—more than ever. It's at the very center of our experience of the Universe. Never before have we been so obsessed with the minutia of time … whether we're honking our horns at the drive-thru window or tapping our toes as we wait on our snack in the microwave. Dinners that used to take hours of preparation now take only minutes, but still we complain! Ever sit through a three-minute commercial break? Or better still, find that you can start a meal, load the dishwasher, rotate the laundry, and check on the kids—all in the space of those six commercials? We are literally obsessed with racing the clock and bending time to suit our needs!

Past, Present, Future

It's no wonder that we struggle to understand some of the bigger concepts when it comes to time and divination. If we are conditioned to think that the 2½ minute wait for a mere television program to resume is eternal, then how can we possibly tolerate having to wait 2 months or 20 years in order to "be where we want to be"?

To the Universe, time is, well, nearly irrelevant. Just consider the vast amounts of time that it's taken to create the universe, form planetary bodies, and explore and discover new solar systems. And if you believe that we souls have many opportunities to reincarnate and "get it right," then waiting (and wading) through the minutia of our daily human travails begins to seem quite insignificant indeed. That is, *if you have the luxury of seeing the bigger picture at all times. (And the Universe has a way of always placing the bigger picture ahead of the minutia.)

Linear time, as we understand and experience it, does indeed exist. *But to the Universe, all events occur simultaneously.* The Universe has access to everything—past, present, and future—at once! From the Universe's perspective, there is both evolutionary progress (the present) and an ongoing record of the past (filed in what Edgar Cayce and other renowned seers called the Akashic Records; see Chapter 5), as well as future potential.

One way divination tools and intuitive professionals do their work is to tap into the Universe's perspective, going outside of our idea of Time altogether to access the Higher Truths. For example, there are times in Laura's readings when she must distinguish between past events and future ones in this present lifetime. This is because during a reading she gains the Universe's access to all of them at once, and the events can appear very close together. At times Laura's had to ask clients whether something she's seeing has already happened to them (in which case, it usually turns out to have occurred fairly recently). If not, she knows that it *will* happen and has a form of earthly time reference to the other events she sees. This is also why Laura can define past life events and experiences with such clarity, precision, and detail. Past life events look different to Laura than present life events do.

The concept of the Universe's take on time is something that we, in our linear earthly lives, have difficulty relating to. But isn't that true of life in general? You don't have any real perspective on something while you're living through it. When you're in school, say, it feels like it will be *forever* until graduation day—but when you're donning the cap and gown, all you can think is "Where did the time go?!"

Take Heed _____

Laura has seen many people give up when they were *this close* to making real progress toward their dreams and goals. Earthly time can create quite an illusion. If you feel you want to throw in the towel on your marriage, job, or any major issue in your life, take time to meditate on how you'd feel if you really did walk away. Stretch yourself to look as far as you can in all directions. Use your journal to record your feelings before you make any hasty decisions. Once you've made a fair accounting of all your possible reactions, you'll have what you need to make the right decision.

Changing the Way We Think About Time

One advantage of the Ancient Stardust Directional Cards is that they specifically address the ever-present issue of time and our perceptions of time here on the earth plane (as aspect that many other divination tools do not address). These powerful cards are a channeled invention by our own master teacher and renowned expert in soul work, Laura Scott. All of us have moments when we feel stuck and confused, when it seems that nothing is happening, nothing is moving, and all could be lost. Using the Ancient Stardust Directional Cards can help you see that despite all earthly appearances, things indeed *are* happening, and energy is always at work. The cards are a great tool for measuring unseen progress, allowing you to tap into a higher understanding of the movement of energy all around you. (You'll find more information on the Ancient Stardust Directional Cards in Appendix A.)

The Ancient Stardust Directional Cards are grouped into four basic categories, making it easier to understand the subtleties and nuances of the Universe's energy patterns. There is a category for taking heed, one for taking action, another for rest, and one for release. Each of these categories contains three or four cards that hone in on your personal space. For example, the Take Heed category contains four cards: Caution, Detour, Slow, and Test. Each of these cards defines a different nuance of the energy described by the category. Turn to Appendix A to see representations of each of the cards in the deck. If you are someone who needs to contemplate how time and energy are working with you in your life, these cards are perfect for you.

The Ancient Stardust Directional Cards have four categories: one for rest, one for taking action, one for tak-

ing heed, and one for release, plus two bonus cards.

When Laura's friend, Sally, wanted to know whether she should hire a particular candidate to help with her business, Laura had her use the Ancient Stardust Directional Cards for guidance. Her friend sat quietly for a moment, focusing on her question. Sally then shuffled the cards, spread out all the cards face down in front of her, and selected the one that felt right to her. When she turned it over, she found that she had selected the Caution card. This card invites further reflection. It alerts you that there is more going on than surface appearances suggest, and advises you to take heed. It also indicates a need to reexamine your role, your actions, and the actions of those around you.

Divine Inspiration

You can use the Ancient Stardust Directional Cards to help make specific decisions, as well as for direction and advice on larger or broader questions. They are particularly helpful for times when you feel "stuck," or when it seems that things are working against you.

Sally reflected on the card's message and quickly decided that this potential employee was not the right match for her present needs. As she implemented her decision she felt completely free from worry. Later, she told Laura that the card solidified several misgivings she had been trying to talk herself out of. The Ancient Stardust Directional Cards helped to take the stress and strain out of her decision making and helped her to navigate the situation better. Sally now considers the cards an important companion in her life.

Using the Ancient Stardust Directional Cards

We've outlined for you a step-by-step process for consulting the Ancient Stardust Directional Cards. As always, journaling is an important part of the process, so we've included space to write and some questions to get your reflections started.

1. Sit quietly for a moment, focusing on a specific question that you need guidance on. Remember to breathe deeply and ground yourself with a short prayer. Taking time to do this will strengthen your confidence in the information you are about to receive.

    Write your question here: _____

    _____

2. Shuffle the cards, being careful to keep all the cards facing the same way.

3. Spread the cards out face down in front of you, in a pattern or at random.

4. Place your hands over the cards, just a few inches from them, and allow your hands to "float" above each card in turn. Select the one that feels right or different from the rest, as if it is jumping out at you with an energy force all its own.

5. Turn the card over and read what it says. Notice which of the four categories it is from. Go to Appendix A, find the appropriate card image, and read the paragraphs pertaining to the message the card delivers.

6. Use your journal or the spaces here to record the selection and respond to these questions.

    Category of card chosen: _____

    _____

    Card selected _____

    _____

How does this card relate to your question?_____

_____

How does its message relate to your own intuitive feelings on this subject?

_____

_____

Does the message *conflict* with your own intuitive feelings? How?

_____

_____

Does the message *support* your own intuitive feelings? How? _____

_____

Other reflections? _____

_____

Final thoughts: _____

_____

The Movement of Heavenly Bodies

Time may be an invented way of perceiving the Universe's reality, but it *is* based in observable facts, as we can see in the planets' constant and predictable movements. Astrology teaches us that these movements, along with the movements of the Moon and Sun in relation to the planets and other heavenly bodies, influence us—our personalities, our experiences—and the personalities and experiences of the people all around us.

Let's think for a moment about the finite and the infinite. We hurry about our daily lives on earth obsessing about how little time we have, how much time things take. Speed, details, and precision matter. All the while, the earth is spinning on its axis and revolving around the Sun. The heavenly bodies are always moving, in predictable ways, throughout the cosmos.

Astronomers and astrologers (for centuries of human history, these were nearly one and the same!) have plotted the dates and times for every solar or lunar

Resonances

Sometimes fiction is less strange than truth. The world of *Star Trek,* and many other works in the science-fiction genre, gives us a helpful model of how the Universe operates outside of our standard concept of time. If Trekkies can accept the notions of time travel, warp speed, empaths as crew members, and "beaming up," then why can't the rest of us?

eclipse and predicted accurately the movement of the heavens millennia in advance. If this is true, can astrology tell you what will happen in the future? Astrology can help give you an indication of what is coming up for you, as well as insights into the predictable patterns in your life. Astrology is great for pinpointing those inevitabilities, especially the fixed destination that we call our destiny. But remember, you will always have free will to maneuver.

We'll have an exercise later in this chapter where you can examine your astrological birth chart—the map of the heavens at the precise moment and place of your birth—and begin to interpret the signs and symbols that can help you plot your unique course through life. How you use your birth chart map, to set in motion the chain of events, the path that will take you from this moment to your destiny, is totally your choice. That's where free will—yours and that of others—enters in. It certainly keeps life interesting!

The Continuum of Time

"What's that, ensign? You wore your Starfleet uniform when you time-traveled back to nineteenth-century America?! Oh no! You've disturbed the space-time continuum!"

Yes, it's a beloved device of time-travel scriptwriters: the ol' space-time continuum. If you ever get the chance to go back in time, don't stomp on so much as a prehistoric butterfly—or the human race might never evolve. And, as in the classic time-travel movie *Back to the Future*, you'd better be darn sure never to date your own mother. ("Think, McFly, think!")

But for all its Hollywood hokiness, the space-time continuum is a complex concept integral to the science of physics. We *do* experience time and space as firmly linked concepts. You have an innate sense of the time it would take for you to walk from your home, say, to the nearest street corner; if you took that stroll and glanced at your watch to find that two hours had passed—or, worse, that it was now *earlier* than when you'd started out—you'd be pretty thrown. That's just what makes jet lag so disorienting.

Albert Einstein's famous Theory of Relativity postulates that time does not flow at a uniform speed, and when you throw in the affect of gravity, objects can actually curve *space-time*, elongating or condensing distances. All this, though, can only be detected when a body travels at or near the speed of light. If the "body" traveling is a human being, then the

Future Focus

Space-time is a term physicists use to define the dimensions of time and space in which all physical objects—animate and inanimate—appear.

distorting of time and space would become something the person could see and feel as his or her speed approaches the velocity of light—a short time for our traveler would be perceived as a very long time for Earth-bound loved ones. However, no one to date, at least that we know of, has experienced this phenomenon at light speed!

In our everyday Earth-bound lives, though, we intuitively feel the distorting effects of time and space in all of our journeys, small and large. There is evolution at work as the present morphs into the future, stages of development that must proceed in an orderly way. You can't hit the fast-forward button and make life speed up. That's because, here on the earth plane, between "now" and "the future," you've got to make an infinite number of choices that will propel you from here to there. Those are the optionals, the possibilities, that divination can reveal and guide you through.

Looking Ahead or Just Looking?

When we look into the future with divination tools or via personal readings, we want to know what *will* happen. All of us want to avoid the pratfalls, the heartaches, and the failed business ventures that life can throw us. As you reach for and practice with divination tools, your "percentage" for divining outcomes will get better. Sometimes you can, and will, avoid the chasms in your life. But other times, like it or not, you are meant to experience them just as they are.

Remember, divining the future is not a "pass" card. As we see possibilities, or the potential of future events and developments, keep in mind that free will is at work. Don't forget that our own earthly perspective is limited, and there are infinite options for outcomes beyond the one you might be hoping for.

Resonances
People often make the mistake of thinking that because Laura is a psychic and channel, she will never be tested in her lifetime and can use her gifts to avoid all of life's "trying" events. Not true! Laura must undergo all her own earthly lessons like anyone else … including heartache, failure, and loss. No psychic is exempt from her or his own life work and journey. If that were true, they'd all be timing the stock market brilliantly with perfect relationships and pristine health—and probably the only "work" they'd want to do would be on their tans!

So will those possibilities revealed through a reading or divination exercise *ever* come to be? When a reading reveals that the potential exists for a future development, it will be your free will option to take steps that will allow for the acceptance, or the rejection, of that potential.

You can use Tarot's Past, Present, and Future spread—we'll call it your space-time spread—to help understand the confluence of time in the flow of your life. Tarot imagery is deeply suggestive, frequently drawn from mythology, legend, religion, and dreams. Although individual cards carry a preset or traditional meaning (and most decks come with a book or pamphlet describing them), it's more important to heed the meanings that they carry for you. Use a Tarot deck that resonates for you. If you're an intuitive thinker, Tarot will really play to your natural strengths. If you're a visual learner who remembers more of what you've seen than what you've heard, Tarot imagery is likely to make an impression on you.

After grounding yourself and meditating for a short time, write down your question in your journal or in the following space provided, shuffle the deck, cut it, and deal the cards into the pattern you see illustrated here.

Your space-time question: _____

_____

Meditate on the card's images and what they may have to tell you. Tarot's 22 Major Arcana cards resonate to karmic issues at play in your life, while the Minor Arcana cards represent free will decisions in regard to those larger forces of the Universe!

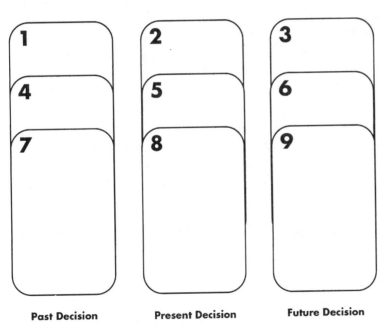

Column 1 shows past influences surrounding your question, column 2 shows present influences, and column 3 shows future influences.

Past Decision   **Present Decision**   **Future Decision**

Divine Inspiration _____

The four Major Arcana suits of the Tarot deck can indicate the potential timing surrounding an event:

Wands   Events occur in days or weeks

Cups   Events occur in weeks or months

Swords   Events occur quickly, within days

Pentacles Events occur slowly, over months or years

Your free will, though, determines when, if, and how the event unfolds in your life's space-time.

Laws of the Universe

In Chapter 3, we talked about the unbreakable rule of the intuitive arts: *If you're meant to know about something, you will know it.* It's just as important, though, for you to remember that there are some things you're *not* meant to know. In other words, it simply isn't always possible to know that, at a certain future moment, a *specific thing will happen.* Why? Not because the Universe likes to surprise us, but because it's part of how we learn! If we knew exactly where we were going, we'd be so focused on our destination that we would miss the journey, in all its wonder (and its annoyances!). And when you get right down to it, the journey is why we're here. We're on this earth, in this lifetime, to learn and to grow, to soak up all we can on our travels. Every experience is something we can, and should, learn from.

Flux and Free Will

The Universe isn't static and unchanging; it's in constant flux, always in progress. We are all, at once, both independent and interdependent. You have free will—and so does everyone else. And that makes change constant!

From Archimedes to Einstein and Carl Sagan

Give me but one firm spot on which to stand, and I will move the earth.

—Archimedes, Greek mathematician

The most beautiful thing we can experience is the mysterious. You live through the darkness from what you learned in the light. All mystical experiences conflict with the "real world." This is their very nature.

—Albert Einstein, physicist

Understanding is joyous.

—Carl Sagan, astronomer and astrophysicist

From ancient to modern times, the quest for understanding moves the Universe. So are empirical knowledge, divination, and faith really so far apart? It's only human: Sometimes we believe in things without really understanding why. We just *know*. Maybe divination tools will help you find your resonance and go with your gut, no matter what the world tells you. You may find that one day, science will back you up!

Ancient Astrology

Ancient sky-watchers didn't have powerful telescopes or blazingly fast computers, but that didn't stop them from creating some incredibly accurate and wonderfully elegant systems for understanding the movements of heavenly bodies. The Mayan calendar is still more precise than ours, and neolithic stone circles around the world light up during the solstices to this day.

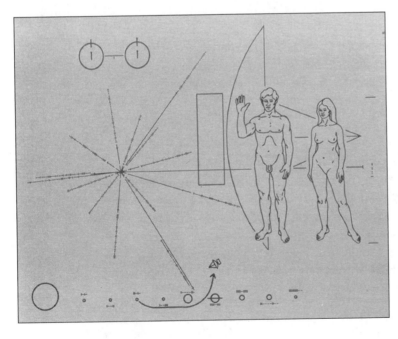

Carl Sagan and colleague Francis Drake look to humankind's future in this plaque prepared by Linda Salzman Sagan and sent into space on Pioneer 10 and 11 satellites. These images are meant to help intelligent extraterrestrial beings to plot a course to planet Earth.

Astrologers today have adopted the most modern technologies, allowing them to create detailed, personalized *birth charts* in minutes. (Of course, interpreting and analyzing a chart takes considerably longer.) You can have your birth chart done for a nominal fee at many metaphysical bookstores, or you can check your local phone book or the Internet for websites that generate birth charts and licensed astrologers who can assist you in interpreting their meanings.

When you're ready to order your chart, be sure to have the following information:

- Your date of birth (yes, including the year—this is no time for vanity!)

- Your place of birth, both city and state or country

- Your time of birth, as exact as possible

Future Focus

Your astrological **birth chart** is a literal map of the heavens at the precise moment and place of your birth. You are a living metaphor for the Universe!

All these factors are critical to the calculations necessary for an accurate chart, and you might have to do some sleuthing to find them. Time of birth can be especially tricky. In the past, this fact was not required on many birth certificates, so many of us don't have an official time to go by. Be ready to ask family members or seek out childhood memorabilia to get at least a general idea. (Co-author Mary Kay is grateful that her very precise father took charge of her birth announcements. There was her time of birth right next to "Weight" and "Length," on a stork-shape card pasted into her battered old baby book!) But don't despair if your information isn't perfect. Some astrologers can "work backward" to pinpoint a time of birth according to events that have happened in your life. Just remember that the better your facts, the more accurate your chart.

To see what an astrological birth chart looks like, we've included one here for someone we feel is very connected to Universal energy—humanitarian and peace advocate Mahatma Gandhi. Looking at Gandhi's birth date, October 2, we see he is a Libra, the zodiac sign of balance. In interpreting a birth chart, astrologers look at where the planets appear in the astrological signs and houses at the precise moment and place of your birth. The symbols you see on the outside of the birth chart are the signs. The 12 slices you see are the astrological houses. The symbols within the slices are the planets, along with their degrees of placement within each house. The lines and symbols you see in the center of the chart indicate the *aspects* or relationships that planets make to each other in the chart.

There are many astrological books that give detailed information on how to interpret birth charts. We recommend *The Complete Idiot's Guide to Astrology, Third Edition*, by Madeline Gerwick-Brodeur and Lisa Lenard. We'll return to Gandhi and his birth chart in Chapter 22, but for now, we want you simply to look at this astrological map of Gandhi's personal moment and place of manifestation on the earth plane. Before doing any research to identify what each symbol and its placement means, meditate on what this map of Gandhi says to you, and record your impressions in your journal.

Once you have your own birth chart in hand, do the same meditation. How does the chart look to you? Are symbols clustered together or spread out? Are some houses full or empty? How much activity do you see in the center of the chart? Before you begin research to unlock the meanings of the symbols in your birth chart, record these early responses you have to the image of your astrological birth chart map. Later, when you've learned more about astrology, you can return to these comments and see how revealing they are on an intuitive level.

Mohandas Gandhi

Natal Chart
Oct 2 1869 NS
7:11 am LMT -4:38:24
Porbandar INDIA
21°N38' 069°E36'

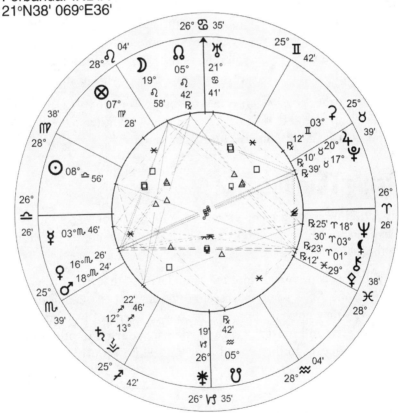

The birth chart of humanitarian and peace advocate Mahatma Gandhi.

Modern Physics

Relativity. Fractals. Quantum mechanics. The deeper our scientific understanding goes, the more the Universe seems to expand. Is there any limit? Or is the Universe's infinity only a matter of our own ability to grasp it? Big questions—too big for most of us to even want to ponder. But maybe we can get an idea of the Universe's outline if we consider something many of us have come to use regularly, if not every day: the Internet.

E-mail, instant messages, websites, home pages … is there any end? Even if you *could* count up all of the Internet's components, all you'd have to do is post a message announcing the number—and you'll have added one more to the total.

Do you have to know every site, message, and URL to use the Internet? Of course not. You just have to tap into it at one point to gain access to the whole. Because, in theory (and as long as you can devise a server powerful enough), you can always add *just one more*; the Internet is, for all intents and purposes, infinite. It offers us unlimited access to information. What we do with that knowledge and power is up to us.

The Universe is the same way. It is beyond huge. But you can access its energies, even if you can't comprehend the whole. You can even tap into its power with the force of your own free will. What you do with it is up to *you*.

Just Passing Through

So consider: How active are you in your own life? Do you make things happen, or do things happen *to* you? Are you fully here in this present moment? Or are you just passing through?

With any luck, you are now beginning to understand that it's a little of all that wrapped into one. Sure, some folks seem to be content just taking things as they come. But they may not have the same lessons to learn in this lifetime as you do. So remember to relax and resist the urge to compare yourself to others as you explore what divination means to the time of your life and how it can improve your experiences day by day.

The Least You Need to Know

- We humans see time as linear. The Universe sees time as multidimensional.

- Even some of the most renowned scientists of our time acknowledge the simultaneous existence of a mystical force.

- Your journey can't be compared to anyone else's!

Chapter 6

Everything Is Energy

In This Chapter

◆ You are made of energy

◆ Your actions affect the Universe's energy field

◆ How colors and objects reflect and affect your energies

◆ Chakras and your personal energy field

◆ Integrating Eastern and Western medical ideas for better health and greater well-being

The crackle of static electricity. The little "spark" you feel when you touch a light switch or another person. The flyaway hair just after you've brushed it. Your own personal energy is a physical phenomenon you can experience on any given day.

This chapter is all about the energy that forms us, binds us, unites us, and affects us. Everything and everyone is energy, and the better we understand that, the better we can use it to know ourselves and divine the future!

From the Big Bang to Feng Shui: How Energy Shapes Our Environment

Our Universe was born in a burst of energy. NASA cosmologists have used data from a robotic probe looking deep in space to calculate the birth of the Universe: about 13.7 billion years ago. We call that birth pang the Big Bang, and although we don't know everything about it (or exactly what caused it in the first place), some of humanity's most brilliant thinkers are constantly measuring, theorizing, and observing in an attempt to understand it better.

The Big Bang was an explosion so powerful that today, an almost unimaginable number of years later, its force is still expanding. It was so powerful that its energy imbues all of us and all that has ever existed. Not to get too cosmic here (although we can hardly help it!), everything from the table and chair beside you, to the building around you, to your body itself is made of atoms, the stuff of the Big Bang. Every atom has its own positive or negative charge. And all those component charges together create an energy all their own. Everything that we can see or feel or sense is energy.

The same is true for every thought you form, every intuition, and every emotion. They, too, have positive or negative charges. Your mind, your soul, and your body all combine to create an energy that is uniquely yours. Because we are made of energy—and all around us is energy, too—there are ways you can improve the quality of your life by manipulating the objects around you and the energy flow within you. You can affect the overall *feel* of things if you know how to work with their energies.

Those of us schooled in a Western worldview are only just beginning to understand this idea. But in Eastern philosophy, it's been known for thousands of years. In Chinese, the concept is called *feng shui* (pronounced *fung shway*).

Future Focus

Feng shui is the Eastern art of placement. In feng shui, it's thought that energy flows in a physical environment the same way it flows through the body. Anything that impedes the energy flow throws off the feeling of a room, building, or garden (and can even have a negative impact on it). Feng shui practitioners work to encourage positive energy flow through design and decoration.

The basis of feng shui rests on a simple principle: that the exterior both reflects and influences the interior. From that has grown a complex system of placement that, many believe, will allow positive energy to flow throughout any environment.

To improve feng shui, professionals combine the intuitive arts with architecture, interior design, and landscaping to create spaces that people can operate in more peacefully and productively. Their spaces work, practitioners say, because energy flows through them in ways that strengthen the positive influences and banish the negative ones. Many Asian businesses and families consult a feng shui professional whenever they buy or build a new home or office—the same way Westerners would call in a building inspector or an architect.

Resonances

You don't have to remodel or redecorate to influence the energy flow in your personal spaces. Sometimes, a small change will make a big difference. For example, Mary Kay had set up her laptop in what she thought would be a cozy corner to work on this book. But she soon found her ideas dead-ending, and writing feeling like a chore, every time she booted up. When she looked at her workspace through the prism of feng shui, the problem was instantly clear: She'd literally boxed herself into a corner! All she had to do was pick up her laptop, move to a more open space, and voilà— creativity began to flow again.

Of course, energy continues to flow in all spaces, whether or not the principles of feng shui have been applied there. See if you can become more aware of energy in the environments you encounter every day. Gauge how a space makes you feel. Are you at ease there, or on edge? Take note of the colors and textures around you; notice how the furniture is arranged, especially in relation to any doors or windows. Can you see paths where energy can flow freely, or blockages where energy will be stopped? Are there soothing background noises, like flowing water or stirring leaves?

Design isn't everything, though. Even a well-organized space can feel wrong to you because of energy influences under the surface. For example, some people hate to go shopping because of the jangled feeling they get after just a few minutes in the mall— "mall buzz," you might call it. The behind-the-scenes energies in a large enclosed space like a mall are just too much for some of us: the sound systems, the electrical wires, the colors, the smells, the *people*—all that energy combined makes some people very uncomfortable. (No matter how many water fountains the designers put in .... Have you noticed that every mall has a fountain? And more often than not, the fountain's energy in this environment becomes confused, noisy, and, well, splashy instead of a calming, centering flow.)

That very same boxed-up mall energy gives other people a positive mall buzz, making them feel excited and happy. What is sensory overload to one person is exhilarating fun to another. Either way, it's the energy flow that leads to the feeling.

On the Move: A Placement Exercise

Feng shui can have a dynamic effect on the intuitive feel of an environment. But before we get into the basic principles of feng shui, try this exercise to experience the effect of changing the energy in your environment. When you've completed the exercise, we'll give you another one that uses feng shui to look at your space. We'll see how closely your untrained intuitive radar in this exercise hones in naturally on areas of your life where you want to influence your future for the better.

1. Choose a room that you can rearrange without inconvenience to others. Home or office, any space will do.

2. Move as much of the furniture as you can into a completely new arrangement. Move decorative objects, as well, including pictures, plants, and mirrors.

3. Live with your new room for a day or two. Then take a few minutes to ground yourself and use your intuition to explore the space. How does energy move here? What is the room's metaphysical texture? Does it flow easily, or do you bump into that end table? Move your eyes around the room and see where it gets "stuck." Record your thoughts. _____

   _____

4. Now move everything back the way it was (pictures, plants, and mirrors, too!).

5. Live with the old arrangement for a day or two, then revisit it with your intuition. Ground yourself and experience the space anew. Does energy move differently now? Does the room feel more or less comfortable to you? Do your "old" items suddenly have a new life? Are you able to see that painting for the first time in months? Can you pinpoint the differences? Record your thoughts.

   _____

   _____

6. Give thanks for all your insights, and compare your writings. How did placement affect your feelings in the room? How many things seemed new after simply shifting their placement?

Using Baguas

Okay, now let's apply feng shui to your room or house's energy. We've created this map using feng shui's energy centers, or *baguas*. According to feng shui, each room or house contains nine areas, or *guas*, where a particular kind of energy dwells. Each gua is related to the energy of a unique set of life experiences. To influence your life experiences and bring them into a new balance, you need to focus on the gua that shapes the flow of the particular energy surrounding your situation. Each bagua has its own color energy as well.

Bagua	Color
Reputation and fame	Red
Love and partnership	Rose
Fertility, creativity, and children	White
Travel, and generosity and help from other people	Silver
Life work, career, and life path	Black
Knowledge, learning, and wisdom	Blue
Family and grounding relationships	Green
Abundance and prosperity	Purple
Health	Yellow

To look at the feng shui energy your room or house is manifesting as a whole, simply take the energy map we've created in the following diagram and stand in the main doorway, facing inward. Use our energy center map as an overlay on your room or house and examine each gua. Are there windows and open spaces? Blocked-off or neglected corners? Clutter? Objects you use frequently or unused objects? Hard, glossy surfaces? Soft pillows? Mirrors that reflect the energy back into the room?

Future Focus

A **bagua** is a feng shui map of your room or house that helps you focus on the energies of your life as they relate to the space you live in. The bagua delineates nine **guas,** or energy centers located in specific areas of your room or house, that relate to specific life situations.

Next, you can begin to look at the areas of life you want to know about and improve. How do those guas appear in your room or house? Do these areas truly reflect your inner hopes and intentions? What can you do with this space to open and release the positive energy that will help you to manifest changes in your life? For example, if you are looking for a new career, you might decide to move your home office out of the spare room upstairs located in the gua of fertility and children and move it to the life work gua or the fame gua, if that is what you are wishing for! Begin to see how you can put your personal space in tune with the energy guas. How closely does your space—the way you have it right now—*really* reflect what you want for your future?

To tune into the energy guas, you can perform a simple meditation exercise to feel the energy of that particular space and intuit within yourself whether the flow of manifesting potential is moving freely and powerfully, flowing sure and steady, trickling, meandering unfocused, or just plain blocked. Place a scarf or piece of cloth in the color of the gua energy as close to the center of the gua space as you can get, and stand in yoga's mountain pose or sit comfortably in a meditation pose on the color surface. Close your eyes and breathe deeply, harnessing the energy with this spoken affirmation: *I am one with the flow of energy in and through the space of my life.* As you breathe in, feel the quality and movement of the energy enter around and through you as you become one with the space. In this way, you will reach an inner seeing that will help you—perhaps more than your visual assessment can—make changes that *feel* right and move your energy with a new and profoundly beneficial pattern, flow, and direction toward the future you want to live in.

Divine Inspiration

In Western houses, it's common to open up the front door and be greeted by a staircase. Feng shui experts advise against this because, in energetic terms, energy will literally run down the stairs of such a house and out the front door. But don't despair! For just a few dollars you could hang a lovely mirror in the entryway to deflect the energy back inside your home. That's a whole lot cheaper than moving an entire staircase!

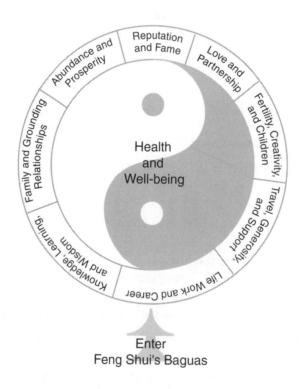

Enter
Feng Shui's Baguas

The Universal Energy Field

When you add up all the energy generated by you and by me and by all the people, creatures, and things in the Universe, you've got a pretty awesome whole. That's the universal energy field, which links all of us into a tremendous, interdependent system. Remember "the Force" in the *Star Wars* movies? Once again, science fiction hits close to the mark. Philosopher Immanuel Kant called this force the human collective unconscious. Because all of us help to create the universal energy field, each of us can affect it, tap into it, and draw upon it for strength and deeper understanding.

It may seem beyond belief that any one of us, in all the vastness of the Universe, can make much of a difference. But remember that you are an integral part of the great energy system, no less important than any other. One single snowflake is unique in all the world. It has its own energy charge, but all alone it won't make much of an impression on the landscape. But billions of snowflakes—now you're talking blizzard! The more unified our energies become, the more powerful we all can be.

Buddhist practitioners believe that humanity must work for the benefit of all sentient beings, that is, all beings that live. In the Buddhist spirit, practice support for the universal energy field by repeating this affirmation upon rising in the morning or as a prayer before bed: *Today, I wish joy for all sentient beings and harmony in the Universe.*

The Fabric of Existence

Our knit-together energy lays down something like an equal playing field on which we can all act. It's the basis to the world we know, the fabric of our existence. And if we all are made of energy, and our energy combines to create a universal energy field, all of us are part of it. We all help create it; we all have an equal capacity for tapping into it.

In the world of physical energy, we know that an object in motion tends to remain in motion, but an object at rest tends to remain at rest. (That's inertia, or the second law of thermodynamics, if you've forgotten your Newtonian physics.) Metaphysical energy is the same way. If the space around you is in chaos, your thoughts and feelings will be affected by that confusion; you're likely to feel chaotic inside, no matter how peaceful you try to make your thoughts. It's not enough to have your consciousness in order if you'd like a more peaceful life. Your actions and your environment have to be in harmony, too, as you learned by looking at your living space through the lens of feng shui.

All Is One and One Is All

Individual components of the universal energy field hold their own energy—energy that you can pick up on, whose texture you can actually *feel*. When you perceive the distinctive energy of a person or an object, you're usually responding in your own way to its metaphysical texture. Your intuition is tapping the universal energy field to glean this information.

We've talked about telekinesis, the power to intuit facts about an object just by touching it. Telekinetic experiences like these happen when you sense the object's energy. Have you ever gone furniture shopping and tested out a few different chairs? The one you bought probably just felt right to you. In part, you were responding to the chair's own energy as you made your choice.

In some cases, though, you can see the physical effects of an object's energetic presence—just as you can see the effects of static electricity, such as flyaway hair or sparks in the dark. In a manufactured object, the energies of its physical materials and the people who worked on it combine to give the product its own distinct energy. Some cars, for example, seem to collect negative energy throughout Their production process. When they roll off the manufacturing line, *nothing* works right: their batteries die, their belts snap, their engines stall. "It's a lemon," we say, and there are consumer laws on the books to protect us if we should buy one. That's because manufacturers and lawmakers know that you can't ever fix a car like that. (But now *you* know why!)

Again, all these energetic influences work under the surface or behind the scenes. Because we're all bound together, our energies work on one another in myriad ways.

You can experiment with this concept by exploring your own telekinetic abilities. Begin by touching or holding objects in your home that belong to you or to someone close to you. Close your eyes, ground yourself, and begin to feel the energy of that object. What images, sounds, feelings, and messages are evoked? Then, turn to the outside world. See if you can pick up the energy of places or objects you visit regularly or are intrigued by. Or ask a friend to let you hold an object important to him or her, or something that was inherited or owned by a deceased relative to see what energy rises there and whether you can identify correctly the meaning or history the energy of the object holds within it.

The Personal Energy Field

Of course, a human being is much more complex than a manufactured object. That means your own personal energy is much more flexible and changeable, shifting with your thoughts, emotions, and actions. It's something that you're always adjusting, either consciously or not, in response to your inner landscape and your outer surroundings.

Remember that you are made of atoms, the stuff of the stars. (It's one of the reasons why Laura's website and divination cards are named "Ancient Stardust"!) Each atom has its very own charge—and each atom is always in communication with the atoms around it. Every part of your body is humming with energy: energy that you can redirect, change, *use!* How? By adjusting your environment, changing your thought patterns, opening your intuition.

The following exercises are designed to help you get in touch with the energies at work within and around you.

Favorite Shirt: A Color Exercise

Color affects us in all kinds of ways. According to feng shui, areas in our personal space correspond to the energy of different colors. But we all have colors we are drawn to or repelled by. Often, the colors of the clothes we choose each morning reflect both our inner energies and the energies that can be seen in our outer auras. We may not realize how much those colors will impact our feelings all during the day.

1. Choose two shirts of similar styles (two sweatshirts or two T-shirts, for example) but of different colors—the more different, the better. Have a pen or pencil handy.

2. Put on one shirt and set the other aside.

3. Sit comfortably and ground yourself as you would for any meditation, with a few deep breaths and a quieting of the mind.

4. Use your intuition to focus on your feelings and emotions *right now*. Write whatever comes to you at this time. _____

_____

5. When you feel ready, stop writing and give thanks for the insights you have gained.

6. Now, change shirts and go through steps 3 and 4 again, re-grounding and re-focusing on your feelings *at this moment*. Write whatever comes to you at this time. _____

_____

7. Stop writing when you feel ready and again give thanks.

8. Compare what you've written. Did you notice any differences? How did the colors affect your mood or your energies?

Foundations: Your Chakras

As we've seen, your thoughts and your physical body both have energies all their own. Your body, as a physical entity, derives its energy in part from the atoms that comprise it. But your body also has energy centers that are constantly at work. We call these energy centers *chakras*.

Chakras can be envisioned as nerve centers, on a purely physical level. But metaphysically they're much more. They're the spinning cyclones where our energies live.

On a physical level, your chakras are energy conduits that correspond to nerve centers.

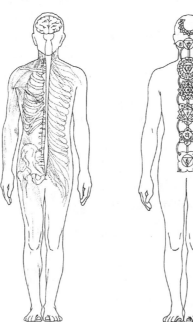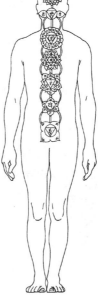

There are seven primary chakras in the human body. They run through our very core, along the spinal column. Each of the primary chakras carries its own associations—with body parts, numbers, colors, planets, and more. (In this way, we can connect astrology, numerology, and other divination systems with the body's energies. See Appendix C for more information.) For now, though, we're going to focus on the physical nature of the chakras and their spiritual effects.

- The base or root chakra is at the very base of your spine, between it and your pelvic bone. This is where your power and your sexual energies live. Maintaining and creating physical life is the base chakra's mission.

- The second chakra is centered behind your internal reproductive organs. Emotions are processed here. Your passions and your sexuality emerge from your second chakra.

- The third chakra is just behind your navel. This is the realm of the intellect, where thoughts, opinions, and judgments are generated. (And you thought it was all in your head!) Your sense of self and your conscious choices are ruled by the third chakra.

- Located behind the heart in the center of your chest, the fourth or heart chakra rules our dream life. It is our bridge between the physical and the spiritual.

- The throat chakra, fifth in the progression, rules our powers of speech and self-expression. We derive philosophical concepts like justice, truth, and perfection from the throat chakra, which is the spiritual mirror of the physical body.

- The sixth chakra is often called the "third eye." Located right between your eyebrows, it is the center of clear perception, that which allows us to "see the light." This is the source of your intuition.

- The crown chakra, the seventh, is at the very top of your skull. This is where your spiritual life resides, the center of enlightenment.

We'll be talking more about the chakras, their associations, and using them to divine messages about your body's energy flow in future chapters. For now, just remember that your personal energy—your life force—is generated mainly by these seven wheels of light within you.

Your True Colors: Your Aura

You have other chakras, too—thousands of them, located all through your physical body. All these secondary chakras generate their own energy. Eastern medical techniques such as acupuncture work mainly with the secondary chakras. And these secondary chakras have another important function: They generate your *aura*.

Future Focus

Your **aura** is your external personal energy field that both protects you and reflects you. It is the last layer of outer energy that surrounds your body. All living beings have an aura, including plants, animals, and humans.

When we talked about furniture shopping, we said that the chair you buy is the one that just feels right to you. In that case, you're responding to the energy of the chair.

In the same way, you can get a feel for people—whether they're friendly or threatening, peaceful or agitated. What you're feeling is the other person's aura, the energy that his or her body generates. The aura surrounds a person's entire body. You can sense it when someone is physically present, and sometimes even when he or she is elsewhere. But it is there to be felt with your intuition.

When people talk about auras, they usually refer to them as having color. Indeed, many of those with a good intuitive sense of auras can even associate emotions and health issues with particular aura colors. But color is not the only way that auras are sensed. You might perceive aura as a shape, a texture, or a brightness. We don't want to limit your exploration of auras by imposing meanings on specific colors or qualities. By concentrating on seeing and feeling auras, you will learn to reach associations that are meaningful to the issues surrounding the places or people whose auras you want to experience.

The seven primary chakras and myriad secondary chakras throughout your body generate the energy that creates your aura.

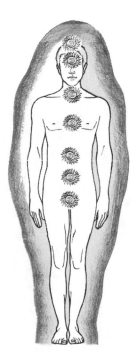

Your aura and the auras of those around you are always changing as energies ebb and flow during the course of each day. That's why intuitive professionals can use auras to understand, or "read," their clients. It's also how you can tell when your partner or friend is not feeling well or has had a bad day, before either of you has said a word.

As a shortcut in the pursuit of your exploration of auras, you may want to consult an intuitive professional to "get your aura energy and colors done." What does this practitioner see? And how does their vision of your aura resonate for you? The information you get will help you to develop a better understanding of your own power colors and how to use them in your wardrobe and physical environment to enhance the quality of your aura and your life.

When Laura's aunt had her colors done, she went from looking and feeling tired and drawn to looking youthfully energized in a matter of a few moments. When you understand the impact that color has on your inner psyche and outer aura, you'll find that people will often respond to you in a new and more positive way. They may not know it, but what they are really reacting to is how your selection of colors either enhances or drains the energy field that's always around you.

Inner Vision: Your Intuition

If everything is energy, intuition is a Geiger counter. It's the way to gain awareness of your own energies and the energies all around you.

Intuition doesn't have to be a massive blast of lightning. It can be as subtle as a single atom of energy coming through. But whether it's a whisper or a scream, after you've become attuned to your intuition, there's no denying its force.

Life Force, Eastern View

Eastern philosophy has, for thousands of years, acknowledged and embraced the notion that the Universe's energies flow around and through us all. Yogis, Indian spiritual masters, have long used yoga to support the primary chakras. Chinese doctors work with the body's *chi*, or life force, to support the health of the whole person, not merely to treat specific symptoms. They use various techniques to manipulate the body's energies into a state of wellness.

Chinese medical professionals often use aura readings and other intuitive methods to help in diagnosis and treatment. And it certainly does seem that the Eastern medical philosophies are very successful, in terms of the longevity, health, and general wellness of those who use it.

> **CAUTION**   **Take Heed**
>
> In Chinese medicine, the principle of "perverse chi" holds that illness enters the body through the neck chakra, in the area between the ears and the shoulders. Next time you feel a cold coming on, wrap a scarf around your neck to protect the fifth chakra and help ward off the perverse chi that leads to chills and sickness. Feel better?

Chi and Prana

As we've said, chi is energy, the life force. To a Chinese medical practitioner, checking the chi is as basic as checking the pulse.

Prana is a Sanskrit word for the movement of chi, the life force, through you. Prana is the energy that gives life to all living things. Some call it the soul of the Universe. Your prana is a rhythm that moves through your body. If it's in tune with the rest of creation, you'll feel united, whole, healthy, and well. If your rhythm is out of step, though, you'll feel uncomfortable, even sick. The goal of Chinese medicine and other Eastern healing methods is to get the body's energy back in tune with the Universe's. In yoga, prana is connected to the breath and breathing exercises, called *pranayama*, that harness the energy of the breath for the benefit of mind, body, and soul.

You can connect to the prana life force right now by doing this simple breathing exercise. Lie on your back on the floor (not on a bed, couch, or other soft surface). Breathe out fully and deeply and hold the stillness for a moment of grounding and centering. Now, inhale slowly to a count of 10, filling your body with air beginning at the lowest point in your abdomen and moving upward until your lungs are full. Let your torso rise and expand with the breath, but keep your shoulders down. At the full count, hold the breath for another moment of stillness. Then, reverse the pattern and exhale to a count of 10, breathing the air out at first from your head down through your abdomen. Repeat. As you do this exercise, feel the breath, your prana life force, moving into all parts of your body.

Energy Meridians

The secondary chakras, the body's thousands of smaller energy wheels, are arranged in a pattern along your energy meridians or pathways. When Chinese doctors treat a condition, they never deal with the symptom alone. They believe that illness or pain emerges when the body's energy system is out of balance, so they treat the body as a whole by redirecting energy along their meridians.

When Western thinkers picture needles, they usually think of large, scary, dull, hollow ones like those you see at a blood bank. But in Eastern medicine like acupuncture, it couldn't be more different! *Acupuncture* is the comfortable insertion of thin needles (as fine as a human hair) to change the body's energy flow. They are not hollow. Although they barely penetrate the surface of the skin, acupuncture needles touch energy points all over the body, and serve as conduits or tuning forks to balance energy and release blocks of chi. They often have an immediate effect on many health conditions, and leave patients feeling deeply relaxed after treatment.

As you begin to work with your body's energy, an acupuncturist is a wonderful professional to consult about your body's energy flows and blockages. Be sure to choose a practitioner who is fully licensed and experienced, as this person will be able to give you knowledge, information, and exercises to benefit your body's energy balance.

Life Force, Western View

Western medicine is logical, clinical, and linear. Where Eastern medicine analyzes your body's energy systems and feels the quality and flow of your pulse, Western medicine quantifies and examines body parts and systems in isolation. Eastern medicine treats the body's whole system. Western medicine cuts to the chase and operates.

Western medical philosophy understands the body as a collection of interrelated, but distinct, systems. The respiratory system takes in oxygen and disposes of carbon dioxide; the digestive system processes food into nutrients; the circulatory system sends the oxygen and nutrients to cells throughout the body. And so on, and so on. Even though the systems must work together for the body to function, each is seen as a separate entity: If a patient comes in with a stomachache, a Western doctor will focus on the digestive system to the exclusion of the others.

And the life force that's so central to Eastern thought? Western doctors might talk about brain activity or heart rate (both of which are electrical, or energetic, impulses … hmmm …) or respiratory function. If you've got those, you're alive. If you don't, you're not. Simple as that.

Or is it? Not too long ago, before brain waves could be detected, people were regularly declared dead just because their hearts had stopped or they couldn't breathe on their own. Today, it's not uncommon that someone is revived after a heart attack or emerges from a coma. Is it so far-fetched to imagine that perhaps Western medicine has more to learn about the energies that constitute life?

Life Force: A New World View

Here's the reality: We need both Eastern and Western medical knowledge! Only then can we leave the bonds of linear thinking behind us and connect to the greater truths of our energetic, interconnected Universe.

If you fall down and break your arm, you need an x-ray and a cast. That's the Western medical approach. But did you know that you may be able to cut your healing time in half, as well as reduce pain and any permanent side effects, by adding Eastern practices to the treatment plan? It's true. In medical facilities all over the world, this new line of integrated thinking is quickly emerging and has a growing number of sound studies and evidence to back it up.

Both the Eastern and the Western medical systems have a great deal to offer us, philosophically and physically. When we combine them into a system that supports our whole selves, the physical and the energetic, then the outcome is greater health and balance for us all. Those ancient ideas that were once labeled by Western doctors and scientists as "alternatives," are now seen as valid and are being embraced as "complementary" or "integrative." And that's a win-win situation for us all!

The Least You Need to Know

- Energy is within you, comes from you, and is all around you.

- All the objects around you have energy.

- Colors and objects reflect and affect your energies and personal energy field.

- Your aura both protects and reflects you energetically.

- Integrative medicine—a combination of Eastern and Western medical techniques—is the cutting-edge care of tomorrow.

Chapter 7

Science Meets Skepticism: Where's the Proof?

In This Chapter

- ◆ Doubt: It's only human
- ◆ Let your journal be your proof
- ◆ How to test yourself—and how to practice
- ◆ The case for intuition: hard evidence

You're with us so far in our journey through the many methods and tools we have to divine the future. But we bet that at some point along the way you've had a question or a nagging doubt: Can this be for real? Is it all true? And how can I be sure?

We may not lay all your doubts to rest in the next few pages. But we'll show you how others have grappled with these questions, and give you a focus that you can use to start finding your own answers, your own truth about divining the future.

Appearances Can Be Deceiving

Questions. They're part of what makes us human. When the great French Baroque philosopher Descartes declared "I think, therefore I am," he showed us how central doubt is to our very essence.

So it's perfectly okay to approach divining the future and the intuitive arts with curiosity, skepticism, and even challenges.

At the same time, though, we have to acknowledge that although there are some things that can be proven, other things are less defined—or defin*able*. We can root some aspects of the intuitive arts in science, but other facets are nebulous and always will be. After all, intuition is knowing something without knowing how you know it.

In other words, there are some things we've got to take on faith.

Divine Inspiration

What role does faith play in divining the future? Plenty. One example involves an expression many people still use today, though they may not be conscious of its origin. Any skeptic might be called a "doubting Thomas," a name that comes from a Bible story. Thomas, one of Jesus' followers, just couldn't bring himself to believe that his teacher had risen from the dead. It took a lot for doubting Thomas to come around, the story goes; he had to actually touch Jesus before he could make that leap of faith.

We know of many out-and-out skeptics, whose perspectives change in the face of evidence they can't refute. But that doesn't necessarily change their questioning natures! Like writer Bob Olson, a former detective who, after a mind-blowing session with a psychic medium, decided to use his skills to launch a three-year investigation of mediumship. Could there be people who truly possess the gift of communicating with spirits? Today, Olson is convinced there are indeed individuals who possess special gifts in the many fields of the intuitive arts—as well as those who are not tremendously gifted, or are outright frauds! Olson's website, www.OfSpirit.com, is the result of his journey of investigation. It is a wonderful source for qualified intuitive arts practitioners in fields as diverse as Reiki, music therapy, Tarot, flower essences, psychics, and more.

Certainly, though, there are some charlatans out there, in part because the "truth" of intuitive experiences can be so difficult to quantify. Of course, the frauds make it that much harder for some people to believe in those whose gifts are real. And then remember the fate of poor Cassandra gifted with prophecy. According to Greek myth, after spurning Apollo's advances, Cassandra found herself cursed by the god so that, although always true, mortals would never believe the veracity of her prophetic visions and insights.

Another difficulty is the nature of proof itself. What pushes a skeptical person over the boundary from doubt to belief will be one thing for you, something else for your brother, and something else again for your friend. Proof is different for different people, and there are some people whose specifications are very hard to meet! You might be satisfied with a dream that "comes true," your brother with an intuitive feeling that turns out to be accurate. But your friend might still be suspicious even if a professional psychic gave her a written report describing the travel plans she just booked for next month and accurately predicting some of the experiences she would have on the trip! You just can't force faith.

> ### Resonances
>
> Laura will never forget the client who wanted to communicate with her mother, who had passed on. "I see a woman with short curly hair, bright blue eyes, wearing a red checked dress," Laura told her. "She has a raised mole on her left cheek, about an inch from the corner of her mouth, and she's playing with it. She says she's your mom." "Yes, that's how she looked, mole and all," said the client, "and that was her favorite dress. But ..." Long pause. "How do you know it's really *her?*"

All of which leads us to yet another reason why it's so important for you to develop your own intuition as you delve into divining the future. Your intuition can be your armor that protects you from fraud, and your guiding light through the thickets of doubt. If you can learn to trust your own inner sense of what is true and what is not, your way to the truth of the future will be clear.

The Quest for Quantification

When research scientists are at work in the lab, there's one piece of equipment they're never without: not a supercomputer, not an electron microscope, but a simple notebook. Scientists must keep meticulous notes and records of data as experiments are performed to chart their progress and to document their results. If others question their conclusions about an experiment, lab notes are often the first piece of evidence to be examined. Without this empirical, evidential data, science simply doesn't happen.

You're a scientist yourself, in a way: a researcher of the intuitive arts. And you, too, will need to keep "lab notes" and clinical records on your "experiments" in your journal.

If you're looking for proof through the intuitive arts, journaling your own experiences is the only real way to get it. You can formally test your abilities, you can wait for a revelation, you can find a guide or a guru. But for most of us, it takes a lot of convincing, a lot of little "hits," before we can trust and believe.

Your journal is the place where you put all your experiments and experiences together so you can begin to make sense of them. We're not talking about a diary wherein you record the minutiae of every day. ("Got up. Brushed teeth. Went to work ....") We're talking about a *tool* that is set aside exclusively for the details of your intuition's work. Your journal will help you determine the patterns of your intuitive experiences so you can identify the future's potentials.

These can be dreams, a meditative vision, or a "feeling"; they can be the result of a particular reading, or just a note about how you called a friend and she told you how she'd just been thinking of you. If you're investigating your own intuition like a scientist would, every experience is relevant and every piece of information becomes data to consider.

If you think of your journal as a "lab notebook," you'll quickly see the logic of formatting your pages for best use. Start every entry on a fresh page, begin with the date, and leave wide margins around your notes. And perhaps most important, leave some blank space at the bottom of each page.

A page from one of Laura's intuitive notebook journals.

> 8-12-90
>
> I have been helping Leoni the past few days and feeling pursued by the letters C L + R. Each day it seems to be getting stronger + louder. (It is almost annoying!) This morning, before I head over to Leoni's house again I am hit by waves on other things. Knowing. It feels like anticipation + excitement like when someone you enjoy is coming over. Maybe someone is? Someone that I need to meet? But where? When? At Leoni's? I will ask her today if these pesky letters (C L R) mean anything to her, and try not to frighten this 86 year old woman in the process!
>
> Amazing! C, L, R! I asked Leoni if she knew anyone with these initials — said no, but — her eyes grew larger + she said her great niece CLAIRE is one of the group coming over tomorrow that we have been preparing for. She wants me to meet her!
>
> 8-13-90 meeting Claire today was like meeting someone I already knew we talked + talked + had so much in common!

Now go collect some highlighter pens of various colors. After a couple of weeks, pens in hand, go back to an old journal entry. Read it over. Did a dreamed event actually happen? A hit! Highlight it in yellow (or whatever color you choose for precognitive experiences). Then use the page's blank space to jot down a note about what happened.

You can use your highlighters to flag hits and misses, various types of intuitive experiences, or anything else you want to track. Our point is simply this: *Use your journal.* Don't scribble your notes and forget them. Go back to them, meditate on them, and learn from them as a scientist would. At the front or back of the journal leave room to create a color code key, so that you can easily keep track of the meanings you assign to colors or other text marks such as underlining or circling information.

You may start slowly, but many people find that intuitive experiences build on each other. The more you focus on them by writing them down, the more you'll recognize them for what they are. You'll be surprised at how quickly you fill up that notebook that once seemed so blankly empty!

> ### Resonances
>
> Laura's earliest journal included all sorts of experiential data that became a valuable tool to document her awakening progress. In one entry she wrote about a dream in which she was handed a credit card. The next day has a new notation: "Credit card arrived in the mail."

How Do You Measure the Intangible?

Not with a ruler or a scale, that's for sure!

Since time immemorial, people have tried to prove and disprove intuitive experiences. And no matter how well designed the experiment, every one of them leaves room for doubt, one way or the other.

That's a testament to the difficulty of quantifying the intuitive arts. They simply can't be proved or disproved to everyone's satisfaction. When it comes right down to it, it's just a matter of belief. (And often the skeptics seem every bit as faith-driven as the believers are, but in the opposite direction!)

It's Elementary, My Dear Watson

Your mission: The truth.

Your method: Experience intuitive arts, apply intuition, achieve understanding.

Simple. Yes, really!

Sherlock Holmes, for all his fictional brilliance, had a similarly simple crime-solving method. He took in every detail, like a human camera. Then he used those basic observations to ferret out the bare truth of a seemingly complex case.

That's your mission in a nutshell. You're not out to convince the world of the truth of divination. You don't even have to convince a single other person. You just have to find those basic, telling details that will convince *you* that there's meaning and purpose Out There.

The truth exists for you to find. But you're the only one who can find the precise way that it will speak to you. If you go out expecting some grand revelation, you may be disappointed. If you've got your eyes peeled for *little* revelations, though, there'll be plenty there. Keep it simple! Write it all down in your journal, and you will see.

Subjective Evidence

Ask the most happily married couple you know why they decided to spend their lives together. We'll bet they won't come up with a laundry list of logical reasons. "Oh, I don't know," they'll say (holding hands and gazing into each other's eyes, no doubt). "It just felt right."

A seemingly subjective way to make such a major decision, but there are so many details below the surface of this couple's intuitive response. Let's be honest: Evaluating data subjectively is the way we live our lives, for the most part. Subjective evidence is true only from a certain point of view, or only from within yourself. From choosing a career to finding a home to shopping for jeans, we may use a lot of sensible criteria along the way—but to make that final decision, we usually go with our gut, with what *feels right*.

Intuition is about as subjective as anything can be. Remember, intuition is knowing something without knowing *how* you know. In that way, the intuitive arts are pretty well in line with much of the rest of what we do in our lives. Divining tools can help you identify your gut feelings, name them, understand them, and act on them.

So can these subjective, anecdotal results of your intuitive explorations be regarded as "evidence"? Strictly scientifically speaking, no. But if you've recorded your experiences as they happen in your journal, subjective evidence is all you need to build up your own case for the meaning of intuition in your life.

Divine Inspiration

Want a quick test of your intuitive skills? Laura once had a client who was also a research scientist. Given his methodical mind, it did not surprise her when he insisted on opening their first session with a three-question pop quiz:

◆ Do you have a good sense of direction?

◆ How would you categorize your sense of smell—is it poor, average, acute, or keen?

◆ Do you like dogs?

Satisfied with Laura's answers, he continued their session. At its close, he explained that all the genuine intuitives he'd consulted had three things in common: They all have an inherent sense of physical direction, they all have a keen sense of smell, and they all connect with animals!

So how did you do? Would you pass?

Objective Evidence

On the other hand, plenty of objective evidence in favor of the intuitive arts has been amassed over the years. Objective evidence is what we'd call "scientific." It is observable, repeatable, consistent, and holds true from any point of view.

The intuitive arts that involve measurable effects or physical objects have been tested in many ways. Graphology (handwriting analysis), for example, is used by criminologists to create a profile of a person from handwriting alone. It's so effective, many criminals avoid using their own writing at all (hence those pasted-together ransom notes you always see in the movies).

But it's not only professionals who have access to objective evidence in favor of the intuitive arts. If you dream about something over which you could have no possible influence (like, say, the name of the next hot reality show's winning contestant) and then it comes to be, you've had an objectively verifiable precognitive experience. Hope you wrote it down in your journal!

Test Your Talent

As we've said, everyone's naturally intuitive—maybe a little, maybe a lot, but the potential is within us all. And in the intuitive arts, as in everything, practice makes perfect.

There are many simple exercises you can do to gauge your natural talents. If you try them often, you can learn to shift your brain out of its usual analytical mode into the intuitive plane. You can train your intuition to come to the fore as needed, to help you focus on what's important and cut out the "static" that your more Earth-bound senses are constantly sending out. That alone can improve your natural intuitive abilities!

Here are a few of our favorite ways to tone the ol' sixth sense.

TV Time

Just about every entertainment news show includes a "pop quiz" segment. The host asks a question, the screen displays three photos or answers or silhouettes, and the show cuts to a commercial while the audience ponders.

For this exercise, ignore the question. (It may help to turn off the sound entirely … and the closed captioning feature, too!)

1. Relax your mind.

2. Focus on the multiple-choice possibilities as images. Don't think of them as "right" or "wrong" answers. Just gaze at them.

3. Allow one of the possibilities to separate itself from the others. It might seem to pop out of the screen, or sink into it, or even light up in your perception. However it singles itself out, that's your choice. Write it down.

4. When the break is over, watch for the answer. Were you right?

If you watch a show that offers quizzes like these regularly, keep a running total of your hits and misses. You could see yourself improve dramatically over time!

Guess Who?

You might be able to try this exercise several times a day, depending on your phone usage (or your popularity with telemarketers).

1. Whenever the telephone rings, relax your mind.

2. Concentrate on the caller and try to gather a mental picture of that person. Be as nonlogical as you can; just grab an intuitive sense of who is reaching out to you. If you draw a blank, try noticing how you feel about this incoming call and the energy it generates. Do you have a feeling you shouldn't pick up the phone? Or do you feel in your gut it's no problem?

3. Only then, answer the phone. Did you "know" exactly who was calling? Or was your mental picture accurate—did you draw an absolute blank and it turned out to be an absolute stranger? Or if you used feelings, did you pick up the phone

against your better instincts only to get talked into joining the PTA by a pushy neighbor? Field a call from your boss when you were supposed to be "in bed with the flu"? Or was it your dear college friend that you've been wanting to connect with again? Sometimes the feelings are easier to pick up than the faces, but try them both and see what works best for you. (P.S.: Yes, it's cheating to use caller ID! That is, unless you only look at it *after* you've listened to your inner vibes.)

Take Heed

Do you notice a pattern where you will lose a phone connection regularly during repeat phone calls with the same person? For example, one time the cell phone battery runs out, another time your cat chews on the phone cord, another time the other person drops the phone, or the line just mysteriously gives out. Is this a bad thing? Well, it could be a very *good* thing. Sometimes the energy of your connection to the person you are speaking with is so intense that a mere phone line is too weak to sustain it!

Intuit-a-Crostic

For this exercise, seek out word search puzzles—the ones that hide complete words in a grid of seemingly random letters. (Many newspapers run them, or you can find books of them at newsstands and collections of them online.)

1. Look at the grid of letters as a whole entity. Don't search for any particular words, and don't run your eyes along the lines in an orderly fashion. Just gaze at the grid.

2. Do any words pop out, sink back, or otherwise draw your attention? You've done it! Your intuition has tuned out the static for you so you could see what's important. How many words can you find with your intuitive powers alone?

Intuit-a-crostic reminds us of the scene in the movie *A Beautiful Mind* where Russell Crowe as mathematician John Nash solves the meaning of a complex encoded numerical grid by staring at it. Even brilliant, beautiful minds make intuitive leaps in gathering data for interpretation!

Putting Technology to the Test

Over the past decade or so, scientists and medical doctors have become more willing to discuss the mind-body connection, and have been experimenting with ways to quantify it. It's become generally acceptable for our most objective thinkers to agree that the human mind is much more powerful than was once thought possible. After all, it's common knowledge that "we only use 10 percent of our brains"—maybe the other 90 percent is reserved for our untapped metaphysical powers!

That's exactly why some scientists have been studying those powers, and embracing their potential, for much longer than the last 10 or 20 years.

Brain Waves and Vital Signs

Today, thanks to electromagnetic sensors, we can "see" brain activity—even in people who seem to be completely unconscious. Patients in deep comas, even those who can't breathe on their own, can have a great deal of brainwave activity. Their physical bodies expend little to no energy while their minds are clearly at work. Where are they? What are they doing?

One thing's for sure: They're not dead, at least not the way we understand the term today. Our definition of "life" is dramatically different from what it was just a few decades ago. Your heart can stop, your lungs can be stilled, but if doctors can measure your brain waves, you're still with us. (Or we intuitive types might say, your soul remains.)

Researchers are exploring brain wave patterns as we move, talk, eat, sleep, and dream. Findings from extended studies of the brain activity of meditating Buddhist monks are integral in the effort to understand the nuances of function in specific brain centers, as well as find clues to the cure of neurological conditions, the reasons for behavioral habits, and physiological processes. From an intuitive perspective, this becomes an exploration of the profound union of mind, body, and spirit.

Covert Operations: Remote Viewing

For the past 30 years or more, it is said, government agencies—including those of the United States—have experimented with what they call *remote viewing*, a process by which a sensitive observer can "see" any physical place, at any distance or at any time, and document ongoing or even future events or projects.

Telepathy? Astral projection? Yes, in all but name.

There's some historical evidence that researchers in the former Soviet Union pursued remote viewing techniques for use in Cold War espionage operations. In response, it has been reported, the United States began its own programs. Some claim that the American intelligence community retains remote viewing experts, along with technologies like spy satellites and observation aircraft, in its espionage arsenal. Although TV documentaries and news programs have featured stories on remote viewing, hard evidence of it is tough for nonexperts to come by.

In any case, it's safe to say that remote viewing has been investigated by scientists the world over.

Future Focus

Remote viewing is the process by which a seer in one location can intuit an event, place, or action as it unfolds, in the present or in the future, at some location other than where the seer is.

No Secret Codes Needed: ESP

Far better documented are the many experiments that have been done to establish the validity of extrasensory perception, or ESP.

ESP is a popular term for all the intuitive gifts we discussed back in Chapter 3, including clairsentience, telekinesis, clairaudience, and clairvoyance. But most people use it as a synonym for "mind reading," or telepathy—the ability to send and receive mental messages or images.

The classic ESP experiments used a special deck of cards called Zener cards that display simple geometric symbols. Two people, a sender and a receiver, would work together (although they would not necessarily be physically close to one another). The sender would draw a card at random and concentrate on the image. The receiver, concentrating on the sender, would name the symbol he or she intuited.

In color, the Zener cards show a red cross, blue waves, black square, orange circle, and green star. You can use markers and heavy paper stock to make your own Zener cards.

Though success rates varied, many people were found to do much better on these tests than chance alone would predict. Interestingly, it was found that many others were able to improve their scores with practice! (Remember when we called it "strengthening the intuitive muscle"?)

You can easily recreate the classic ESP experiments on your own. But you don't need special cards, if you don't have time or crafts skills to make them. All you need is yourself, a friend, and a couple accurate watches.

1. Prearrange a time for this two-part test to take place, and decide how long it will last. (Two to three minutes for each part is fine.)

2. Decide which one of you will be the first "sender" and which will be the first "receiver." You don't have to be in the same location for the experiment to work—in fact, the farther apart you are, the more interesting the results might be!

3. Finally, establish a limited set of images you'll each be able to choose from. For our example, let's say you'll use primary colors—red, yellow, and blue—as your first test set.

4. At the agreed time, both partners, wherever they are, should ground themselves and get centered.

5. First sender, begin concentrating on the primary color you privately chose. Immerse yourself in the feeling you get from that color: Imagine yellow's warmth, the sensation of the yellow sun on your skin, yellow sand on the beach, bright yellow daffodils ... whatever yellow connotes to you. "Send" those images, ideas, and sensations.

6. First receiver, try to pick up on all the feelings your partner is experiencing—not just the color alone. Write down all the images and ideas that come to you.

7. When the first part's time is up, switch roles and repeat steps 5 and 6.

8. Compare notes and prepare to be amazed!

Mind over Body? What About Spirit?

All the research into brain activity, ESP, and so on shows us that the physical and the metaphysical sciences have had a long relationship. It's a relationship we can see within our very selves: the intimate tie between body and mind that we call the "body-mind connection," linked by spirit.

Yogis, people who are expert in the practice of yoga (although we believe any serious student of yoga is a yogi!), have a long tradition of using their minds to come into a perfect union with their bodies' physical potential. In Sanskrit, *yoga* means "union." Mind and body, like the ancient Chinese concepts of yin and yang, must live together in balance. Throughout this book, as we've done already, we'll show you yoga poses and meditation exercises that enhance your body-mind union and nourish your soul.

The practice of yoga encourages a perfect balance of mind and body, linked through spirit, here embodied in the symbol for yin/yang harmony.

Too often, though, people view the mind and body as adversaries in a struggle for dominance of your spirit. That's not what is true! Your body isn't merely a vessel for your mind or your mind merely an engine for your body. Honoring the whole of your essence is the beautiful expression of what it means to be a living human being. Body and mind in harmony through spirit—that's a worthy goal, one that the intuitive arts can help you achieve.

Meditation

Meditation, in its many forms, is a time-tested path to enlightenment and understanding. For most of us, the body is usually in the driver's seat, guiding us through our daily lives and all the world's sensations. Meditation gives the mind the keys and puts the body in the passenger's place for a while. Chanting, lotus-sitting, *labyrinth*-walking, structured prayer—whatever the method, meditation centers the spirit while the mind and body concentrate on sitting or moving in a focused union. It's like a workout that tones the mind-body while setting the spirit soaring.

When you meditate, you deliberately don't "think" in the conscious way we're used to. You don't start with a problem and puzzle out a solution. In fact, *non*thought is the goal. Without thought, your mind can just *be*. And there, where your mind just peacefully exists, it can be most powerful! Total self-awareness comes in the mind's resting state.

Future Focus

A **labyrinth** is a one-way path that makes patterned twists and turns toward the center of a circle and then back out again. Labyrinths have been used for centuries as a pathway to reflection, prayer, and divination.

Breathing Through Life's Twists and Turns

The first step in meditation is to center your mind and your body on the act of breathing; prana is the life force that fills your spirit. Whether in walking or seated meditation, use the flow of breath in and out to find your rhythm and bring you in tune with the universal energy flow around you. If you have access in your community to a labyrinth, take the time to visit and explore the labyrinth walk.

Or use the image here to trace the labyrinth's pattern, breathing slowly and deeply as you navigate its course. If you want, go to a photocopy shop and have the labyrinth image enlarged to poster size. Then, with the poster hung on a wall so the center of the labyrinth is at shoulder level, sit in meditation and extend one arm fully with fingertips extended and trace the pattern, once again breathing deeply and fully, timing the space between inhalations and exhalations with the turns and directional changes the labyrinth holds. What thoughts, sensations, and feelings arise during your labyrinth walk or meditation? How do the twists and turns of the labyrinth mirror your own life experiences, false starts, and new directions? You'll learn more about the labyrinth as a self-knowing tool in Chapter 14.

The labyrinth at medieval Chartres Cathedral.

The Least You Need to Know

◆ It's okay to doubt and question—it's only human! Let your journal be your lab notebook, your clinical records of the messages you receive.

◆ You can use everyday happenings to practice your intuitive abilities.

◆ Meditation and yoga promote mind and body union through spirit.

◆ Researchers have found compelling evidence in favor of the intuitive arts.

Chapter 8

Credibility Central: Trust Yourself

In This Chapter

◆ The truth is already within you

◆ A deeper understanding of the future and the present

◆ Getting past your filters

◆ Grounding as a foundation of trust

◆ Runes for exploring life's issues

Research results and experiments are all, well, scientific, but they can distract you from the real focus of your pursuit: *you*. Divining your best future is what your intuition is all about. There are lots of ways to access and free your intuition—tools, meditation, professional guidance. But whatever the method, all of them can work to scrape away your mental clutter and reveal the inner truths and potentials that already live within you.

Sometimes, the truths we bury—that are yearning to break out into the open—are uncomfortable ones. Your intuitive work may uncover ideas that seem risky or scary to your conscious, "thinking" mind. So when your intuition turns up this kind of information, your first reaction will probably be "No way! That can't be right!" And yet, it *is* right!

Revealing What You Already Know

So what part of a message about your future do you trust, and how do you know what it means? Well, that's another matter where your intuition can enlighten. As information is revealed, you have to run it through your own intuitive "truth detector."

Take some time to quiet your mind and focus on the message. Don't think about it logically. Just hold it in your mind. Now consider the following:

- What's your immediate physical reaction to the information?

- What's your immediate intuitive reaction?

- Do you nod "yes" or shake your head "no" in response?

- Do you have a gut feeling when you think about it?

- Does the information lead to doubts about yourself?

- Would your closest friends say that this information fits with what they know about you?

You may find that a message or piece of information keeps coming back up, no matter how many different readings you do or how many different intuitive tools you use. If the information still doesn't sit right with you, it's time to ask yourself some tough questions: What am I blocking? Why am I resisting this message? Is my intuition really telling me "no," or am I just afraid?

Resonances

When Laura was still discerning the path that led her to intuitive work, she had her astrological birth chart drawn up. The astrologer told Laura that in a few years she would be led into the public arena. That made Laura dismiss the chart out of hand: "Politics? Me? Never!" A long time passed before Laura realized that the chart held the truth—it was Laura's interpretation that was wrong. Today, she's not a politician, but she *is* a public figure!

Remember, time is your friend in situations like these. Rarely do you have to make rash decisions just because something "tells" you to. Take the time to make sure that your choices are right for you in every important way. Follow the cardinal rule: *When in doubt, don't.* If you do feel pressured to make a decision, consider using a tool, such as the Ancient Stardust Directional Cards (see Appendix A), for the valuable insights it can offer on matters of timing and energy.

Guidance from Intuitive Tools

Divination tools can be a great way to uncover and honor the intuitive knowledge you harbor deep inside you. A well-chosen tool, one that suits your own personality, can help you tune out all the sensory static and listen, just deeply listen, to your intuition.

What's in Your House for the Year Ahead?

There are many spreads you can use with Tarot cards, but one of the most popular blends the cards with astrology's zodiac wheel to contemplate a 12-month period. To lay out the Houses of the Year Spread, the Querent (or questioner—that's you!) chooses 12 cards and lays them out in a circular pattern, corresponding to the 12 houses of the zodiac. The cards reveal the patterns and powers that will be at work in the coming year, and can give some idea of the times of their emergence.

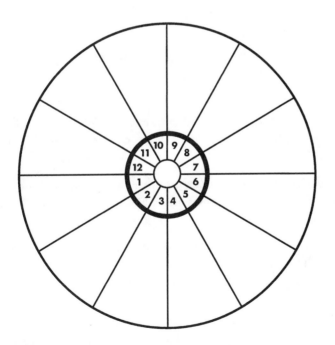

The Houses of the Year Spread combines Tarot and astrology to give you answers about the upcoming year.

As the New Year approached, Mary Kay wondered about what it would hold for her. She knew certain transitions were on the way, and she wanted to know how she could best respond to them. The cards she dealt were telling. In September, Mary Kay's youngest child would be going off to school; the 4 of Cups in the Ninth House seemed to predict a need for inner work on Mary Kay's part in response. But the rest of the year would bring loving help, new projects, and transformation (Page of Cups, Ace of Swords, and Death—which really *isn't* a bad card, no matter how creepy your deck's artist might have made it look!), so it seemed that the transition, given time, would be successful.

But the "Whoa!" moment in the reading came with the Seventh House. This was the King of Cups, which connotes devotion, introspection, kindness, and emotional understanding; it's also strongly ocean-related. Mary Kay had been thinking of going on a family retreat during the summer, and hadn't really followed up on it. But as the retreat house is at an ocean beach, and the card's positioning related to July … well, that was confirmation enough to get her to send in a reservation!

Divine Inspiration _____

In Tarot, no matter which deck you use, the four suits carry signature energies:

Wands	creativity
Cups	love and Emotion
Swords	action
Pentacles	abundance

Consider these energies in your readings and how they resonate to your intuitive sense of the future.

What does your year have in store? Begin with a moment of silence and a few deep breaths. As you begin to shuffle your Tarot deck, focus on the question: "What can I expect in this next year?"

When you feel ready, divide the shuffled deck into three piles, then choose the pile that feels right to you. Set the other two piles aside, and deal out the top 12 cards in the spread pattern.

Now look at your chosen cards as a group. Are the cards upright, or *reversed* in certain positions? Notice where each card has fallen. Each position is associated with a month of the coming year, as well as with an astrological "house," according to the following chart.

Astrological House	Astrological Influence
First	Physical self, personality, early childhood
Second	Possessions, earnings, self-esteem
Third	Knowledge, siblings, environment

Astrological House	Astrological Influence
Fourth	Home, family, life's foundations
Fifth	Creativity, fun, romance, risks, children
Sixth	Personal responsibilities, health, service to others
Seventh	Primary relationships and partnerships
Eighth	Joint resources, sex, death, rebirth
Ninth	Education, philosophy, law, religion, travel
Tenth	Reputation, career, social responsibilities
Eleventh	Goals, groups, friends
Twelfth	Your subconscious: privacy, secrets, the past

To analyze your cards, you might want to use one of the many books on Tarot inter-pretation. We recommend *The Complete Idiot's Guide to Tarot, Second Edition*, or the booklet of card meanings that probably came packaged with your deck. Alternatively, you can meditate on each card in turn, focusing on what its images mean to *you*.

Record the cards in your reading, along with your findings, or your feelings, in your journal.

By the way, if cards in a Tarot reading come out "upside down," leave them that way. Reversed cards carry their own messages, and often represent the mirror energy of the card when it is upright. In your journal, denote a reversed card like this: "Hanged Man R" or "4 of Swords R." Just because a card is reversed does not mean the energy it carries is negative. Many times reversed cards will indicate delays or problems, but they can also indicate decisions made and forward motion, too. It depends on the card and its context in your reading!

In Your Hand: A Palmistry Exercise

Your hand is a map of your inner self, and it is constantly changing as you change. Reading that map is a skill you can learn over time. The better you know your hand's hills and valleys, the better you'll understand its meanings.

Set aside some time to really examine your hand. (Your dominant, or writing, hand is the one that's usually used for palmistry readings.) Find a quiet place where you can concentrate, and—this is important—where you'll have a good source of light. A bright desk lamp, or a window where natural light streams in, will do nicely.

Take a deep breath, quiet your mind, and focus on the question: "What does my hand have to tell me today?"

Now start to look, *really* look, at the features of your hand, both the palm and the fingers. Examine the shape of your palm and fingertips, the skin between your finger joints (or *phalanges*), and the spot on your palm where each finger connects to the hand (or *mounts*). Look for any colored dots, which may be red, white, black, or blue. (No, ink spots don't count!) Finally, look at your hand's lines. Are there many of them or few? Are they well defined? Do they form patterns?

When you've looked carefully at every inch of your hand, you can personalize the following diagram by drawing or writing in your observations to create a written record of *your* hand.

Now compare your diagram with your hand. Are there any other features you hadn't noticed before?

You can use your final diagram as a baseline. In the next few days, scan your hand at various times. Have any of your diagrammed features disappeared? Have any new ones shown up? The human body is constantly changing and evolving; what appears in your hand on one day, may not appear in the next day, week, month, year, or beyond! Compare your hand's features to the following diagram, which shows the planetary influences that your features signify.

Every area of your life can be seen in your palm. Compare your hand's major features to the following chart. Can you see the relationships between your hand's map and your life?

Astrological influences in your palm. The first phalange represents psychic intuition; the second phalange represents logic and reasoning; the third phalange represents physical energy and the material world.

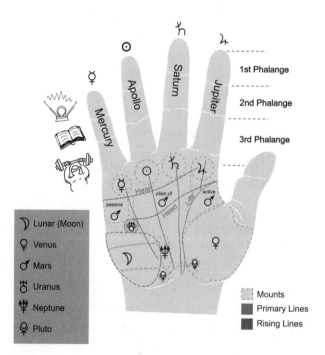

Astrological Planet	Planetary Influence in Your Palm
Mercury	Communication, commerce, healing
Apollo	Creativity, vanity
Saturn	Rules, responsibilities, law and order; relationship with father
Jupiter	Optimism, leadership ability, charisma, relationships
Venus	Generosity and matters of the heart
Mars	Temperament, resilience, assertiveness
Uranus	Inventiveness, ideals
Neptune	Large-scale creations, travel, career
Pluto	Transformation; relationships with siblings
Luna (Moon)	Nurturing, receptivity, dreams, imagination; relationship with mother

Entire books have been written on palmistry (check out *The Complete Idiot's Guide to Palmistry* for starters!), but this exercise is a great way to begin your own exploration. As the days go by, track changes in your palm as they correspond to the changes in your life.

Learning to Tune In: Filters and Focus

The ideas are so common they've become stock phrases: "That just doesn't sit well with me." "I'll have to sleep on it." You may not be used to calling on your intuition in a conscious way. But when it kicks in on its own, it just can't be denied. When you're truly tuned in to yourself, you free your intuition so that it can inform you when you need it to. That's a tremendous asset in all aspects of life, whether your intuition is helping you understand divinatory messages or helping you understand a co-worker. So set your intuition loose! How? By making it your business to listen to it, and learning to trust its messages.

Filters are the lenses through which you perceive the world around you. Ever wonder why witnesses to an accident all tell slightly (or even radically) different stories? It's because each witness's filter system blocks and colors different kinds of information, affecting what people see—or *think* they see.

All of us have our own predispositions. We've collected them in response to our experiences, our personal histories, the things we've read and heard and seen, even our parents' attitudes. When we say that someone sees life through rose-colored glasses, we're talking about their filter system (in this case, an unrealistically optimistic one). And someone who's prejudiced about a certain group of people can see them only through a narrow filter.

We all use filters every day to make assumptions about people. For example, we may assume that someone is wealthy because she is well dressed, or assume that another person is poor because he is poorly dressed. To really excel at intuition and divination, you have to learn to suspend your pre-existing filters (which tend to be limited and narrow) and to replace them temporarily with new, expanded ones.

Why might you need new filters?

♦ To permit emotional detachment

♦ For protection

♦ For guidance

♦ To permit only the highest and the best to come through

♦ To help set aside your pre-set opinions

♦ To help calm the mind

Grounding lets you open up your expanded filters safely to allow all kinds of information in—even things you might consciously block in ordinary circumstances. That's one of the many reasons why we encourage you to ground yourself well before you venture into the intuitive arts.

With only our limited "everyday" filters in place, divination can be difficult or impossible to do. Laura's own astrology experience from several years ago shows how powerful our limited filters can be. When she heard that she'd be "in the public eye," her filters classified that as "politics" and her predispositions said "No way!" Those filters caused her to reject the whole reading. Of course, Laura found her path regardless—destiny won out!—and when she came across that astrology reading recently, she had quite a chuckle. It was correct, down to the very dates!

Take Heed

Many people are so eager to open up to the intuitive arts that they rush in, asking questions and collecting answers in a state of desperation. They will eagerly accept information from anyone or anything. Using proper grounding and filtering rituals assures you that you are only letting in the "highest and best" information possible and that *you* are always in control.

Your basic filters can really skew how you receive information, making it next to impossible for you to be impartial and to set your emotions aside. Expanded filters invite in only the highest and best information, enabling you to trust the results.

If you want to get past your innate limited filters, remember to take the time to do your grounding rituals so you can put your new filters in place. Remain focused on the essential information. This is an ongoing, never-ending job as you work with your intuition. You can't help but be emotionally invested in your own life, after all. And, living as we do within the strictures of linear time, it's tough to shake off the boundaries of cause-and-effect thinking. But that's what good professional intuitives do every day: They suspend their linear thoughts at will and turn off their ordinary assumptions. You can do it, too.

What if you've expanded your filters, but your reading still doesn't feel right to you? Sometimes, when a reading challenges you, it's a sign that you *need* to be challenged. If your gut tells you to run from what you're hearing, maybe your resistance is masking a fear that you must overcome. The more grounded you are when you begin a reading, the safer you'll feel as you explore your message and its true meanings.

Getting Grounded: Grounding and Filtering Exercises

In Chapter 3, we sketched out two simple grounding exercises. But just as there's a divination tool for every personality, there are hundreds of grounding rituals that can settle your spirit and put you in the right frame of mind for intuitive work. Now that you understand the importance of filters, you can experiment with the following exercises to expand and redefine your own.

The Mighty Tree

1. Sit (in a chair, not on the floor) and quiet yourself.

2. Make sure your legs and arms are uncrossed, and place your feet flat on the floor.

3. Take a few deep breaths.

4. Close your eyes and imagine that attached to your feet is a powerful root system that goes way down, deep into the core of the earth. Picture the roots, and feel their strength running through your legs, anchoring your feet to the floor. The surface winds may blow, but you know that with a root system like this, you will bend and sway and never break.

Yoga's tree pose is a standing variation of a rooted, grounding exercise.

The Plug

1. Sit in a chair and quiet yourself.

2. Uncross your legs and arms, and place your feet flat on the floor.

3. Take a few deep breaths.

4. Close your eyes. Imagine that attached to your body is a powerful electrical cord. See yourself taking the plug end and inserting it into the power source (whatever you imagine that source to be like). Once the connection is made, imagine the current "booting your systems up" with your new and expanded filters.

Ritual Card

Use an index card to write out your own prayer to the God of your understanding for protection, grounding, guidance, and information. "Dear God, please help me to receive that which I need to know. Let only what is in my highest and best interest come through. Please always keep me safe. Thank you, amen."

Flex Your Intuitive Muscle: A Filtering Exercise

This three-part exercise is adapted from one that Laura does with her classes. It's a great way to "shock" your mind out of its usual linear thought patterns.

Part 1: Suspending the Mind

Read the following trivia questions, and write your answers in the spaces that follow the quiz. As you can see, your "knowledge" is no good here—because we haven't given you the answers, just their multiple-choice numbers! Focus on the numbers themselves and choose the one that seems to "pop out" of the page, or seems to "sink into" it, or otherwise singles itself out.

A. What is the only insect that produces food humans eat?

   Answer: 1 2 3 4

B. What day of the year are all race horses considered to turn one year older?

   Answer: 1 2 3 4

C. In what direction does the leaning tower of Pisa lean?

   Answer: 1 2 3 4

D. What license must Californians acquire before they can legally set up a mouse-trap?

   Answer: 1 2 3 4

E. What outfit held its first plenary session at San Francisco's Opera house in 1945?

   Answer: 1 2 3 4

F. What is a Munich resident suffering from if he has a Katzenjammer?

   Answer: 1 2 3 4

G. What is the largest U.S. city to be hit by 16 earthquakes registering between three and five on the Richter Scale from 1850 to 1995?

   Answer: 1 2 3 4

H. Every minute, how many cells are estimated to die in the human body?

   Answer: 1 2 3 4

I. What is the largest population on the planet?

   Answer: 1 2 3 4

   J. What south Atlantic group of islands boasts 338 sheep per human?

   Answer: 1   2   3   4

A. ____   F. ____

B. ____   G. ____

C. ____   H. ____

D. ____   I. ____

E. ____   J. ____

Part 2: Challenging the Linear Mind

Now answer the same questions again—this time, with the answer choices supplied. But we ask you to fight your analytical mind, despite the answers' presence. Select your answers based on intuition alone. Which choice singles itself out to you? Write them in the spaces that follow the quiz.

   A. What is the only insect that produces food humans eat?

   1. The June bug

   2. The worker ant

   3. The honey bee

   4. The bumble bee

   B. What day of the year are all race horses considered to turn one year older?

   1. September 1

   2. April 1

   3. May 1

   4. January 1

   C. In what direction does the leaning tower of Pisa lean?

   1. North

   2. West

   3. South

   4. East

D. What license must Californians acquire before they can legally set up a mouse-trap?

1. A trapping license

2. A hunting license

3. A fishing license

4. A gaming license

E. What outfit held its first plenary session at San Francisco's Opera House in 1945?

1. The National Baseball League

2. The Society of Architects

3. The Screen Actors Guild

4. The United Nations

F. What is a Munich resident suffering from if he has a Katzenjammer?

1. A stubbed toe

2. A sexually transmitted disease

3. A nosebleed

4. A hangover

G. What is the largest U.S. city to be hit by 16 earthquakes registering between three and five on the Richter Scale from 1850 to 1995?

1. Seattle

2. New York City

3. Washington, D.C.

4. Los Angeles

H. Every minute, how many cells are estimated to die in the human body?

1. 300 million

2. 1 million

3. 10 million

4. 20 million

I. What is the largest population on the planet?

1. Amphibian

2. Plant

3. Insect

4. Human

J. What south Atlantic group of islands boasts 338 sheep per human?

1. The Falkland Islands

2. The Premoria Islands

3. The Great Barrier Islands

4. Greenland

A. ____   F. ____

B. ____   G. ____

C. ____   H. ____

D. ____   I. ____

E. ____   J. ____

Part 3: The Score

Now you can score Parts 1 and 2, based on the answer key that follows. Which test produced the more accurate results? How did the forced filter in Part 1 affect your answers?

Answer Key

A. 3   F. 4

B. 4   G. 2

C. 3   H. 1

D. 2   I. 3

E. 4   J. 1

Lessons of Life, Lessons of the Soul

All that you experience in your life, the joys and the sorrows alike, are part of what make you *you*. They inform you, and form you, as you choose your paths on your journey. Your life's lessons are your soul's lessons as well. If you remain conscious of this, and trust what you discover, you will learn much more from these lessons! Remember as you make your journey that it's you who creates it. Your own free will gives you the power to enact change, to reach for goals, to choose the roads that will take you to your destiny. Intuitive arts tools can help you understand the messages of the spirit and make the choices that are best for you.

Uncharted Territory

As you continue to explore the intuitive arts, remember the cardinal rules we talked about in Chapter 3:

◆ If there's something you are meant to know, it will be revealed to you.

◆ If you're not meant to know something, it will remain hidden.

◆ Some things can only happen as a result of choices you make.

So don't be discouraged if your divination method of choice "fails" you by not telling you clearly what to do. That's not what divination is meant to do! Your tools are not in control of your life. *You* are. Only you can make the choices and take the actions that will make your future happen. Your tools can help you map the uncharted territory that is your future, but you have to decide where to carry them.

> **CAUTION** **Take Heed**
>
> There's a fine line between trust and surrendering your power. If you consult an intuitive professional whose messages don't jibe with your own intuition, walk away.

Seeking Answers: A Rune Exercise

Runes are an especially useful tool to consult when you're wrestling with the larger issues of your life. Each rune is inscribed with a letterlike symbol derived from the ancient writing systems of northern Europe. Runes have a tactile power are bodly graphic. If you are drawn to Celtic tradition, runes might already be a part of your heritage.

Ann had gone back to school to pursue a Master's degree in theater, and had been asked to work as a teaching assistant in the upcoming semester. Ann knew that this position would tell her a lot about how she might use her degree in the real world. As she put it, "This is going to be a time of mutual testing—I'm trying teaching out, and teaching is trying me. I want to stay aware of my feelings toward the job, whether I'm interested in doing this long-term and whether I'm any good at it." So Ann centered herself with a few deep breaths and focused on her issue, which she worded this way: "The issue is my new teaching assistant position." She then drew three rune stones from the bag and laid them out in a row, right to left. They were Eihwaz, defense; Sowelu, wholeness; and Hagalz, disruption.

The first rune Ann drew gives an overview of the situation. Eihwaz, defense, connotes a need for patience. Sometimes delay is okay, Eihwaz counsels, just as you wait to receive your passport before you can travel the world. Look toward the goal, and persevere through any difficulties, because growth is happening.

Ann drew Sowelu, wholeness, as her second rune. In this spread, the second symbol points to the challenge inherent in the issue. Sowelu is linked to the right or true path, to self-actualization. But it counsels humility as the path is sought.

Take Heed

Divination tools can be addictive! If you find yourself growing dependent on your favorite tool (if you can't go out for a cup of coffee without consulting your runes first, for example), take a time-out. Your tool can help you access your intuition, but it shouldn't be used as a crutch.

Hagalz, disruption, was Ann's third rune. The third symbol in a three-rune spread is a call to action. Hagalz is all about change, and forceful change at that. When Hagalz appears in a reading, brace yourself for some elemental power that strips away the old to make way for the new. Hagalz can mean a change within oneself, or a change that comes from the outside. But it also reminds us that we have inner power of our own, and Hagalz can be a call to begin to wield it.

Ann was impressed at how aptly the reading spoke to her own tendencies, and to her hopes for the future. "I do expect things to go right on the very first try, and I get terribly frustrated if they don't," she said. The overall message she got from the reading was "Have patience, be humble, because change is coming." Ann knew herself well enough to hear the wisdom in this message. Her natural instinct would be to judge the whole enterprise quickly and then to decide that teaching wasn't for her if the first few days went badly. The runes' message was just the reminder Ann needed to hear. Sure in the knowledge that she was on the right path, Ann approached her new job with hope and humility, knowing not to jump to quick conclusions.

The Runes

Symbol	Name	Meanings
ᛗ	Mannaz	The self
ᚷ	Gebo	Partnership; a gift
ᚠ	Ansuz	Receiving messages or gifts
ᛟ	Othila	Separation; gain through loss
ᚢ	Uruz	Strength; old life must die so new ones can begin
ᛈ	Perth	Secrets; hidden forces of change at work
ᚾ	Nauthiz	Need to deal with constraint, pain
ᛜ	Inguz	The completion of a new beginning
ᛇ	Eihwaz	Patience in the face of obstacles
ᛉ	Algiz	Control of emotions
ᚠ	Fehu	Fulfillment; conserve your gains
ᚹ	Wunjo	Joy; clarity in attainment of a goal
ᛃ	Jera	Harvest, beneficial outcome
ᚲ	Kano	Opening; begin a new endeavor with seriousness
ᛏ	Teiwaz	Active energy from deep within
ᛒ	Berkana	Growth, rebirth; gentle flow into a new form
ᛗ	Ehwaz	Transit, transition, physical movement

continues

The Runes (continued)

Symbol	Name	Meanings
Laguz	Laguz	Fluidity, rhythm, cleansing
Hagalz	Hagalz	Elemental disruption, great change
Raido	Raido	Communication; unity at journey's end
Thurisaz	Thurisaz	Gateway between Divine and mundane; call to contemplation
Dagaz	Dagaz	Time for breakthrough, transition
Isa	Isa	Time of gestation
Sowelu	Sowelu	Time to seek wholeness
		Death (literal or figurative); giving control to the Divine

The three-rune spread that Ann used is great for a concise analysis of any issue that may be before you. Be sure to formulate your question in terms of issues, avoiding specific yes-or-no questions. Remember, runes are best for helping you understand the forces at work behind the scenes and within your spirit. Here's how to do your own three-rune spread:

1. Gather your rune stones in a bag or bowl.

2. Ground yourself with one of the exercises we've outlined, or with several deep breaths, focusing on the issue at hand.

3. Draw three stones, one at a time. Place them before you, face up, in this pattern:

Three-Rune Spread.

Rune	Rune	Rune
3	**2**	**1**
Action	Challenge	Overview

If any of the symbols fall "upside down," leave them as they are. These reversed symbols carry their own meanings.

4. Use the table, or the information that accompanied your rune stones, to meditate on your reading. What do these runes mean to you in relation to your issue?

The Least You Need to Know

◆ Intuition can free the truths already within you, so you can see the present and divine the future with confidence and clarity.

◆ We all have our own pre-existing filter system.

◆ New filters are important allies as you explore your intuition.

◆ Use intuitive tools to practice, practice, practice!

Reading the Body

Of all the energies we work with in our lives, physical energy—the energy of the body—is the one that most of us know best. But that doesn't mean we know it well. From divining methods as diverse as chakras, medical intuition, graphology, and affirmations, there's so much to explore as we learn to understand and communicate with our bodies.

Chapter 9

The Body Beautiful

In This Chapter

◆ Intricately connected: body, mind, and spirit

◆ Restoring health imbalances

◆ How to receive and interpret your body's messages

◆ Your body trusts you!

If someone asked you to describe your physical appearance, what are the very first words you'd be likely to use? Would you stick to the basic driver's license facts—gender, height, eye color? Would you focus on your best features—"I've got a friendly smile and chestnut hair"? Would you be self-deprecating—"Oh, I've got a few pounds to lose"?

Or would you just change the subject?

Our society has a less-than-healthy obsession with the body's outer appearance. We judge people on their beauty, their weight, their clothes, even their height. But at the same time, we neglect our bodies in some important ways. Our bodies aren't just physical entities; they're made of energy, too. Wherever you go and whatever you do, whether you're out competing in a sport or home on the couch watching the game on TV, your body is always humming with energy. Its intricate interconnections are continuously on and firing, even when you're asleep. Your body's always "on."

For all this constant effort, you'd think we could show our bodies a little more gratitude. But most of us don't. Many of us neglect our bodies, or push them too far, or take them for granted. Some people even feel as if they're battling their bodies, or that its needs are somehow secondary or unworthy.

The Vessel of Life

Your body is a wonder and a gift! It is more than merely a shell for the spirit to live in; it's precious and powerful, with a beauty all its own. And if you can learn to listen to its messages, your body can illuminate your past—and can guide you into your future.

There's another major benefit to understanding your body's signals: You'll be healthier all around. Modern medical science is wonderful, and it's improved all our lives in so many ways. The trouble is that its complexity and technology are so overwhelming that it's easy to find yourself at its mercy—to let your doctor make decisions for you. All too often, we walk into a doctor's office and just present ourselves to "be cured." The doctor is the expert; we are merely the patient. And patiently we wait for the expert to fix whatever is wrong.

Although an expert might have access to a great deal of technical information, you have access to the most important facts: the ones that your body gives you. You're not a number or a statistic. You're a unique individual, and your responses to the world are subtle and unlike anyone else's. *Because you live in your body, you know it best.* And if you trust what your body knows, if you can "read" your body's messages, you become a *partner* in your own health. Become part of the decision-making process, and your health care will be much better suited to your body's true needs.

Sustaining Your Health and Well-Being

If you've ever owned a car with a persistent problem, you know that moment when you feel like even Houdini couldn't divine the source of its signals and get that car fixed. Should you keep on driving? Or do you need to pull over? As its owner, you know that you're responsible for the car's maintenance—and you spend a lot of time, effort, and money to diagnose and repair your car's every whine or hesitation (with or without professional assistance). You know that if you don't, you might end up stuck in the breakdown lane of the highway one day.

Well, you're responsible for a machine just as complex as a car: your own body. Your body fires off signals just as unmistakable as dashboard lights and billowing smoke. Sometimes your body's signals are subtle, a twinge here or an ache there. Other times, its signals are an undeniable cry for help—an illness or an injury. If you want your body to run well long into the future, you'd better pay close attention to what it's telling you *now*, and be willing to respond.

All of your systems—body, mind, and spirit—are equally beautiful, valuable, and important. Each of them deserves your loving attention. Each needs to be strong and supple if they're to work together—and they do need to work together, in a balanced way, for you to feel healthy.

Resonances

So often, when Laura works with a client who has physical health problems, she will see energy blockages in their mental or spiritual systems as well. That's because physical illness is usually more than just a physical problem. If your body lands you in the "breakdown lane" of life, you might need to do some work on your mind or your spirit before you can feel better. Similarly, if your spiritual health seems to be flagging, you might have to pay some attention to your body!

Learn to look beyond the body's surface appearances to understand the energies at work in your life, and you'll know what kind of "maintenance" you need.

Physical Fitness

Your physical body has certain basic needs. Food and rest are two of them, and they are easy (even pleasurable) for most of us to supply. But your body has another critical need, one that we're often reluctant to fill: exercise. Ahh, the dreaded "e" word!

Your body—every body—has to have activity on a regular basis. Without even the most minor movement and exertion, a body feels cramped, polluted, clogged up. Tensions mount and stress increases. Muscles will atrophy, contract, and even stop working. This is why those suffering from paralysis must still have regular physical therapy, to keep their bodies from losing even more ground, and to help them function on a daily basis. But many of us tend to think of exercise as a matter of reps and miles and workouts. You're not exercising, it seems, unless you're up before dawn and feeling as uncomfortable as possible.

The good news: Your body doesn't much care when or where or how you move it, it just knows that it needs to move. You're in your body all day, every day—you take it with you everywhere you go (something that's easy to forget when we become too detached from our physical selves). Why not keep it moving? You might be surprised how many miles you can walk in an average day, or how many muscles you can stretch and tone while gardening. Just being *aware* of your own body as it performs its regular tasks can go a long way toward getting the activity you need for good health.

The goal isn't to bench-press a certain weight or run a set number of miles; it's to be able to live in your own body with joy. Some people seem to be able to do this naturally. Think of someone like Goldie Hawn, who's been in the public eye for years—and always looks as if she's enjoying every minute of it! Her verve and zest for life shine through in the way she moves and carries herself. (Interestingly, she's a big fan of yoga and Eastern philosophy. Once she even got Oprah Winfrey's studio audience to spontaneously do some yoga stretching on the show.)

Being present to yourself, honoring and loving your body, will bring you a long way toward overall health. In your journal, take a full day and write down everything you eat and how your mood or level of physical energy is affected that day. Begin to experiment with foods in this way to determine what makes you feel best—body, mind, and spirit. The results may be different than you expect; for example, that ice cream or double espresso may *seem* best, but, in reality, some low-fat chips and salsa or a cup of green tea actually produce the longed-for effect.

Divine Inspiration

We're holding out hope that the next wave of dieting will be an acknowledgment that fad diets do not produce life-long, life-enhancing results. If fad diets worked, obesity would not be one of America's most life-threatening illnesses (it's right up there with lung cancer and heart disease) and there would be no weight-loss industry waiting to take your money with every new diet that comes along. Be aware enough of your own body to understand your unique reactions to food. Focus your mind to recognize how different foods make your body feel, and avoid foods that are unhealthy *for you*. A well-nourished body feels good and energized, and it's integral to strengthening your intuition!

Emotional Nurturing

A healthy mind is one that is aware and in tune with its emotions. Sometimes we have to remind ourselves that there's no such thing as a good or a bad emotion. Emotions can't be judged; they just *are*. Once you accept your feelings as valid, whatever they may be, you can begin to deal with them in a constructive way. Ignore your emotions, or deny them, and you're setting yourself up for destructive behavior—and for negative effects on your physical and spiritual health, too.

Connecting to your emotions means recognizing and honoring how you feel about the people, places, and situations around you. If you've ever avoided someone because you always feel tense around them, you weren't being rude; you were connecting to your emotions in a self-protective way. In your journal, reserve a page to write down the emotions and physical responses you feel when encountering specific people, places, or situations. Looking at these connections on paper may give you some revealing information you're not now consciously aware of.

Time spent with friends can be very nurturing, both emotionally and physically. For women, especially, connecting with friends is not just optional. Studies have shown that women who make close emotional connections with friends are healthier and fight illness better—and the more opportunities they have to talk with their friends, the stronger the illness-fighting effect. So yes, you might really *need* that leisurely lunch every now and then! Call a friend and book one today.

Spiritual Evolution

Appearances can be deceiving. You are so much more than what you appear to be. Your size, your looks, your income, your diet—all that is incidental. You are spirit, too. And to be truly healthy, you need to be well connected with your spiritual side. Daily spiritual practice works like regular exercise to strengthen and stretch the soul. It reminds you that appearances aren't everything: that you're far more than your outer body can ever reveal. Your efforts to learn how to divine the future are an integral part of your spirit, or soul, work. Your active curiosity puts you in tune with that universal energy we are all a part of.

What Your Body Says About You

Remember, some appearances can be and *are* deceiving! The runway image isn't all it's cracked up to be! A person can *look* slim and healthy but have a sky-high cholesterol level. He or she might suffer severe halitosis, anxiety, or stomach ulcers, and have muscles that are underdeveloped through underuse! Another person might not have a Hollywood physique but be more active, fit, and healthy. There are all kinds of bodies and all of them are beautiful when eating and moving in healthful spiritual balance. Here are some physical clues that the body can give us to a person's internal emotional or spiritual state.

Straighten Up!

Picture meeting someone who is habitually slouched, curling up the body almost into a question mark. Does this look to you like a positive, confident person, or like a timid, self-conscious one?

Now picture meeting a person who strides up to you and makes immediate eye contact. How do you think this person feels inside? And which of the two would you rather try to make conversation with?

Lift up your heart and see what change it produces in your body, mind, and spirit.

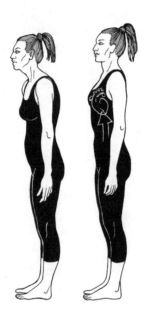

The messages you send out to the world through your appearance, your bearing, and your general manner aren't always the same as those you tell yourself in your head. But very often, those outer messages are revealing. Body language, after all, is a huge part of any human conversation. Sometimes, your body tells the world things you won't admit even to yourself. For example:

◆ A wrinkled brow can signal worry.

◆ An erect posture connotes self-confidence.

◆ Nail-biting can be a way to control stress and emotional pain.

◆ Folded arms equal skepticism or closed-mindedness.

◆ Pinched lips can be a sign of disapproval or holding back.

◆ Squinting may have nothing to do with poor eyesight; it can signal confusion, frustration, fear, or hesitancy.

Reading Your Body's Signals

Stop reading and notice your body's posture and physical feelings right now. Are you hunched forward? Standing with your weight on one side or the other? Furrowing your brow with worry? Now think about the body you're carrying around with you. How are you holding it at this moment? Does your head feel heavy? Are your eyes dry? Are you hot? Cold? Thirsty? Hungry?

Write down as many observations as you can. _____

_____

This is the first step toward true body consciousness: the ability to identify how your physical self feels and what it's doing at any given moment. Only then can you slow down enough to understand and interpret your body's messages and what they signify for the future. At any time of the day or night—on waking, at mealtimes, or whenever it occurs to you—take a minute to observe your body's feelings and actions, and write them down in your journal. You'll soon find your body awareness increasing dramatically.

Once you've begun to focus more attention on your body's signals and sensations, try this exercise to help you when you are having difficulty making a tough choice.

1. Write out two or three options you are faced with right now in making the decision or choice at hand.

   Option: _____

   Option: _____

   Option: _____

2. Take a moment to ground yourself, using any technique you prefer.

3. Tune in to the first option, or possibility, and "try it on." Imagine how you'd feel making this decision. Write down how your body language and body energy changes when you "try on" this scenario. Don't analyze your reaction; just write it down. _____

_____

4. Now do the same for each of your other options. _____

_____

5. When you've finished writing, read each of your reactions. This is a great way to use divination to connect to your body's innate wisdom and energy. How has your body guided you?

Messages You Can't Ignore

Body awareness is a fabulous asset in maintaining your overall health. If you're conscious of your body's needs, you can take care of them quickly, before they turn into problems.

Your body has a great system of communication all its own. When something within you is off-balance, your body begins sending out subtle symptoms. Overtiredness (or insomnia), lack of appetite, and unexplained rashes or aches are little changes that are often the body's first signals that something's out of whack. If you catch these signals, sometimes all it takes is a little simple nurturing—a day off, a nap, some extra nutritional support, more fluids, or just a meditation session—to get your body back in balance again.

But if you miss the signs—and that can be so easy to do, if you're as busy and stressed as most of us are nowadays—your body's communications will become more shrill. What started out as a subtle message can build and build until you experience pain, injury, illness, or breakdown.

Illness is a way your body *forces* you to take care of yourself—its way of screaming "Pay attention to me!" Have you ever suddenly gotten sick at the beginning of a vacation? Your body just needed some TLC, and knew that that was the only time you'd slow yourself down enough to get it!

Guided Imagery

Guided imagery is a visualization and meditation technique. It's a kind of defined quieting of body and mind by way of specific, intentionally focused images. The images are meant to lead you toward a particular outcome. A guided meditation is, in essence, a deliberate act of weaving together the body, the mind, and the spirit. It often leads you through a chain of images, with a definite progression of beginning, middle, and end, to establish a new way of thinking.

Guided imagery has been used with demonstrable success in drug-free childbirth (the mother visualizes the smooth, painless birth of a healthy baby), in cancer treatment (the patient visualizes healthy cells growing and kung-fu-fighting white blood cells battling a tumor), and in overcoming addictions (the person visualizes the benefits of a smoke-free, drug-free, or alcohol-free life). It has also been used with much success in post-surgical healing. Patients who use guided imagery prior to their procedures have been found to have fewer complications, and quicker recovery rates than those who did not.

Guided imagery is a great way to reprogram the mind and help you react calmly to otherwise challenging situations. Folks who use guided imagery feel more empowered and at peace in stressful situations, because in essence, they have prepared themselves ahead of time to accept a good outcome.

You can have someone talk you through a visualization exercise (Laura has a wonderful healing tape for just this purpose; see the order form at the back of the book), or you can use a tape on your own schedule. You can even make up a visualization routine of your own. If you are visually oriented, you may want to draw your visualization as a way to give your desired outcome a tangible representation from your mind, through your hand, and onto the paper where your spirit can explore what you wish to manifest.

> **Take Heed**
>
> Some people begin a guided meditation exercise with the best of intentions—only to fall asleep halfway through the tape or the session. Don't sweat it if this happens to you. While your body is sleeping, your brain's still awake! It will hear and understand the message.

Your Handwriting: Imagery That Defines You

We can find another kind of imagery in something most of us do every day (though perhaps not as often in this computer age): write! The intuitive art of *graphology* involves looking at an individual's handwriting to divine information about that person. Handwriting is hard to fake or manipulate without tremendous conscious effort; in that way, it becomes a terrific barometer for our moods, feelings, and physical states.

Examining the appearance of the words that come from our hands can tell us if we are happy or sad, well or ill, confident or wary. Your doodles and spontaneous scribbling are also tangible messages your body and mind send to your spirit. Do you draw geometrical shapes and mazes (no way out!)? Or do you draw cartoons of people in situations (sarcastic or sweet …)?

> **Future Focus**
>
> **Graphology** is the intuitive art devoted to interpreting your written words and marks to reveal information about your moods, feelings, and physical states.

Graphology expert Anna Koren, consultant to businesses, governments, even law enforcement agencies, supports the following general characteristics of handwriting analysis:

- Small writing indicates a writer with mental focus and analytical thinking.

- Large writing indicates the writer's wish for attention and admiration, as well as the need to show love in return.

- Left-slanted writing indicates a writer who is self-conscious and/or introverted.

- Right-slanted writing denotes a writer who shows the potential for sociability and extroversion.

- Upright writing denotes a writer who is an independent, objective thinker and balanced decision-maker.

- Heavy pressure denotes a writer who pushes insistently and tries to persuade.

- Medium pressure denotes a writer who goes to no extremes but maintains a friendly balance.

- Light pressure denotes a writer who chooses carefully, is wary, and is sometimes overly sensitive to perceived slights.

What message is your hand sending *you* through the imagery of your written words and marks?

Mind-Body Empowerment from Prayer

Researcher Larry Dossey has publicized numerous scientific studies that confirm what religious faiths have taught for thousands of years: that prayer has power, and that its effects are real. Dr. Dossey concluded that …

- The power of prayer does not diminish with distance.

- Prayer can be continuous.

- There is no one right way to address God.

- Relinquishing prayers work best.

- Love added to prayer increases its power.

- Prayer is outside of time.

- Prayer is a reminder that we are not alone.

The "prayer studies" not only give credence to long-held religious traditions; they also point to the reality of the mind-body connection, and indeed to the interconnectedness of all life and all creation. Prayer can be an incredibly empowering tool, especially when you or someone you love is facing health problems. There *is* something you can do on a spiritual level to affect the outcome for mind and body!

Restoring Balance

Good all-around health happens when we understand that we are equal parts mind, body, and spirit, and that we need to find peace in all three of these aspects of ourselves. There are millions of ways you might choose to find that peace. Going to church every Sunday is enough for some people. Daily meditation works for others. Still others need yoga sessions, regular retreats, or divination tools. The possibilities are endless. Here's a technique that anyone can use to bring a little balance back, whatever your other activities.

Breathing: The 4-7-8 Exercise

Unless you're a trained vocalist, you probably don't pay all that much attention to your breathing. Even though we're doing it 24/7, we Westerners are not very conscious breathers. We don't often use our full lung capacity. And when we get stressed, we tend to send all our energies right up to our neck and shoulders (which is why you often get breathless in times of tension).

Deep, controlled breathing sends vital oxygen to all your cells by enriching your blood. It also redirects energy down to your lower chakras, helping you feel more balanced and secure. This breathing exercise is easy to remember, and it's inconspicuous to perform. Try it next time you feel your nerves heading toward the edge.

1. Sit comfortably with both feet on the floor and your back and neck erect. (Try imagining a string at the very top of your head, pulling you upright.)

2. Breathe in for a slow count of four. *Slowly*—as in "one Mississippi, two Mississippi ..."

3. Hold this breath for a slow count of seven.

4. Exhale for a slow count of eight.

5. Do a minimum of three repetitions of the 4-7-8 sequence; nine reps are even more beneficial.

The 4-7-8 technique is a fabulous stress-buster, and a great way to "get back in your body" when tension or worry has jolted you out of it. Remember, breath is prana, the life force. Connect yourself to that, and you are accessing a powerful tool to reach for the Divine, the source of all wisdom.

Your Body Hears Everything You Say

Your body is very trusting. It only knows what you tell it, consciously or unconsciously. And it believes everything it hears.

Tell your body, "Every winter I get a terrible cold" ... and obligingly, every winter your body will give you a terrible cold. Tell your body, "I'm so clumsy, such a klutz" ... and your body will obediently trip over the next thing in its path. Tell your body, "This chore is a pain in the neck!" ... and guess what you'll get?

As the metaphysical teacher and guru Louise Hay says, you just can't detach from your body. Your mind, your body, and your spirit are so closely integrated that they cannot be separated. And they are always listening to one another.

The tapes we tend to run in our heads over and over, the ones that make up our self-image, were mostly "recorded" for us in childhood. Much of what we think we know about ourselves comes from that formative period of our lives.

But that doesn't mean you're doomed to live out the messages your parents and peers gave you years ago. You can record new messages over those tapes, if you choose to. You can tell your body new messages. And guess what? Your body, bless it, will believe them, too! In your journal, reserve a page to write positive affirmations for your body's health and well-being. Start with this one: *Every cell in my body today vibrates with vitality in harmony with all that is. I am alive!*

Think healing, think positive. You *are* alive, and your body is here to walk you joyfully into your future.

The Least You Need to Know

- To be truly healthy, all your systems—body, mind, and spirit—need to be balanced and strong.

- Your body communicates with you through posture and attitude, as well as through pain and illness.

- The spirit of your handwriting and spontaneous scribbling illustrate your body's moods and your mind's preoccupations.

- Guided imagery, conscious breathing, prayer, and meditation can all restore a healthy balance to your life.

- Your body believes whatever you tell it, positive or negative.

Chapter 10

Inner Workings

In This Chapter

- ◆ Your body's chi, or energy
- ◆ How energy meridians reflect and affect your health
- ◆ How health intuitives identify energy blockages
- ◆ Improving your energy flow—and your health

Your body has a higher intelligence all its own, and you can see it in action every day. If you cut your finger, platelets and white blood cells swarm to the site to fight infection and stop the bleeding. When you eat, all the parts of your digestive system work in concert to squeeze nutrients from the food and send nourishment where it's needed.

You don't have to make these things happen; your body's systems know what to do all on their own. And when your body is reasonably well balanced, a state doctors call *homeostasis*, it all just works, every day and 'round the clock, fired by physiological mechanisms we simply take for granted.

But if you stop to think about it metaphysically, you've got to be amazed. *How does my body know how to do that? Where is the spark that fires my existence?* Answer: It's all in the energy!

The Body Magnificent

Your body's many systems work so smoothly and communicate so elegantly because they're connected by the energy that flows through them all. You can't see this energy in the ordinary sense, but it's there. And it can be sensed—through intuition.

It's like the way you can't see your blood flowing, but if you stop, center, breathe deeply, and concentrate, you feel your pulse moving as your heart beats—or how you can't ordinarily view your brain at work, but you sure can "see the gears turning" when someone else is deep in thought. Intuition gives us the ability to sense the body's energy, and especially the way that its energy moves. Once you understand how and why this can be done, you have that much more power to affect your energies for the better.

Chakras, Meridians, and Health

As we said in Chapter 6, your body's energy field is generated by your chakras, the whirling wheels of light within you. The seven main chakras run from the base of your spine to the crown of your head. But all throughout your body are dozens upon dozens of smaller chakras. These work together to generate your aura, the energy field that surrounds you at all times.

According to yoga theory, chakras release and channel prana, your life force, moving it upward—ever higher toward enlightenment. The metaphor of the lotus blossom, which is rooted in mud but flowers in brilliant beauty at the water's surface, is the one yogis use to describe how releasing the free flow of prana in your body can lead you to bliss.

A few names for the universal healing energy in other cultures:

- In India: *Prana*

- Polynesian Hunas: *Mana*

- In Native American Iroquois tradition: *Orenda*

- In Hebrew: *Ruach*

- In Islamic countries: *Barraka*

- In Japan: *Ki* (Reiki is named from this word.)

- In China: *Ch'i* or *chi*

Use this tai chi movement to feel the energy of your heart chakra. Begin with your hands outstretched, and as you move them together, feel the energy warm and gather between your hands until you hold your heart within them.

Prana, chi, or energy, moves along a path of *meridians* to flow throughout the body. Over thousands of years, Eastern medicine has pinpointed the placement and purpose of these meridians and learned how working with those meridians can ease pain or restore health. In acupuncture, for example, several fine needles are precisely placed along specific meridians to remove energy blockages or to redirect chi in healthier ways. Chiropractors manipulate your spine. In Western medical terms, what chiropractors do is free and restore the full connections of your nervous system; from an Eastern perspective, they open energy pathways to release chakra energy.

Future Focus

Meridians mark pathways of energy through the body, which health practitioners, both alternative and intuitive, can use to release and restore the body's life force.

Energy Flow

Your energy meridians work in much the same way as your body's circulation system (though their pathways don't necessarily coincide). Meridians move energy through your body the way your blood vessels ferry oxygen and nutrients through your body. Both your energy meridians and your blood vessels are part of your body's overall communications system. When everything is working properly, both energy and blood can flow through your body freely, and all is well.

That's how the inner life force works!

Meridians mark pathways of energy through the body.

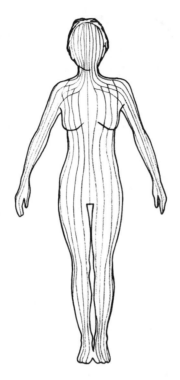

Energy Blockages

When there's a blockage in any part of your body, your life force energy stalls or becomes stagnant and health is affected. A medical doctor can identify from certain telltale symptoms a blockage in the circulation system—like a particular heart sound or a weak pulse. Sometimes those red flags are the first indications of a problem. That's because the early physical symptoms of circulatory trouble can be so slight, as subtle as a vague dizziness or a bodily ache.

It's the same with alternative and intuitive health practitioners—from massage therapists to radiant healers. Although alternative practitioners, such as massage therapists, feel the energy blockage with their hands, intuitive practitioners, including radiant healers, *sense* an energy blockage. They use their gifts to pinpoint the blocked meridian's physical location, in the neck or the foot or wherever it happens to be, and direct healing energy to restore well-being (perhaps also facilitating a trip to the massage therapist, acupuncturist, or chiropractor!). When Laura sees health blocks, certain systems flash to her, as if on a giant circuit board.

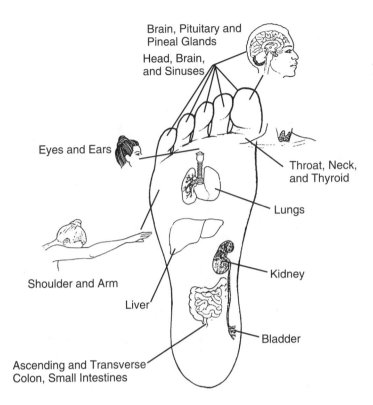

Brain, Pituitary and
Pineal Glands

Head, Brain,
and Sinuses

*Reflexology, a form of foot
massage, connects pressure
points on the foot to areas of
health throughout your body.*

Eyes and Ears

Throat, Neck,
and Thyroid

Lungs

Shoulder and Arm

Kidney

Liver

Bladder

Ascending and Transverse
Colon, Small Intestines

Often, the symptoms of energy blockage are subtle, too, and may not present them-selves as physical problems. Blocked energy can result in an emotional reaction, a spiritual reaction, *or* a physical reaction—or any combination of these. When a health intuitive makes a diagnosis based on energy flow, it's often a multileveled one. Laura will often define imbalances to her clients by describing the location of the main source of system stress, be it physical, mental, or emotional.

Energy blockages can be very profound, or quite transitory. They can come of a long-term life imbalance, or just arise on the basis of a passing emotion. Either way, energy healing can be very effective because it treats all levels of the problem—physi-cal, spiritual, and emotional.

Working with Body Energy

Unlike the standard pulse rates or normal body temperatures that Western medicine uses as its baselines of health, each person's energy system is entirely unique. The way prana manifests in you is an energy all your own, which works in a customized way for *you*. Its flow can change in reaction to the things you encounter in your daily life, an ongoing work or family situation, or a passing mood, even as it is set by such per-manent factors as your personality and history.

Divine Inspiration _____

Did you know that the "normal" human body temperature of 98.6 degrees is based purely upon averages? Your own body temperature on a "healthy day" is likely to be higher or lower than that somewhat arbitrary number. Try taking your temperature on several different "healthy days" to find your own average. How far above or below 98.6 degrees is it? Knowing the subtle nuances of your own body can help you to better understand how it works, and it can also teach you which clues and symptoms indicate the need for some support.

Interestingly, when you consult an intuitive health professional, not only your own energy but also your *practitioner's* energy comes into play. These two independent energy systems inevitably overlap as you work together, and they affect each other—creating a synergy of healing power. Here, again, is why you need to bring your own intuitive strengths into any encounter with a practitioner—actually, *any* health practitioner, whether it be traditional, alternative, or intuitive.

Think about just who it is who'll be laying their hands on you. Is there some resonance between you? How do you feel about this person on a gut level? You need to find a practitioner you're completely comfortable with, so it's okay to go beyond the factual into the territory of the emotions. Tune into the practitioner's energy, because it's just as important as your energy is.

Here's a list you can use to gauge how a health practitioner's energy and your own energy might overlap. This list works for choosing both mainstream and intuitive practitioners.

◆ Do you like the sound of his or her voice?

◆ Does the person make eye contact? If so, how do you feel about that contact?

◆ Do you resonate with the things or principles the practitioner is saying?

◆ Is the practitioner focused, or does he or she seem scattered or unprepared?

◆ Do you feel you've been heard as an individual or lumped into a generalized statistic?

◆ How good are the practitioner's references?

◆ Is the practitioner forthcoming about training and licensure or certification in his or her field of healing?

◆ How many people with your condition does the practitioner treat each year, and how does he or she track the effectiveness of treatments?

◆ Does the practitioner believe in your power to heal?

♦ Are you considered an equal participant in the healing work?

♦ Is the practitioner open to your unique choices for creating a healing team? Will the practitioner be able to support and respect these choices?

Revelations Without Invasion

Although energy work and intuitive body healing are physically noninvasive, in some ways they can be more personal than any medical procedure you've ever had! That's because they affect your body's essential energies, your life force. Your practitioner will focus on the mental and spiritual aspect of your energy flow, as well as on the physical side.

For example, you might go to an intuitive professional for help with a nagging neck pain. You've never had whiplash or any other neck injury, you've tried four different pillows and three kinds of mattress, you've gotten various ineffective diagnoses and treatments from various doctors, and the pain remains. An intuitive might tell you, "This is not really a physical problem. It's emotional. You're bottling up your voice with someone in your life, keeping all your feelings hidden. Your throat chakra energy needs to be released. You need to own your own voice in this situation."

A diagnosis like this one—even though it may be spot-on—may not be enough to stop the pain. You might need to combine healing methods, integrating your own experience of traditional medical, complementary therapies, and intuitive techniques as you explore the source of your disease within your mind, body, and spirit. When it comes right down to it, you are responsible for your health. Optimal health comes with a balance, a homeostasis, of mind and body, and we would add, spirit, as well.

The more you develop your own intuitive knowledge of all three of these elements— mind, body, and spirit—the more accurately you will be able to divine and direct your life force energy and live a vital future.

Health Intuitives

Health intuitives are practitioners with the ability to tune into a person, look within them, and see or sense their energies. Generally, a health intuitive can get a snapshot of what's going on in the physical body. A skilled and sensitive health intuitive like Laura not only senses or "sees" physical symptoms, but can also make connections between those symptoms to draw conclusions about your health. For example, she might say something like "You have a deep pain in your upper left side," or "You're walking around in a daze, almost faint; you seem to have a blood-sugar problem," or

"Your body is sensitive to certain foods. Here are the ones that are causing trouble." Laura's descriptions can be very accurate, but she always emphasizes the need for proper medical testing and follow-up. When her dear friend Jen wasn't feeling well, Laura told her that she had a hot gallbladder and needed surgery, fast. Jen listened, and did her best to patiently follow her HMO's frustrating red tape and slow testing procedures. It took another week before Jen was rushed into the ER in agony and had that emergency gallbladder surgery.

Some health intuitive professionals are known specifically as *medical intuitives*. These practitioners may be more clinically trained in the physical workings of the body. They may focus more on the scientific and clinical aspects of physical health, in keeping with their knowledge and training.

But good health intuitives train as well. Many study anatomy and the body's systems and work with traditional physicians to help improve their accuracy and their interpretations of what they see. They might also work at helping you integrate this information with the mind, body, and spirit.

Of course, *intuitive practitioners are not medical doctors*, as any reputable one will be quick to tell you. But by tuning into your energies, they can see past the surface symptoms to help pinpoint physical imbalances. With that information, you can choose the right medical professionals and coordinate further care.

Intuitive X-Rays?

So how do health intuitives do it? Do they just scan the body like a human x-ray machine and see what's going on in there? Do they do a prana MRI?

Actually, there are as many ways to do an intuitive health reading as there are health intuitives! As everyone's inner energies are unique, and as every intuitive health reading involves two individuals' energetic forces, it's impossible to generalize about what any reading will be like.

Health intuitives are good at identifying multipronged medical problems: those that stem from multiple insults to a person's system or are rooted in emotional or spiritual imbalances. Intuitives can be very helpful if you're living with symptoms that have been misdiagnosed in the past, or that have been treated many times without relief.

A good health intuitive should ideally be able to give you a sense of the urgency of a medical situation, like Laura did with her friend Jen. Your reading should clearly indicate if the problem is a low-grade or slow-developing one, or if you should see a doctor *this minute*. An intuitive should also be able to steer you to the right medical practitioner for your problem, and often will give you suggestions for ways you might use integrative medical techniques in your healing process.

Health intuitives work in all kinds of ways. Many will want to see you in person. Some of those who do so will wish to lay hands on you, or will "float" their hands several inches above your skin to get a sense of your aura. But other health intuitives, like Laura, can do a reading just by talking with you on the phone; others will focus on a photograph of you; still others can work via the most impersonal means, like e-mail, and need nothing more than your name.

Before you dismiss any of these methods out of hand, remember that there are a lot of doors into the clubhouse! All a health intuitive really needs is to get a bead on your own uniquely flowing energy. As we're all intercon-nected, energetically speaking, a health intuitive just has to "plug in" to that universal energy system to get through to yours. That's why any of these methods—and dozens more—can be valid. What's important is that you find a practitioner whose methods and manner feel right to you.

Edgar Cayce, for example, used nothing more than a person's name and age to plug into his or her Akashic Record and do a health reading in a trancelike state—often from hundreds or thousands of miles away from the recipient. So although you may think it's more accurate to have a health intuitive read for you in person, remember, it's not always necessary!

Take Heed

We wish we didn't have to say it, but sadly, we do: There are bogus health intuitives out there, so be cautious when you choose a practitioner. Be especially on guard if a health intuitive ever promises that he or she can cure you. Healing your body is within *your* power, not anyone else's. A legitimate health intuitive will offer insight and guidance—not cures.

Metaphorical Messages

Once your chosen health intuitive has "plugged in" to your energies, the messages received are very individual to the way the intuitive intuits and to the energy sur-rounding your unique situation. Some health intuitives are especially straightforward, seeing the physical body just as it is, cells, blood, bones, organs, and all. Others might receive their messages via images or metaphors. See the following examples:

◆ A fractured bone might be "seen" as a simple image, two lines jaggedly broken apart.

◆ A stomach problem might temporarily give an intuitive the same sense or physi-cal sensation in his or her own body.

◆ An image of a bowl of rocks in the belly could lead an intuitive to identify indi-gestion, as well as validate the client's own perception of the problem.

- An intuitive might "hear" his or her spirit guide saying that a client has an ear infection.

- A "hot" sensation may be mirrored in an intuitive's body as he or she scans your painful knee.

- Scar tissue may be "seen" by a health intuitive as a cloudiness or thickening in an area.

- Based on an understanding of chakras, an intuitive might see and sense blocks in different regions of the body that correspond with the client's emotional body.

Just as different people experience pain in many different ways, health intuitives sense the body's energy in highly individual ways. That is another reason why it's such a good idea to talk with a potential health intuitive about how he or she sees and interprets messages. Make sure ahead of time that you're comfortable with how your practitioner works.

Feel the Healing: Intuitive Touch

Intuitive touch, or radiant healing, is the name we give a range of healing techniques that take their cues from your energy field, your aura field, and your chakra points. Intuitive touch methods are hands-on (or hands-above, in the case of Reiki), requiring physical closeness between practitioner and client.

Reiki

Reiki is a Japanese technique of energy medicine that has been practiced for hundreds of years. It is used primarily for healing and for pain relief, but as it deals with the inner energy system it can also be used to bring emotional and spiritual comfort and peace.

The life force is called "Ki" in Japanese (it's the same idea as the Chinese *chi*). Reiki—pronounced *RAY-key:* "ray" like the sun's warmth, "key" as in the key to your body's energies—is a way of manipulating the energies past blockages, back into their free-flowing channels.

Reiki healers often sense ki and move ki in the form of heat in their hands and bodies. In an in-person Reiki treatment, the practitioner might lay hands on you, or might move his or her hands several inches above you when working over chakras in the chest and pelvic regions. Through their hands, they serve as conduits for Universal Energy to move through them and into your energy field. The energy will go where it needs to, whatever the client's physical position or limitations.

Reiki also transcends distance. Many practitioners participate in long-distance healing work (similar in some ways to a prayer chain) and use special symbols to send energy to people who've requested healing in locations all over the world.

What does a Reiki treatment feel like? Many clients feel a soothing transfer of heat as the practitioner works—even if the practitioner never actually touches them. (Laura's clients often refer to her hands as "mini space heaters.") Others feel warmth moving through their bodies. Many clients report a very soothing feeling of calm and peacefulness. Some will fall asleep, often free of the pain that has dogged them relentlessly. Essentially, Reiki is an ancient healing technique of universal energy transference, so the sensations are as individual as you are!

Reiki practitioners must all undergo study, practice, and the passing of attunements to open up the healing channels and currents. Practitioners go through various levels of attunement before they are certified to practice Reiki. When you receive an attunement, it is thought that your ki ascends.

Resonances

Next time you're enjoying a hot cup of coffee or tea, try this little sensory experiment. Set your mug or cup down and slowly draw your hand close to its side—close, but without touching it. At what point can you feel the heat of the liquid radiating out to your hand? You don't have to touch the mug to feel the warmth. That's a lot like the way Reiki practitioners can move energy without touching you: The energy just radiates outward from their well-attuned hands.

You can use this higher ki to heal yourself, or you can turn it outward to bring healing to others, or to your pets. Many people, just for self-help purposes, become attuned at the first or second level; it isn't an arduous process, and it brings relief in so many situations of physical or emotional distress. You may want to look for Reiki teachers at holistic centers in your community, if you are interested in exploring your own healing Reiki talents.

Studies have shown Reiki to reduce post-surgery recovery time by up to 30 percent. Because it's noninvasive, Reiki is an excellent complement to Western medical practices. Many integrated hospitals around the United States are now encouraging Reiki before and after surgical procedures as a valid method of pain management and as a way to reduce complications, avoid side effects, and speed healing time.

Because of their attunement with the universal energies, some highly attuned Reiki practitioners experience an increase in their own intuitive capabilities. If this sounds interesting to you, be sure that you choose a practitioner or a Master who not only understands the Universal energy, but also has a good sense of boundaries and ethics when it comes to accepting and "sharing" these intuitive bursts.

Shamans, Psychics, and Soul Workers

Shamans, traditional healers in many societies, are often deeply connected with animal energies and the influence of the natural world. When a person with a health problem consults a shaman, he might be advised that he "needs more bear energy"— and this prescription is well understood, metaphorically, in the context of their shared culture. Shamans make good use of trance states, meditation, and dreams, interpreting the animal spirits' metaphorical messages in much the same way health intuitives do. Increasingly, shamans are bringing the knowledge of indigenous and ancient cultures, such as Mayan and Native American, to new relevance in our mainstream experience.

Psychics also understand health issues, though not to the level of a true health intuitive. But as psychics are drawing from the same energy stream, as it were, they can give insight into medical matters.

Soul workers go beyond the limits of psychotherapy or counseling to help you connect with your divine purpose. They encourage you to consider the impact you are to have on the earth, and to act for the higher good. Soul workers can get in touch with your energies and help you "tune in" to a higher frequency. When they work with your energies, they encourage physical healing, as well.

Enjoy exploring the many ways you can divine—how you can get to know—how the life force flows through *your* essential self. Direct that energy to bring your body, mind, and spirit into harmonious balance.

The Least You Need to Know

- Your body has a higher intelligence: its energy, or life force.

- Energy flows freely through your body when you're well-balanced.

- When your energy flow is blocked, you can experience physical, emotional, or spiritual problems.

- Health intuitives sense your energy flow to pinpoint blockages and spot medical conditions.

- Other intuitive professionals—such as Reiki practitioners, shamans, and soul workers—also work with your body's energy to promote health and balance.

Chapter 11

Signs and Messages

In This Chapter

- ◆ Being intuitive about your own health
- ◆ Astrology's Chiron and Tarot's healers
- ◆ Auras and your subtle bodies
- ◆ Yoga's mind, body, spirit triangle
- ◆ Understanding and honoring your body

When you want to serve as your own health intuitive, divination techniques and tools really come in handy. In this chapter you'll find lots of exercises and suggestions for using divination in matters of physical health.

Remember, each of us has our own background of knowledge and learning when it comes to medicine. If you excelled in chemistry and biology in your school days, or if you've been a caregiver for an elder relative, or if you've had medical training of any kind, your health intuition will be wired along the lines of what you already know. So pay close attention to the images you receive in your intuitive work. How do they tie in to your knowledge or experience?

Be Your Own Health Intuitive

Your body is always giving you signs and signals, miniature news bulletins on the state of your physical health. Sometimes these signs are subtle, hard to identify or even to notice. Sometimes they're major and impossible to ignore. And sometimes, you know that symptoms are there, but you push them away with over-the-counter medication or the simple force of will—until they resolve themselves, or develop into something more serious.

On the other hand, when the trouble signs are slight, you can genuinely miss them. Illness can sneak up on you sometimes, no matter how intuitive or self-aware you are. So pay attention to your body's signals and signs—but don't blame yourself for an ailment if one should develop. Instead, you might ask yourself: "Is there something I need to learn from this experience?"

Future Focus

Hypochondria is a mental affliction, in which sufferers believe everything is going wrong in their bodies. Intuitive knowledge of physical problems is something different entirely!

Follow your intuition if you "just know" that something is specifically wrong with your health, even though your doctor can't pinpoint any problems. Thyroid imbalances, for example, are often extremely difficult to diagnose and treat effectively without great attention and care on the part of your physician. You may be ill, but you're certainly not a *hypochondriac!* Intuitive knowledge of a health problem is specific, not a cloud of fear. Be persistent about seeking care until the source of your medical problem is uncovered.

Now's a good time to try an intuitive health scan on yourself. Have a pen or pencil handy and use the space provided to write. Or you could use your journal. Give your brain the task of being your scribe; if it's busily occupied with writing, it won't be able to get in the way of the message your body needs to send to you.

1. Sit comfortably and quietly, feet on the floor, arms and legs relaxed.

2. Breathe deeply and ground yourself, using whatever technique you prefer.

3. Assess how your body is feeling right now. Starting with your toes, focus your intuition's attention on the parts of your body—your feet, your calves, your knees, and so on—up to the top of your head. Continue to breathe deeply as you ask yourself:

   Does this body part feel heavier than others?

   Is this part in pain?

Do you feel any achiness, numbness, or tingling?

Does this body part feel hot? Cold?

Do you feel tight and claustrophobic?

Is your breathing shallow or full, fast or slow, regular or labored?

Are you breathing from your abdomen, watching your belly move in and out with each breath? Or are you breathing from your chest, causing your shoulders to rise on each inhalation?

If you place a finger over your right nostril to close it, can you breathe easily and fully through your left? If you close the left nostril, can you breathe easily and fully through the right? Which is better?

Overall, how do your clothes feel on your body?

Overall, how is your posture? Are you sitting as straight as you can?

If you stretch your arms and turn your head from side to side, is movement easy, or does it feel restricted, tight, or painful?

Record all your observations in your journal, even for those areas in which you have "nothing to report." (You might note "feet—fine" or "lower legs—okay.") It's a good way to get into the habit of slowing down and systematically checking every part of yourself, head to toe.

4. Read over your notes as dispassionately as an intuitive medical practitioner would. How do your body's physical sensations relate to other aspects of your life?

5. Now go back to the body observations you wrote in Chapter 9. Do you see similar notes? Do the repetitions point to an area of concern? Or are your observations wildly different?

The more frequently you perform a "body scan" like this one, the more accurately you will be able to divine and interpret your body's messages.

> **CAUTION**
>
> **Take Heed**
>
> Intuitive techniques will go a long way toward creating a healthy life, but don't overlook all that Eastern and Western medicine have to offer. If your intuitive work indicates a physical problem, please seek appropriate medical attention and testing from a licensed health professional right away.

Mind, Body, Spirit

When you're working in health intuition, stay aware of the three-part nature of good health. Your physical, emotional, and spiritual energies all play a role. Because these energies are so closely intertwined, all of them have to be strong and balanced for you to be truly healthy—and any of them can give you clues to whatever may be ailing you.

Your physical energy can give you evidential clues: medical symptoms, observable facts that can be seen, heard, or measured. Your emotional and mental energies can help you understand connections between your body's sensations and your mind's work. (If your ankle hurts and you haven't injured it, are you resisting movement for some reason?) Your spiritual energy hones in on interpretations of your sensations: how you feel in terms of energy. For example, if a sore throat feels hot and angry, your spirituality can help you identify what aspect of your life is making you feel the same way.

Edgar Cayce's Messages for Health

Edgar Cayce's legacy lies in his 14,600 channeled readings, as well as the Association for Research and Enlightenment (A.R.E.) he helped establish a few years before his death in 1945. The vast amount of information that Edgar channeled included specific health regimes and treatments for each of the 14,600 individuals he read for. The A.R.E. still exists today, and is run by the Cayce family (www.edgarcayce.org) to continue Edgar's work.

Resonances

Laura receives her information through channeling, the flow of information from the "ethers" through a honed source, as Edgar Cayce did before her. Based on their level of trance, individuals who work as channels serve as conduits for information to pass through them. Those who go deeper into trance may show significant changes in their voice, posture, or energy. Both information and entities can be channeled. Some channels have no recollection of these deep trance states, but others do.

At the A.R.E. Clinic in Phoenix, Arizona, doctors use castor oil for virtually every aspect of health. Edgar Cayce recommended castor oil packs over the liver in 545 of his readings as a treatment for the liver and digestive system. Healers from many cultures have used castor oil for more than 3,000 years, but Cayce's work helped bring its benefits into the modern era.

To support the work of the Cayce readings, a company called Heritage Products created an entire product line based on his work. The Heritage Company is recognized by the A.R.E. community as the source for pure Cayce products. Their health line reflects the breadth of Edgar Cayce's readings—with products ranging from tooth powder to muscle massage ointment to Aura Glow oils to mouthwashes to shampoos to castor oil packs.

Cayce's work has stood the test of time; many holistic and homeopathic remedies in wide use today come from his insights. After decades of dependence on manufactured drugs, research has now begun to document the medical value of Cayce's more natural remedies—something the A.R.E. has known since the 1940s!

By focusing so strongly on the equal importance of our physical, emotional, and spiritual energies, Edgar Cayce blazed the path that health intuitives today still follow. (We can only wonder what other important health knowledge we would have today if Edgar Cayce had only listened to his own body's messages and avoided such an early burnout.)

Health in the Stars and in the Cards

Astrology's charting of the planets reveals so much about our lives and health, and none more so than the asteroid Chiron ⚷. Chiron, often referred to by astrologers as the "wounded healer," can help you identify areas where emotional, physical, or spiritual healing needs to occur.

In larger planetary cycles that affect us all, Chiron aspected to Uranus indicates a radical shift of thinking, such as the movement toward integrating traditional, alternative, and intuitive health care. Chiron conjunct to Neptune shows the mystical investigation of spiritual beliefs. Chiron and Pluto, joined in a cycle that began in December of 1999, promise transformation and higher truth. On a personal scale, Chiron's placement in your astrological birth chart can show you how you can harness and direct healing energies in your own life.

Whatever deck you choose to work with, the symbolism and images of the cards make the Tarot a good intuitive tool to receive primary messages relevant to medical issues. Some cards to consider:

♦ The Chariot often points to physical well-being—strength, vigor, and good health, if the card is dealt upright, or weakness and poor health if the card comes up reversed.

♦ The Devil frequently relates to addictions of any kind—even an addiction to a physical ailment. If you're hanging on to an illness for emotional reasons, the Devil might point this out to you. (Chains, in Tarot imagery, connote self-imposed restrictions. Are you holding yourself back from good health?) Reversed, the Devil can indicate an addiction you're overcoming.

♦ The 4 of Swords tells you that you need more rest! If you've got an illness that you just can't shake, maybe you're not giving your body the time and peace it needs to recover. The 4 of Swords might well come up in your reading to tell you to go a little easier on yourself.

◆ The 9 of Swords points to distress of any kind, either physical or mental. When you're in the throes of illness, the 9 of Swords illustrates the depth of your pain and confusion. Conversely, the Ace of Cups indicates the flow of healing energy.

◆ The 2 of Pentacles and the 7 of Wands indicate stamina; the 8 of Wands indicates ease and comfort.

Just about any Tarot card can relate to an aspect of a health issue. It all depends on the question you have posed and the relationship of your chosen cards to one another in your spread. Try this Seven-card Health spread; it looks at the roots of the health problem, the nature of the problem, and its future resolution—important aspects of any health situation.

1. Sit comfortably at a table, center yourself, and relax.

2. Begin to shuffle your Tarot deck, clearing your mind of all thoughts but the issue at hand. (Try phrasing your question openly, such as, "I want to know more about my medical condition.")

3. Whenever you feel ready, stop shuffling. Divide the deck into three roughly equal piles.

4. Choose the pile you feel most drawn to and set the others aside.

5. Deal the top seven cards in this pattern:

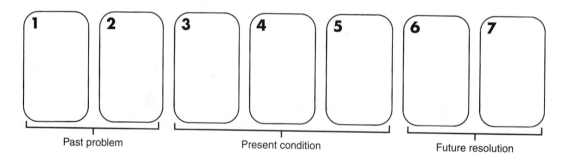

| Past problem | Present condition | Future resolution |

6. Study the cards, each one in turn. Try not to analyze them for now. Just consider what the imagery says to you. You might also like to consult a Tarot reference book, such as *The Complete Idiot's Guide to Tarot, Second Edition* for more ideas on the subtleties of each card's message. Write down your thoughts about the spread's message for your health.

Cards 1 and 2: The past roots of your health problem. _____

_____

Cards 3, 4, and 5: The present situation surrounding your health problem.

_____

Cards 6 and 7: The future resolution of your health problem. _____

_____

Getting in Touch with Your Subtle Bodies

Your subtle bodies are the layers of energy that surround and envelop your physical form. Generated by your inner energy sources, your chakras, the subtle bodies are another way of looking at your many-layered aura. Your mood, your daily experiences, your physical well-being—all these aspects and many more can make your subtle bodies full and expansive, or shallow and tight.

♦ The _physical body_ is just that, the physical vessel for your life force energy.

♦ The _astral body_ is the vessel for your mind.

♦ The _causal body_ is the vessel for your spirit.

In an ever-widening circle, your subtle bodies interpenetrate and carry the life force that is you. Here's a simple way to sense your own subtle bodies:

1. Take one hand and place it a few inches above any part of your body (bare-skinned or clothed, it makes no difference).

2. Slowly move your hand downward, without touching yourself. At what point do you feel a sensation in between your hand and your body?

3. Now make a gentle patting motion with your hand, still without touching your skin or clothing. Can you feel the energy in the space between?

You can also practice sensing subtle bodies with a partner:

1. Begin on opposite sides of a room.

2. Slowly move toward one another, making a gentle patting motion outward with your hands.

3. At what point can you feel one another's energetic presence?

Resonances

Have you ever noticed how contagious applause can be? That's because when people start clapping, they're not just expressing themselves, they're exponentially expanding their energy in an explosion of joy. When you feel that expansive energy coming your way, you want to send your own energy out to meet it—so you clap! An ovation is born!

What Your Aura Reveals

As we've seen, auras are more than just pretty colors. In fact, not everyone who "sees" auras sees them in color. Many people sense auras as texture or shape. An aura can be fluffy like a cloud of cotton, or tight and smooth as a glass shell. It can "feel" prickly, bumpy, or soothingly soft. It can even have holes—often just above a body part that has been injured or is in pain, or if you've had some jarring or shocking news. And your aura changes all through the day as you experience new moods, feelings, and needs.

Your aura can reveal any of the following:

- Your energy level (chi)
- Sites of physical trauma
- Energy blockages
- Depression
- Pain
- Satisfaction
- Worry
- Pride
- Anger
- Joy
- Inner peace
- Any human emotion or sensation

Divine Inspiration

Everything and everyone has an aura, humans and animals alike (not to mention inanimate objects and plants!). Have you ever seen a sleeping cat jump up in alarm as you silently approached it? That's because cats are especially sensitive to auras—especially when it comes to sensing intrusions into their energetic space.

It's possible to analyze your aura on your own, and your journal is a wonderful tool to use for this purpose. Just make a practice of observing the feel of your energy, exactly as it is, and writing your notes in your journal. (Try doing it first thing in the morning or last thing before bed, just to get into the habit.) What word would describe your mood? If you were a color, what color would you be? If you could stroke your emotional state, how would it feel? Over time, you'll get to know the signals and signs of your particular energy field.

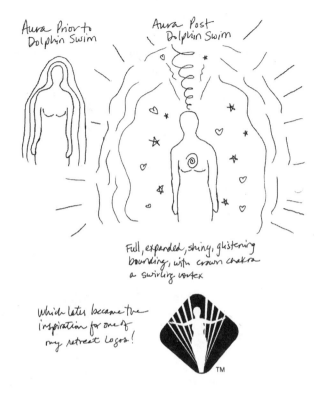

Aura Prior to Dolphin Swim

Aura Post Dolphin Swim

Full, expanded, shiny, glistening bounding, with crown chakra a swirling vortex

Which later became the inspiration for one of my retreat logos!

Still, it isn't easy to "see" your own aura—for the simple reason that you're *inside* it! Aura analysis is usually best done by someone who can observe you from a distance. And remember, unless your "helper" or practitioner uses metaphors that resonate for you, what they see won't make a lick of sense! So if you sense your moods in terms of color, someone who sees colored auras could be a good match for you. But if you feel your aura as a sensation, you might do better with another practitioner.

Listen Close, Listen Deep

The insights of Eastern philosophy have a lot to offer us when it comes to health intuition. After all, the entire system of Eastern medicine is built on an intuitive understanding of energy flow!

Yoga Union: Mind, Body, and Breath Work Together

The combination of mind, body, and energy consciousness are what make yoga practice so much more than a stretching routine. Yoga's not just exercise; done well, it strengthens your energy as it tones your body and mind. Yoga is a wonderful meditation technique—and the peace and centeredness that meditation encourages is a pillar of all-around good health. The best yoga teachers help students to learn to work within their bodies' limitations, and to use their breath to help their bodies shift into poses and postures they might have initially resisted.

Practice yoga's triangle pose and celebrate the triad of mind, body, and spirit focused in balance and harmony. When doing triangle pose, work to keep your hips in alignment with your head, shoulders, and feet. Avoid over-reaching; wherever you are, that's fine! Hold the pose as you breathe deeply and fully from your abdominal center.

Yoga's triangle pose, shown here modified, unites mind, body, and spirit.

Meditation, Mindfulness, and What Your Brain Is Doing

The number one reason why most people have trouble with meditation is pretty simple. We just can't get our minds to shut up! Your brain is like a hamster on a wheel, constantly running in place. Your intuition is more like a flowing stream, moving gently but with purpose. Their movements are so at odds that the brain rebels when confronted with intuition. It fights with its greatest strength: the force of its chatter. Your brain just interrupts. And interrupts. And interrupts.

How loud is the noise in your head? Try this quick exercise to find out:

1. Take a few deep breaths and settle yourself down.

2. Close your eyes and try to think of nothing. A blank screen of nothingness. Try to stay in this state for a few moments successfully.

3. How long does it take before your brain interrupts and reminds you to pick up the dry cleaning, mail the credit card bill, send a birthday card to your niece, deposit your paycheck, and hey, let's not forget telling you to check your watch and pay attention to the time!

Meditation seeks to direct the brain's flow of thoughts. That's why it can feel like it takes a Herculean effort to just sit still and focus in meditation. Some people even experience headaches when they first try to meditate. Opening up that healing "third eye" (remember astrology's Chiron!) can really seem uncomfortable. So in frustration, many of us just give up.

If you are new to meditation, or have already tried it and "failed" more than once, keep at it. Remember, not all forms of meditation are for everyone! Chanting helps some people's brains relax; drumming does the trick for others. Even something as simple as staring at a fixed point can help. If you looked throughout the world you'd find hundreds and hundreds of different forms of meditation. And each of these can have countless variations, so that no two meditation techniques are alike, nor are any two meditation experiences alike.

Even those who are devoted to daily meditation practice find that each experience, although similar in theme, is completely different in content. Native Americans have a saying for this: "You cannot step in the same river twice."

Not only is the water ever-moving, but so is the air and the earth. So, too, is your own energy constantly shifting.

Here are some basic "rules of the flow" that Laura gives to her meditation students to help them enhance their practice:

♦ Absolutely no drinking or drugs.

♦ Eliminate stimulants from the diet (caffeine, excessive sugar).

♦ Establish a meditation routine.

♦ Wear comfortable, nonbinding clothes for meditation.

♦ Turn off distractions such as the TV, cell phone, pager, or computer during sessions.

As you meditate, feel your body relax, your shoulders lower, your breath deepen within you, and as you reach to an awareness of your pulse moving, repeat this mantra: *River flow. River flow. Ommmmmmmmmm.* Meditation prepares your mind, body, and spirit to clear so that you can hear their deeper messages.

Interpreting Your Body's Messages

Once you've begun to listen to your body and receive its communications, you've got another task: understanding what the messages mean.

Your intellect won't always serve you well in this. For one thing, your thought process is always influenced by your first reactions to new information. For most of us, when we stub a toe or bang an arm, the immediate impact is followed by a shouted "ow!" Actually, this is the brain's conditioned response to an event. In truth, the pain is optional.

Try this, the next time you have a minor stumble. Instead of just reflexively shouting "Ouch!" reframe your initial reaction this way: "Wow, that's a lot of sensation." Because you're not immediately labeling the event as good or bad, your brain must become alert to what else is going on. Notice how your body response changes. Instead of pain what do you feel? Heat? Pressure? Agitation? Sympathy? Understanding? Energy? Do you notice that you "get over it" a lot faster when you've disengaged from labeling your reaction as pain?

If you want to get to the truth of your body's responses, free yourself from any preconceived labels or expectations about what you are experiencing physically, emotionally, and spiritually. Health intuition, the key to understanding your body's metaphorical code, the "language" it's using to speak to you, rests in giving yourself the freedom and opportunity to hear and assess the "data" you receive. Use your journal to record all that you discover.

Resonances

Most of us have suffered a headache at one time or another. How would you categorize your headache? Is it sharp? Dull? Clustered? Does your head feel like it is being squeezed, or like it's been pierced by an arrow? Is it worse when it's cold or hot out? Is it worse in the morning or evening? These are just a few of the questions a homeopathic physician would ask in order to prescribe the precise treatment or remedy for you. By paying close attention to the information your body is giving, you can hone in on relief—and answers—faster.

Is It Serious?

Grounding and filtering can help you gauge whether a health condition you're intuiting is minor or demands immediate attention. A good way of doing this is by asking your body to use a symbolic image to characterize the seriousness of what you're seeing.

Decide on a series of symbols that would make sense to you. For example, if you drive a lot you might imagine a traffic light in this role. A green light would symbolize a minor or benign condition; a yellow would be more guarded; and a red would tell you to get help quickly. Meditate on your chosen symbol system to "teach" your body how to use it.

Once you've intuitively pinpointed an area of health concern, visualize your traffic light in regard to it. With your symbolic language in place, your body will tell you how serious the problem is. You might even use your traffic light to make a quick check on your overall health from day to day. And if you feel a cold coming on, meditate upon your traffic light—it'll tell you if you need a whole day in bed or just some extra vitamin C and a scarf (remember that perverse chi!) to head off the illness.

"My Body Has Nothing to Say!"

Yes, it does. Every body has plenty to say, and says it, all the time. Concentrate on every part of your body, top to bottom, and listen.

Honoring Your Body During a Health Crisis

Of course, it's best if you can pay attention to your body's needs before you ever get to a crisis point. But that doesn't always happen, and that's when you can get sick.

During a health crisis, it's more important than ever to give your body a chance to communicate with you. Slow down: Tear yourself away from your regular schedule, and don't feel guilty about it. Perhaps a divination tool or meditation session can help you settle your mind and listen. Then do the things you need to do to heal, and don't let your mind talk you out of it! Extra rest is okay. A food craving is okay. Maybe postpone running that marathon. Honor your body, and respect its needs.

Unless, of course, you *want* to get sick … and sometimes you do. We'll talk about that more in Chapter 14.

Understand Your Options

You are the team leader in any health crisis. You can have doctors and nurses and intuitives and therapists on your team, and all of these experts have important skills and knowledge to offer. But none of them is in charge. It's *your* health; you're the boss.

Of course, when you're feeling lousy to begin with, it can be tough to summon up the energy to take the reins. (That's the other reason why so many of us cede too much power to our doctors.) If that's the case, it's time to add another member to your health-care team: a support person just for you. Ask a friend, a relative, or a colleague to be with you as your backup. Your support person can take notes for you, stick up for you, or just remain with you and hold your hand. It's amazing how much stronger you feel when you know that someone's got your back.

A health crisis of any kind can upset your life's apple cart in myriad unexpected ways. The people who care about you are going to want to help, and they won't know how. Invite them into your experience. Let them support you at a time you need them most. You won't get any medals for going it alone!

Leading Your Body, Mind, and Spirit to Whole Health

Whatever treatment options you might choose, be mindful that a health problem is rarely a matter of the physical body alone. Just as your energy intertwines many threads, your health is many-faceted, too. Pay attention to your mind and your spirit. Strengthen them as your body heals, and you'll be *truly* healthy, learning to divine and interpret the messages that lead to well-being.

The Least You Need to Know

- Divination tools and techniques can help you be your own health intuitive.

- Intuitive messages have validity; don't be put off by doubting medical pros.

- Edgar Cayce's work as a medical intuitive and channel lives on through the Association for Research and Enlightenment, providing healing support and remedies to millions.

- Honoring your body's messages and limits will help you to be aware of any serious health issues, and provide support to you while you heal.

Chapter 12

Healing and Health

In This Chapter

- Angel cards and healing lessons
- Ancient healing instruments
- The Native American Medicine Wheel
- Colors, flower essences, magnets, minerals, and more

Healing is so much more than our limited, earthly assumptions about physical wellness. In the larger reality, healing is one of the Universe's words for progress. It's about letting in the flickers and flashes of greater Truth that can move us to new levels of understanding. Sometimes, the very illnesses and health problems that challenge you most are what reveal these truths to you.

In our society, physical vitality is our only measure of what it is to be healthy. Of course your body is important! But it's only one third of your whole being. True health is a question of balance, of integration of the mind, spirit, and body.

Healing Doesn't Always Mean Curing

It can be frustrating to feel that physical health is being denied to you. Often, people in this position end up feeling angry—at themselves, at the God of their understanding, at the Universe as a whole.

But if we agree that illness is an experience you can learn from, perhaps we can trade that frustration for insight. When you're feeling physically unwell, instead of asking "Why can't I get better?" maybe the important questions are "What's really going on here? What do I need to learn?" Angel cards, with their gentle imagery and loving messages, are perfect conduits for this kind of insight. Try this exercise:

1. Sit comfortably and ground yourself.

2. Taking your deck of angel cards in your hand, begin to shuffle. As you shuffle, focus on asking your angels: "What am I to learn from the experience of this illness?"

3. When you feel ready, stop shuffling. Then, letting your intuition guide you, choose the card that "feels right" to you from any part of the deck. (Remember, if another card seems to "stick" to the chosen one, it's one that your angels want to be sure you hear. Consider both cards.)

4. This is your angelic message! Sit with the card a moment, reflecting on its imagery and its words. If your angel cards came with an explanatory booklet, you may wish to read the author's comments on your chosen card.

5. Use the following lines to jot down your reflections.

Angels' healing message

_____

_____

_____

Resonances

Just because the body is broken doesn't mean the mind or spirit has to be. Think of all the people, today and throughout history, whose physical disabilities could never contain their energy or spirit. From actor/director Christopher Reeve to cosmologist Stephen Hawking to writer Helen Keller to U.S. President Franklin D. Roosevelt to 12-year-old poet and peace activist Mattie Stepanek: Your body, healthy or unhealthy as it might be, does not have to define you.

Ancient Practices

Non-Western cultures have long acknowledged the importance and the unity of mind, body, and spirit. Divinatory rituals going back to those of ancient Egypt, the Incas, the Mayans, native American Indians, the Japanese, the Chinese, shamans, and more embrace this overall vision. Other cultures have much to teach us about how to use healing energy to live fuller, more integrated, and self-knowing lives.

Ancient practices embraced the nurturing we all need to feel healthy and whole. Bathing rituals, energetic cleansing rituals, dream journeying, and life-passage rituals all serve to connect people to the rhythms of the Universe's life force energy. And in many cultures, aging and illness have rituals of their own—they're a natural part of life, after all. Drawing on the deep wisdom of these practices, whatever your own traditions, is a way of integrating energy that can bring peace and healing.

Tibetan Bowls, Bells, and Other Instruments

Tibetan bowls, bells, and other instruments are ancient, sacred healing objects that work with sound energy to affect your brain's alpha waves. For Buddhists, the sounds can all be traced to the one sound, Om, the signature of the Universe. Bowls and bells are ancient metal instruments with incredible energetic power. The sounds they make throb or ring with a pulsating, self-sustaining energy that can be a call to meditation, a source of strength, or a focal point of physical healing. Because of their resonance and pitch, they are known to alter the state of mind of those playing them or listening to them.

The most powerful bowls (and bells) are made of a series of seven metals, each metal symbolically representing a different kind of heavenly energy. When the bowl instruments are being made, they are hand-pounded into their unique shapes over an open flame while prayers are chanted in an intensely ritualistic process. Each bowl is unique and "speaks" with its own voice, dependent not only on the shape, thickness, size, and weight of the bowl itself, but also on the pressure and energy with which the bowl is played or struck, as well as the size of the dowels used to play it.

The bowls and bells can be rung, as bells are, with a wooden striker. More often, though, you rub the outer edge of the bowl with a striker in a clockwise motion by holding the dowel perpendicular to the bowl's or bell's edge and following its rim evenly and steadily as you balance the bowl itself in the palm of your other hand (or hold the bell by its handle). The longer you rub, the more intense its frequency becomes; a Tibetan bowl's or bell's vibrations can fill your entire body with sound energy waves that you feel deep in the core of your physical being. As the bowls are played longer, and as listeners go deeper into meditation, many report hearing the sound of chanting released in the tones.

In healing rituals, Tibetan bowls or bells can be placed on, over, or around the body's chakra centers and then struck. Other people prefer to have several bowls arranged around their body. Either way, the sound vibrations from these instruments will change the alpha waves within the brain, and work to "tone up" your body's energy, cleaning out the cobwebs, in a way. Most people report a feeling of bliss, or even a "high," after experiencing the sounds of bowls and bells in person—because not only have their chakra centers been energetically cleansed, but their physical brains and cells have responded to the sound stimuli as well.

Authentic Tibetan singing bowls and bells can be quite expensive, and you should always play them before you purchase one. Selection of a bowl or bell is a highly personal task, and it is important to choose the one that sounds the most pleasing to you. For a more affordable alternative, you may want to explore the power of sound vibrations in other ways. *Tingshas*, or farmers' cymbals, are used by many intuitive health practitioners to signal the beginning and end of each session, as well as to listen for blocks in the chakra centers. They resemble two flying saucers, each about three inches in diameter, joined together by a leather cord; they often are decorated with beautiful symbols. Tingshas have a light, ringing tone that's very pleasing, and in comparison with bowls and bells, they are relatively inexpensive. Or you can try the exercise later in this chapter to find sources of sound energy in some unexpected places!

The Spotlight: A Chakra Exercise

When you're feeling good, in harmony with yourself inside and out, your chakras—those seven major energy centers that whirl in place along your spine—are working together, radiating energy all through you.

But sometimes a chakra can hit a speed bump of sorts, throwing its movement out of balance. And then the whole system can be just a bit "off"—enough to make you feel unwell, or unhappy, or simply out of sorts. This is a great exercise when you're just having one of those days:

1. In a peaceful place where you won't be disturbed, lie flat on your back. (Use a yoga mat or folded blanket if you'll be lying on a hard surface.) Let your arms rest alongside your body, palms down.

2. Perform one of the grounding exercises we discussed in Chapter 8: Imagine being plugged into the Universe, surrounded by light, or whatever makes you comfortable.

3. Visualize a spotlight shining down from above you. Its light is warm and golden. Train the spotlight's beam on your root chakra, at the very base of your spine, within your lower pelvis.

4. Concentrate your attention on the source of the light as it widens to cover that one chakra.

5. Feel the light's warmth gently heat the chakra. You may begin to feel a pulsing sensation. As your chakra warms, imagine it begin to spin like a carousel, in a clockwise motion.

6. When your root chakra is warm and you feel comfortable, imagine the spotlight moving up your spine to shine on your second chakra, in your upper pelvis. Again, widen the spotlight until it covers the chakra, and allow its warmth to gently heat your chakra and set it spinning.

7. When you feel comfortable, move the spotlight up to your third chakra, just behind your navel. Let the spotlight warm the chakra and feel it begin to spin.

8. When you're ready, visualize the spotlight moving up to your heart chakra, in the center of your chest. Again, allow the light's warmth to warm the chakra and help it spin.

9. Ready? Move the spotlight up again and focus it on your throat chakra. Pinpoint the light to cover the chakra, warm it, and allow it to spin freely.

10. When it's comfortable, move the spotlight up to your "third eye," right between your eyebrows. Feel the light's gentle heat encourage the chakra to relax, warm, and revolve.

11. Now move the spotlight up to shine on the very top of your head, the crown chakra. Feel the warmth until the chakra spins.

12. Widen the spotlight until your entire body is suffused with its golden warmth. Be aware that while your body is stable and at rest, these points within your body are spinning in harmony.

13. See yourself in peace and light, feeling as if you've been out in the sun (without any risk of sunburn). When you are ready, get up slowly, and do some light, gentle stretching—continuing to enjoy the warmth.

> **Take Heed**
>
> If you're prone to vertigo or dizziness, it might bother you to visualize spinning chakras. You'll get just as much from the exercise if you imagine the spotlight warming each chakra deep down within your body.

Did you notice any of your chakras warming more easily than others? Were some of them spinning already? Were some resistant? You might want to write down your observations in your journal and connect them with whatever is going on in your life.

Healing Power of Energy

Supportive, palliative, preventative—energy has all kinds of healing powers. And, just as your mind, body, and spirit are inseparably woven together, the effects of energy are similarly intertwined. As you learn to direct this energy, enhancing your health and becoming more self-aware, you may find you are eager to share what you know with others to help them divine a vital and healthful future for their own lives.

Vibrational Energy

Sound has an energy that you can feel, as you know if you've ever felt the bass thrum through you at a rock concert or gotten goose bumps on hearing a thrilling high E at the opera. Sound travels in waves, of course, and the energy of those waves can have a physical effect on your body's pulse rate and respiration. Metaphysically, sound energy can relax your mind and park it in neutral. It can have a soothing effect on the psyche and, as new research is beginning to show, an altering effect on your brain's alpha rhythms. When newborns turn with pleasure toward a human voice, and when mothers calm those babies with peaceful lullabies, we're seeing the power of sound in action. And when everyone at a wedding reception taps their glasses and fills the hall with ringing, you know it's time for laughter and a kiss!

Divine Inspiration

The ancient mathematician Pythagoras wrote that the planets and stars were engaged in a great dance, set to the "music of the Spheres." Today, scientific evidence is mounting that sound is a part of the very essence of the Universe, and of our own physical selves. When genetic researchers in Spain decided to see what would happen if they translated strands of DNA into music, they were pleasantly surprised at the lovely results. With the genetic bases transformed into bass notes and melodies written to match them, the DNA music had a New Age feel that the academics who heard it—particularly the psychologists—found very relaxing.

Tibetan bowls and bells, as we've seen, possess especially powerful vibrational energy. These qualities make them precious—and rare. Quartz crystals, glass bowls, crystal goblets, and many other materials can also emit sound frequencies. Because each of us resonates to some tones more than others, experiment to find which ones please you!

1. Look around your home for sound-making objects. Glass and metal are likely materials, and a cup or bowl shape helps to focus and intensify sound waves. Wine glasses, vases, basins, and bowls are all good possibilities.

2. Find a small wooden dowel to use as a striker. (The handle of a wooden kitchen spoon would work just as well.)

3. One by one, gently tap the rim of each object with your striker. Is the sound pure, bell-like, and clear, or dull and thudding? How long does it sustain itself? How do the vibrations affect you? Set aside the objects whose tones most resonate with you.

4. Take the objects you've chosen and, one at a time, gently rub the striker around and around the outside rim. This should produce a more sustained sound. Again, take note of your reaction to these vibrations.

Did one of your objects stand out in your ears? Did its sound make you feel energized, or uplifted, or peaceful? You might want to consider ways to incorporate these sounds into your own grounding rituals and daily meditation practice.

Color Energy

Why are hospitals painting over their pistachio-colored walls in favor of soft shades of rose? Why are so many restaurants decorated in red? Because color has its own energy, and different colors encourage specific effects. Hospitals want people to heal; restaurants want people to eat. The colors in the surrounding environment can help make these outcomes happen.

Take a moment to look around your own spaces, focusing on the colors and the textures you have around you. The energy of color is something that can affect you strongly—and it's one of the energies that you have a great deal of power to change and direct!

Think about what each room in your home or office is meant to do. Then consult the following color chart to decide if the existing colors meet your energy needs—and if not, what colors might be a better fit. Consider, too, the amount of color in the room. Is there too much? Not enough? What's the overall energy like? And, most importantly, how does the room's color energy feel to *you?*

Color	Effects	Helps Heal or Relieve
Red	Lively, vital	Inertia, exhaustion, poor circulation, low blood pressure, malnutrition, anemia, menstrual deficiency
Orange	Mentally and physically stimulating	Catatonia, lung problems (bronchitis, asthma), muscle cramps, kidneys, hemorrhoids
Yellow	Optimism, joy	Depression, mental lethargy, indigestion, constipation, hearing problems, skin problems, liver problems
Green	Relaxing, refreshing	High blood pressure, ulcers, headaches, sleeplessness, nerve disorders, boils, muscle tension
Blue	Hopeful, serene	Sore eyes, earache, sore throat, inflammation, infection, nausea, diarrhea, menstrual excess, skin problems (cuts, burns, itching)
Indigo	Intuitive, soothing	Pain; eyes, ears, nose, and throat problems; lung problems; skin disease; obsession
Violet	Calming, purifying	Neuralgia, sciatica, scalp, kidneys and bladder, rheumatism, neurosis, insomnia, mental disease

Flower Essences

"Treat the person, not the disease; the cause, not the effect." These are the words of Dr. Edward Bach, a renowned English immunologist and bacteriologist who worked in the early twentieth century. Dr. Bach noticed a distinct pattern in his patients: Energetically speaking, many of them had symptoms and signs of energy imbalances long before the physical manifestation of illnesses in the body emerged. So he came up with a system of 38 remedies to correct the emotional imbalances that can lead to physical, emotional, or spiritual illness. Like homeopathy, the Bach system is based on the energies of various plants. Today, his system is in use in many countries around the world.

The Bach essences are based mostly on plants, trees, and flowers, but it's not their scents that are used, as in aromatherapy. It's their energy profile that's important. The essences themselves are odorless and tasteless. You take them orally, just a few drops at a time, and they are quickly absorbed into your system. (Some people prefer to put a few drops on their pulse points.) Because they work on your energy vibrations, the essences affect your spiritual and emotional energy alone; they don't interfere with medicines or drugs, or with any part of your physical body. They're nontoxic and non-habit forming. And as they work to change the aura, they work on children, animals, even plants! You don't need to be conscious of the essence—or even conscious at all—for it to have an effect.

Resonances

Rescue Remedy, the hallmark of Dr. Bach's system, combines five of the Bach essences. It's used to counterbalance any kind of stress. Barbara, one of Laura's clients, keeps Rescue Remedy close at hand wherever her family goes. "We just pull it out whenever anyone gets hurt or feels ill or upset, and I've seen it make a big difference for the kids and for myself," she says. Rescue Remedy helped one of her daughters feel calm before surgery, soothed countless small children's bumps and bruises, even calmed the family dog after she was hit by a bus. "And when I used it myself during childbirth, it really helped me stay focused and peaceful."

Bach Flower Essences are chosen based on various permutations of personality and mood. A skilled practitioner will choose a remedy based on a client's personality and deep needs. These may be ascertained through a personality profile, a careful interview, or sometimes just through intuition. But the system is accessible to anyone, not just professional practitioners. You can read up on it informally, or study it formally in a seminar or course.

Bach Flower Essences are available at any quality health food store and through online vitamin shops. Most health food stores will stock free information pamphlets as well as a large array of books on the subject. Laura will often mix custom remedies for her clients to help them attain balance and healing. The beauty of the Bach Flower System is that if a person no longer needs a particular remedy that's in their custom bottle, it will pass through them with no effect!

This quick quiz, adapted from the Nelson Bach Company's guidelines, isn't as detailed or extensive as one a trained practitioner would give you. But it will help you understand one way that Bach Flower Essences can be selected, and it might even let you narrow the list down to the few that are right for you! Put a check mark next to the questions that you would often or regularly answer yes. The flower essence named after each question works to counterbalance this tendency.

❑ Are you so distressed by arguments that you usually give in to avoid conflict? **Agrimony**

❑ Do you have feelings of apprehension or uneasiness with no obvious cause? **Aspen**

❑ Are you easily annoyed by the habits and shortcomings of others? **Beech**

❑ Are you timid and shy, easily influenced by others? **Centaury**

❑ Do you constantly question your own decisions and judgments? **Cerato**

❑ Do you fear losing control of yourself? **Cherry Plum**

❑ Do you fail to learn from past mistakes? **Chestnut Bud**

❑ Do you need to be needed? **Chicory**

❑ Are you drowsy and listless, sleeping more than you need to? **Clematis**

❑ Are you obsessed with cleanliness? **Crab Apple**

❑ Do you often feel overwhelmed by your responsibilities? **Elm**

❑ Do you become discouraged and depressed when anything goes wrong? **Gentian**

❑ Do you believe that nothing can relieve your pain and suffering? **Gorse**

❑ Are you self-absorbed, concerned only about your own problems and ailments? **Heather**

❑ Are you filled with feelings of jealousy and hate? **Holly**

❑ Are you nostalgic, often living in the past? **Honeysuckle**

❑ Do you often feel too tired to face your routines and responsibilities? **Hornbeam**

❑ Are you impatient or irritable with anyone who seems to be moving too slowly? **Impatiens**

❑ Do you lack self-confidence? **Larch**

❑ Are you shy, overly sensitive, or often afraid? **Mimulus**

❑ Do you have frequent, sudden mood swings? **Mustard**

❑ Do you neglect your own needs to complete a task? **Oak**

❑ Are you utterly exhausted, physically and mentally? **Olive**

❑ Do you set overly high standards for yourself? **Pine**

❏ Are you excessively distressed by other people's problems? **Red Chestnut**

❏ Do you feel terror and panic? **Rock Rose**

❏ Are you always striving for perfection? **Rock Water**

❏ Are you always fidgety and nervous? **Scleranthus**

❏ Have you suffered a loss that you've never recovered from? **Star of Bethlehem**

❏ Do you suffer from extreme mental anguish? **Sweet Chestnut**

❏ Do you feel tense and high strung? **Vervain**

❏ Do you feel the need to always be right? **Vine**

❏ Are you easily distracted by outside influences? **Walnut**

❏ Do you appear to be aloof and proud? **Water Violet**

❏ Do persistent, unwanted thoughts often keep you from concentrating? **White Chestnut**

❏ Do you find yourself in a complete state of uncertainty when it comes to major life decisions? **Wild Oat**

❏ Are you apathetic, resigned to whatever may happen to you in life? **Wild Rose**

❏ Do you have a hard time forgiving and forgetting? **Willow**

Although the quiz approach to diagnosis is user-friendly, it's imprecise. Quiz-takers often find that half or more of the Bach remedies seem to pertain to them! It's best to consult with a trained professional when selecting remedies, and to limit the number of remedies being taken at any one time. Our quiz is only to give you a sample of the Bach method; it's not meant to minimize the nuances of the 38 essences, or their synergistic properties when used together.

When your energy is balanced, your mind is more at peace, and your body will have a chance to recover from whatever afflictions you may be experiencing. Body, mind, and spirit, Bach Flower Essences help people, pets, and plants achieve all-around health.

Divine Inspiration

Next time you've got some plant repotting to do, dose the water with Rescue Remedy, and perhaps some walnut essence. You'll likely notice that the plants look better and heartier despite their uprooting.

Magnets and Minerals

Magnets are effective for healing and for pain management. They work to release energy blockages in the body, drawing out trapped energy to relieve pain and improve your overall health. And they're catching on with professional athletes like golfers and ballplayers, as well as chronic fatigue suffers. Laura uses them to alleviate the occasional muscle knots she gets after overexertion.

The magnets used in healing therapies aren't necessarily large (like the ones used in a MRI machine), and they are usually similar in size to the magnets that are probably hanging on your refrigerator. Therapeutic magnets are thin and flexible. They can be worn on the skin for a period of time, or used in a procedure such as acupressure. Some stick to the skin with a bandagelike adhesive; others rest against the skin inside a clothing item like a waistband or a shoe.

If you want to experiment with magnet use, be careful not to overdo it! This is one of those "less is more" situations. You can actually drain your body's energy if you wear a magnet for too long. Also, ask questions about how the healing magnet is made. Some folks swear by counter-concentric circles, but others disagree.

Minerals have special energies, too. If you know someone who's never without her crystal pendant, she may not just be making a fashion statement! Crystals and other stones can have an effect on your emotions and your health.

Mineral	Effect
Amber	Self-confidence
Amethyst	Harmony
Carnelian	Overcoming depression
Citrine	Calms addictive tendencies
Coral	Devotion, good health
Hematite	Grounding, foundations
Jade	Love, accord
Lapis	Happiness, self-love
Onyx	Counters bad dreams
Rose quartz	Good energy, calm, peace
Quartz	Magnifies whatever emotions you're experiencing

Heal Yourself

If you accept our invitation to take charge of your own health care, you *can* heal yourself (maybe with some outside help, too!). Divination tools can bring to light the hidden causes and meanings of illness. Meditation can open up new pathways for healing. And practitioners of all kinds—intuitive, Eastern, and Western—can work in partnership with you to make you whole again in body, mind, and spirit.

Calling on the Divine: A Medicine Wheel Exercise

The medicine wheel, laid out on the ground and oriented toward the points of the compass, was the Native Americans' heavenly observatory. Many societies constructed wheels to pinpoint the solstices, planetary and lunar movements, and other events for astrological purposes. Eventually, as with the Zodiac, the medicine wheel came to signify the circularity of time and our own relationship to the Universe. The medicine wheel today resembles the face of a clock that lays out opposing and complementary forces. A never-ending circle, it encompasses your life, afterlife, and many paths along the way.

The Native American Medicine Wheel has inspired a whole new set of meditation methods, and a new divination tool as well: animal totem cards. Based on Native American legends and metaphors concerning the natural world, animal totem cards are great for those times when you need to reinforce your physical and spiritual connections to the earth.

This exercise uses what's known as the Butterfly Spread to learn about the outcome of a project or enterprise. If you're undergoing a health crisis or are worried about a medical issue, the Butterfly Spread can give valuable information about the roots of the situation, the choices available to you, and the ultimate outcome.

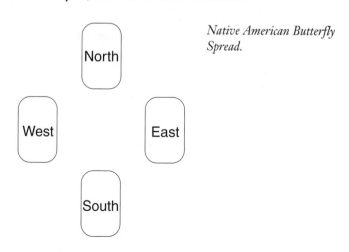

Native American Butterfly Spread.

The spread looks something like a butterfly's body and wings, or like a compass, with one card at each compass point.

The East card is in the Egg Position. This is the nucleus or seed of the issue at hand, the value of its inner core. Every butterfly begins its cycle as an egg, and this card reflects your beginnings in relation to your issue. The Egg card asks, "Is this the medicine that I need at this time and place?"

The South card is in the Larva Position. It tells you what needs to be done, who will take responsibility, and how that can happen. It carries a message of action, just as the butterfly's larval stage is a period of great physical growth.

The West card is in the Cocoon Position. This card points to the situation's higher purpose, just as the cocoon is where the butterfly's inner, hidden development and growth takes place. The Cocoon card asks you to consider your motivations, your goals, and the ultimate meaning of the experience you're going through.

The North card takes the Butterfly Position—the final outcome, the realization of the cycle. What will you gain from it?

To do the exercise, follow these steps:

1. Gather your thoughts and center yourself in a way that's meaningful for you. When you're using animal totem cards, a connection with nature will have special resonance, so consider taking a short walk outdoors, or just sitting with a pet or a houseplant, as part of your preparation.

2. Shuffle the cards as you concentrate on the issue before you.

3. When you feel ready, stop shuffling and deal out the first four cards in the butterfly pattern, starting with the Egg Position (East) and moving around the compass points: Larva (South), Cocoon (West), Butterfly (North).

4. Study your cards for a moment. Then use the following space to write down the cards you've received, their meanings, and what they mean to you.

   Egg Card: _____

   Beginnings; the seed of the issue at hand

   Card meanings: _____

   Larva Card: _____

   Action; responsibility, outer growth

   Card meanings: _____

   Cocoon Card: _____

Higher purpose; goals, motives, inner growth

Card meanings: _____

Butterfly Card: _____

Outcome

Card meanings: _____

Sometimes, the sighting of a live animal can have divinatory meaning. A friend of Laura's called one morning, excited about the weasel she had seen in her back yard. "They're so rare around here!" her friend exclaimed. "What could it mean?" Quickly, Laura looked up "Weasel" in an animal totem reference. "The weasel represents stealth," she read. "Look for hidden sources of energy. Observe who needs attention and offer discreet help. Try alternate ways to work your way into a situation."

It was as apt as if Laura's friend had used a divination tool. She had been unhappy with the options that Western medicine offered as the early symptoms of memory loss appeared in her husband. And her husband had been resisting the existence of the problem. Laura's friend took her weasel sighting as a sign *she* had to get to work, quietly and behind the scenes, to find the answers and help her husband needed.

Calling on Your Doctor

Remember, you're the team leader when it comes to your health. So ask questions, speak up for yourself, and find your own way. Some practitioners trained in Western medicine don't want to hear about integrative or complementary approaches to health. Others are more open. Keep looking until you find professionals you can really work with. And if you're looking for more integrated ways toward attaining good health, don't keep that a secret!

Calling on Complementary Approaches

Today, you've got limitless options when it comes to caring for your health, especially when you consider complementary medical approaches. Health care has broadened to include so many new possibilities—it's like a lazy susan loaded with ideas to try. So try, and try, and try to find what works best for you and for your condition.

There's no reason why you can't combine aspects of Western and Eastern medicine, as well as intuitive approaches, in your life. You don't have to forsake the practitioners and procedures that are comfortable or meaningful to you. Think both/and, rather than either/or, and you can find a balance that's healthy all-around: for your body, for your mind, and for your spirit, too. As you grow centered and stronger, the future will appear with more clarity and direction, because your own life force energy reflects this process.

The Least You Need to Know

◆ Healing is a matter of body, mind, and spirit together.

◆ Energies from ancient cultures—from Tibetan bowls to the Native American Medicine Wheel—are powerful divinatory healing tools.

◆ All kinds of energy—sound, color, plant, mineral—can bring balance to your body's energy system.

◆ Divination can help you understand the meaning behind your health challenges.

Part 4

Reading the Mind

The energy of the mind is the source of our emotions, and we can work with our emotions a whole lot better if we understand the energies behind them. Meditation is one way to harness this energy. Dreams and intuition are the keys to understanding it. Visualization gives us the means to change its direction. This part shows you how to access all these important divining methods, along with a few surprises.

Know Thyself

In This Chapter

- ◆ Exercise the cells of your brain
- ◆ Circle power: labyrinths and mandalas
- ◆ Runes and the *I Ching:* tools for inner knowing
- ◆ How imagination differs from premonition

We've talked about the body. Next up: the mind. Follow us into the labyrinth of emotions and affirmations, the messages we tell ourselves and the messages that others tell us, and all the strengths and weaknesses of the wondrous human brain.

Your brain, like everyone's, is wired for chatter and built for speed. Its running monologue of exploding synapses goes on all the time. It has to! That's just how the brain performs its remarkable job of keeping our bodies alert to danger and open to information at all times—even during sleep.

All these cellular explosions may be necessary, but they sure can seem *loud* sometimes. And it's tough to be peaceful and serene while you're also processing millions of bits of information. That's when your brain seems to trip you up, to get in the way of your spiritual aspirations.

Why Your Mind Does What It Does

Happily, though, there are ways of getting your brain, your body, and your spirit to work together harmoniously. From movement to mandalas, we'll begin to explore how to use your mind to divine the future.

This Is Your Brain ...

Your brain is a unique structure within your body. Unlike your muscles and organs, all of which are responsible for movements of some kind, your brain does its work with tiny internal cells called neurons and the neurotransmitters that carry messages between them. You're born with a full complement of about 12 billion neurons within your brain (there are others along the nerves in the rest of your body). That may sound like a lot of neurons. Unfortunately, though, that's all you get. Neurons can't be regenerated. And you can lose them at any time—a head injury, a seizure, even the slow process of aging can drop a few neurons over the side.

But research does suggest that if you strengthen your neurons and their connectors, you can protect them against future losses. Use it or lose it—that's the idea. And a great way to keep your brain active is by practicing meditation!

If meditation is hard for you, remind yourself that you're not just spacing out or day-dreaming. Try thinking of your next meditation session as a workout for your brain and its neurons.

Where Feelings Come From

The various parts of your brain have specialized functions—there are areas for language, for vision, for scent recognition, and so on. One of its most important functions, though, is multiseated; that is, it resides in many different areas. That function is the generation of emotion.

There's no one "emotional center" in your brain, because feelings are so very complex. Your memories, your senses, your conscious thought processes, your instinctive physical reactions—all these parts, and many more, must work together synergistically for us to "feel" anything.

When you recognize the complexity of your emotions, it becomes much harder to dismiss them out of hand ("Oh, it's just a feeling"). Your brain puts a lot of effort into identifying and naming various emotions, and it uses a lot of information to do so. Maybe we should trust those feelings, and follow them, more often than we do.

Inner Self, Outer Self

So how do I give this powerful mind of mine a good meditative workout, you ask? Maybe you already have! Put a check mark next to any of the questions you can answer with a "yes."

Have you ever …

- ❏ "Zoned out" for a while watching waves crash at the beach?

- ❏ Daydreamed through a class or a speech?

- ❏ Felt your mind can take flight as you washed the dishes?

- ❏ Stared for minutes—or maybe hours—at flames dancing in a campfire or fireplace?

- ❏ Driven a straight or familiar stretch of highway without being fully conscious of the road?

- ❏ Driven home without remembering the ride?

- ❏ Let your thoughts wander as you mowed the lawn?

- ❏ Cleaned house intently to get through an emotional upset or to ponder a problem?

- ❏ Gazed at raindrops falling into a puddle?

- ❏ "Awakened" with a start to find the ironing you'd begun already done?

- ❏ Gardened for hours and completely lost track of time?

- ❏ Sat and watched the wind blow through long grass?

If you've checked even one of these, guess what? You've meditated!

You don't need candles and chants and the lotus position to meditate (although these are great if they work for you!). All it takes is an opportunity to set your spirit free to roam. Sometimes, a repetitive or rote activity does the trick—like chanting "om" or mowing the lawn. Sometimes, a visual focus helps—like a mandala or ocean waves. Whatever works!

"Found meditation" experiences are wonderful. But if you want to make meditation a regular practice, you need to find ways to achieve it intentionally. Rituals, whether they employ movement or divination tools, can really help free the spirit to receive the mind's intuitive messages.

Walking the Labyrinth

In Chapter 7, you were first introduced to the meditative power of the labyrinth. There, you used the labyrinth in seated meditation. When you're physically walking the labyrinth, when your outer physical self is active, your inner self—your mind and spirit—can take flight. Walking through an ordinary environment, even a very familiar one, can call for some pretty conscious footwork if you don't want to trip over unexpected obstacles. That's where labyrinths come in.

A full-scale labyrinth, one that's large enough for you to physically walk through, provides a clear, set path for your body to take. For hundreds of years, people have walked labyrinths in churches, gardens, and palaces as an aid to contemplation or meditation. As your feet just need to follow the path, your thoughts can be peacefully freed as your body makes its steady progress to the center and back.

In Greek mythology, the first labyrinth was built to house the minotaur, a fearsome bull-headed monster. When the hero Theseus walked the labyrinth, he knew that in its heart he would meet his destiny. You won't find any monsters lurking in the hearts of the labyrinths that are constructed today, yet the archetypal story resonates for us still. Walking a labyrinth's indirect paths can bring you close to your deepest truths. It can be a meditative journey to your very heart.

> **Resonances**
>
> On vacation in San Francisco, a couple we know made the pilgrimage to Grace Cathedral to walk the labyrinth together. When they reached the heart of the labyrinth, he surprised her with a marriage proposal! We think this is a wonderful way to celebrate the metaphysical union of two souls sharing life's journey together.

Labyrinths hold this kind of mystical power because their energy mirrors the motion of your life itself. We don't live our lives in a straight line, do we? Our experience is full of twists and turns. There are times when we seem to make good progress—and then there are times when we seem to have landed right back where we were before. But all along, we keep on moving inevitably onward, to the center and back.

Walk the labyrinth with conscious intent to receive a higher message.

To truly experience walking meditation, we recommend seeking out a labyrinth in your own local area. You might find one in a cathedral or church near you, or in a botanical garden or public park. There are traveling labyrinths, too, that take up temporary residence at schools, universities, and religious centers. You might even find a memorial labyrinth near you as the concept grows in popularity. (New York City constructed one such labyrinth to help its citizens recover from the September 11 attacks.)

Found a convenient local labyrinth? Great! Now what? Here are a few ways you can enrich your meditation:

- Set aside plenty of time. You never can tell exactly how much, though! Expect it to take about an hour.

- Try not to squeeze your first labyrinth walk into a fully scheduled day. Knowing you have a dentist appointment in 45 minutes can really tether the spirit.

- As in any meditation, take the time to center yourself before entering the labyrinth. Walking a labyrinth is *not* like running a corn maze! It's not a race, so there's no need to rush.

- There's only one path to travel; you won't be tricked into any blind alleys or dead ends. Don't concentrate on your progress, your direction, or your orientation. (Unlike Theseus, you won't need to unravel a ball of yarn as you go to find a way out! The path will wind you back to an exit point.)

- You may be walking while other people are walking as well. Respect each person's space. You'll quickly pull into your own comfort zone.

- If others are walking the labyrinth while you are there, give them a minute's head start before you begin.

- When you do step into the labyrinth, enter in a spirit of timelessness. Leave your watch behind, and try not to think about how long (or short) a time you're spending on your journey.

- No talking!

You might enter the labyrinth with a particular question in mind: "What is my destiny?" "Is my life on the right path?" Or you might enter in the hope of calming your spirit, of finding greater peace. Whatever your goal is, don't concentrate on it. Let your mind wander free, and your spirit will fly in the direction it needs to go. Remember, meditative walking is about letting answers, insights, and inspirations come in—and for this to happen, you must suspend or relax the mind.

When you emerge from the labyrinth, give yourself some time before you re-enter the "real world." Find a place to sit (you've been upright long enough!) and give thanks for your experience. Jot down a few notes about the insights you gained or emotions you felt during your walk. You brought along your journal, right?

> **Divine Inspiration**
>
> If your labyrinth experience captures your imagination, and if you have the space, it's possible to lay out a labyrinth in a backyard, or in tile on a floor, or in paint on a piece of canvas that you can spread out when you wish. Or go back to the seated labyrinth meditation in Chapter 7. Whatever the format, labyrinth walking is a powerful way to meditate.

Reading the Runes

Divining tools can help you understand the ramifications of your actions, beyond the limitations of your own perception. Tools point out all the ways that events in your life can affect you, both inside and out. Runes, of course, are a time-tested divination method. Rune systems draw on ancient symbolism to make modern divinatory interpretations. Like the labyrinth, there's something elemental about rune stones: They have a connection with ancient ways that you can actually *feel*.

As we've seen, there are many ways to use runes, and different spreads can impart different kinds of information. The Runic or Celtic Cross spread is a great way to get a three-dimensional snapshot of a particular situation in your life.

1. Sit in a peaceful place that has a flat surface large enough for several of your rune stones to be laid out end to end. Gather yourself in readiness for a reading.

2. Run your rune stones through your fingers as you focus on the issue or situation at hand.

3. When you feel ready, choose six rune stones (they might seem to "stick" to your fingers) and lay them out in the pattern and order shown here.

4. Use the following spaces to note the runes you drew. How do the runes relate to their positions in the spread and the question at hand? Refer to Chapter 9 for a list of the runes and their possible interpretations.

Rune 1: The Past—the situation from which you are emerging: _____

_____

Rune 2: You Now—the current situation: _____

_____

Rune 3: The Future—the situation that is coming into view: _____

_____

Rune 4: Foundation—unconscious forces at work in the current situation: _____

_____

Rune 5: Challenge—the obstacles you are facing: _____

_____

Rune 6: New Situation—what will evolve after you've overcome the current obstacles:

_____

You might find great satisfaction—and wonderful resonance—in divining tools you make with your own hands. Runes are particularly good for an "arts and crafts" approach, because their symbols are so graphic and simple. If you love the feel of smooth stone, you can collect a couple dozen water-worn beach or stream rocks and draw or paint the rune symbols on them. If wood has special resonance for you, your local lumberyard can cut a one-inch dowel into disks that you can sand, stain, and carve or paint. Or you can just mold Sculpey clay into flattened ovals, etch the rune symbols into their surfaces, and bake them in the oven to create permanent, usable art. Whatever your craft of choice, a rune set of your own creation is bound to be a special one for you.

The *I Ching*

As a distinctively Eastern phenomenon, the *I Ching*, can be difficult for Western minds to grasp (or Western writers to explain!). The *Book of Changes* has been an active part of Chinese life for 2,500 years, and now it has spread beyond Asia to find a home with spiritual seekers the world over. Even after all this time, new translations and commentaries are constantly being written and published. So before you do anything else, find an edition of the *I Ching* that "speaks your language," as it were. Read a few passages and make sure that the translation and commentary you choose suits your own style and comfort level.

Because—there's no way around it—the *I Ching* can seem pretty esoteric and opaque when you first start using it. But that's really just because the imagery of the original verses is particular to a certain time and culture. The ideas *behind* the verses are timeless. The right edition will draw these out for you. Some people use the *I Ching* as a source for *bibliomancy*—they just flip through the book, eyes closed, and consider whatever page that opens up to be a divinatory message. This simple, elegant process can work beautifully. Let's give it a try!

1. With your *I Ching* edition in hand, sit peacefully for a moment and ground yourself.

2. Hold your question in your mind. (It can be open-ended or very particular. Historically, the *I Ching* has always been used by emperors and generals to divine specific actions. There's no reason you can't do it, too!)

3. Close your eyes and flip through the pages. When you feel so moved, stop.

4. Run your finger down the page you've chosen. When you feel moved, stop.

5. Read your passage (and, if you like, the entire page or hexagram commentary).

6. Meditate on your *I Ching* message.

Future Focus _____

Bibliomancy is the art of divination through a book. Many people use holy or inspirational works for this purpose, such as the Bible or the Book of Changes (*I Ching*), but any book that has meaning for you will do. Simply meditate on your question, close your eyes, open the book at random, and point to any place on the page. This passage contains your message or key word. Holding the message in your mind, you can contemplate its meaning in your life or in regard to your question.

On the other hand, there's nothing like a nice ritual to get the intuitive juices flowing. So here's how to do one of the most popular methods of *I Ching* consultation: the coin throw. In this technique, coins are used essentially as a random number generator. Six coin tosses generate the six lines of the hexagram. And because each toss is completely random, any hexagram of the *I Ching*'s 64 could be created by any set of tosses.

1. Gather your materials: three coins (pennies are fine), a pen or pencil, and your *I Ching* source of choice.

2. Sit peacefully for a moment and center yourself with a breathing exercise or visualization.

3. Take the three coins in hand and focus on your issue or question. When you feel ready, toss the coins gently onto a tabletop. (A cloth or pad can help keep the coins from rolling around!)

4. Look at your coins and note how many heads and how many tails are showing. Tails have a value of 2; heads have a value of 3. Add up your values and use these to determine the first, or bottom, line of your hexagram.

Coin Configuration	Value	Line
Tails, tails, tails	6	— X — (changing yin)
Tails, tails, heads	7	——— (young yang)
Tails, heads, heads	8	— — (young yin)
Heads, heads, heads	9	—0— (changing yang)

5. Draw the first, or bottom, line of your hexagram in the following box.

6. Roll the coins again and add their values to determine the second, third, fourth, fifth, and sixth lines of your hexagram (always counting up from the bottom!). Draw each line in turn in the following box.

Primary hexagram.

7. Use your *I Ching* reference to determine which of the 64 hexagrams your intuition has guided you to. This is your *primary hexagram*. Read the message this hexagram imparts.

8. If your hexagram includes any "changing" lines—that is, any lines with a total value of 6 or 9—you have also been given a *relating hexagram*. This can supply additional information to enhance your reading. Replace any "changing" lines with its opposite and draw your relating hexagram in the following box.

Relating hexagram.

9. Consult your reference to find your relating hexagram and read its message.

10. Meditate upon your hexagram messages. How do they reflect the question you had in mind? Or do they seem to apply to another situation instead?

In our exercise, we created a single hexagram to analyze. This can work fine, especially if you're just dipping a toe into the *I Ching*'s waters. The time-honored method, though, is to create three hexagrams for each reading. (That's 18 coin throws, if you're keeping score at home.) For even more information, skilled *I Ching* users recommend six hexagrams per reading.

Laura advised one of her clients, Francis, to use the *I Ching* to find out more about a new relationship. He had met a woman through his job and was unsure if the "vibes" between them were those of friendship or something more. And, oh yes, both he and she were already married. So Francis wanted to know, "Is this woman interested in me in a romantic way?"

When Francis threw the coins, the primary hexagram he constructed looked like this:

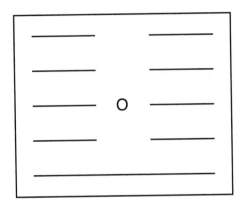

Checking the table in his edition of the *I Ching*, Francis saw that his primary hexagram was Chen, number 51—Shock, or The Arousing. This hexagram certainly does point to some sexual energy! Chen can connote a surprising or uncomfortable shock; it can also, however, reveal inspiration and fertilization, like the return of life in spring. What kind of shake-up was going on here? Francis needed more information.

He found it in his relating hexagram:

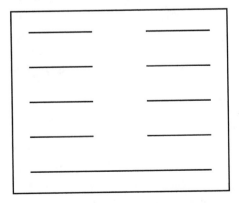

This hexagram is called Fu, or The Turning Point (hexagram number 24). Fu brings a message of renewal, rebirth, and new hope. It also points to profitable business relationships.

Francis's hexagrams confirmed that there was indeed a sexual *frisson* between himself and his new friend. But they also told him not to fear or resist that fact. Rather than running from the relationship, he should look for its benefits—which, in a business sense, were many. It was a nuanced message, to be sure, but on reflection, Francis could see its wisdom.

Gaining Self-Understanding and Insight

We've been talking a lot about using and interpreting ancient symbols and signs. But of course the art of divination is far more than a rote procedure of assigning meaning to a reading or a meditation. It's just as much an internal process—an inner journey of discovery, knowledge, and healing that only you can chart.

Still, everyone needs a little outside acknowledgment of this inner work now and then. We call that kind of pat on the back *validation*.

Sometimes, we don't hear our own voices until we've used them in conversation with someone else. Many people use psychotherapy for just this purpose—to validate their internal feelings. Once they say what's bothering them, and see the therapist accept those feelings, they're no longer burdened. They feel free.

Different "talk therapists" work in different ways, from listening in silence to giving explicit advice. And when the therapy works, it's because the patient's needs have meshed with the therapist's technique. (Perhaps the very best therapists have an intuitive sense of their patients' needs and can match the therapy to them!)

The intuitive arts also offer opportunities for emotional validation. For some people, it's a major reason why intuitive techniques attract them in the first place. Just to have our emotions reflected in a divinatory reading can be greatly comforting for many of us. Our feelings become more real, have validity, when we see them spread before us in the Tarot cards, witnessed in a palm change, or noted on the astrologer's chart. As in talk therapy, this kind of confirmation can be a tremendous release, and it's a great way to mark progress as you work out your own intuitive muscles.

Intuitive professionals offer validation on many levels. A medium can help you contact loved ones on The Other Side, or a channel can connect you with the Universe's wisdom. An astrologer analyzes the planets' and stars' effects on your life. A hands-on healer can help you discover the emotional connections behind your physical symptoms. By respecting the body's signs and messages, intuitive health practitioners can guide your efforts to find, name, and release the sources of physical distress.

Mandala Meditation

Mandalas have been used as focal points for meditation and contemplation for thousands of years, and in numerous cultures. Mandalas are often brightly colored, and the colors and patterns used in them are often symbolically charged. The yin/yang symbol is a mandala. So are the stained glass rose windows found in many medieval cathedrals, Native American medicine wheels, and the Wheel of Fortune card in your Tarot deck.

The exiled Tibetan monks who travel the world to share their culture create exquisite sand mandalas in a striking ceremonial process. The large mandalas, each one unique, are carefully laid out with compasses, rulers, and chalk lines. The art contains 17 or more vibrant colors, all made from ground marble and naturally colored sand. The monks work in groups of three or four for a week or longer until the mandala is completed. As soon as it is finished, the monks hold a solemn consecration ceremony, at the end of which—unbelievably—the mandala is swept into one big heap. This demonstrates impermanence: Everything has a beginning and an end. The sand is placed in an urn or casket and carried to the closest moving body of water, where it is scattered and returned to the elements.

Future Focus

A **mandala** is a patterned design, usually circular, and commonly centered on a single point. Mandalas can symbolize the universe, the "circle of life," or prana, the life force. In Sanskrit, *mandala* means "circle" or "center." The word itself suggests the circular essence of the building blocks of our universe—from atoms to solar systems to galaxies.

Creating a Mandala: An Exercise

Because we draw on the powers of the nonlinear "right brain" to make art, the creative process is a wonderful way to tap into your feelings, and to let your intuition flow. Mandala-making connects the inherent energies of this ancient circular form with forces within you that you might not draw upon too often in our Western, logical, linear society. Here's how to do it:

1. Gather your materials: a piece of good, thick paper 8½ by 11 inches or larger; a bowl, saucer, or dinner plate; a ruler, a compass, and art materials of your own choosing in a range of colors (crayons, pastels, or colored pencils work fine).

2. Position the plate on the paper and trace around it. Within this circular outline you will create your mandala design.

3. Before you begin, take a few moments to breathe deeply and center yourself. Focus on this grounded, centered place. Imagine it as a shape and a color that reflects your feelings at this moment.

4. Recreate that shape and color in the very center of your outlined circle. You can see your centered self in the center of your mandala.

5. Focus your intuition on the environment immediately surrounding you—your home and those who are closest to you in your life right now. If your feelings about these things had color and shape, how would they look? Use your materials to capture that feeling in the area immediately surrounding the shape in the center of your mandala.

6. When this layer is complete, focus your intuition on your friends, neighbors, colleagues, and extended family. Again, imagine your feelings as if they had color and shape. Draw these images in the next layer of your mandala.

7. Keep adding shapes and colors in concentric layers as you focus your inner eye on the emotional landscape that surrounds you, until your outline is completely filled in.

8. Look at your finished mandala as a whole. What draws your eye? What can you sense about yourself from this representation of your feelings? Write your reflections here.

_____

_____

_____

If you don't feel like you're artistic enough to make a mandala from scratch, don't despair! There are lots of ways to experiment and play with mandala shapes. Many educational toy stores carry Pattern Blocks, small flat tiles made of wood or foam. Because they fit together neatly, they seem to naturally fall into concentric mandala patterns as you manipulate them. Pattern Block play can be very soothing—almost a meditation in itself!

A number of companies publish mandala coloring books, collections of outlined mandala shapes that you can fill in with your own choice of colors. Some of these are created with meditation in mind; others just focus on mandalas as artistic or cultural artifacts. Either way, coloring the outlines in is a great way for the "artistically challenged" to create beautiful mandalas of their own.

Using Your Mandala to Meditate: An Exercise

Now that you have your own personal mandala (either created from scratch or colored in), it's time to put it to good use as a meditation tool. And you thought it was just a pretty design!

In all the many cultures that create them, mandalas are used to help focus or center the mind through the sense of sight. A mandala, whatever its origin, tends to naturally draw your eye to the center. Don't fight the flow—it's a great way to begin a mandala meditation.

1. Prop your mandala upright, or tape it to a nearby wall, and gaze at it as you ground yourself.

2. Relax your body and let your eyes float to the center of your mandala. This represents your peaceful, grounded self. Rest your gaze here until your whole body feels just as peaceful.

3. Rest the tip of your tongue on your soft palate, the area just behind your upper teeth. (Keep your mouth closed and breathe through your nostrils.) This opens up an energy flow center that's perfect for meditation; it also relaxes your jaw.

4. With your focus on the inner ring of your mandala, your perception of the outer rings may shift and change. Your peripheral vision of the edges may make the colors and images there seem cloudy—or they may suddenly take on new meanings that you can't see when you look at them straight on. Let your eyes relax in the center as you take in the information from the corners of your eyes.

5. When you feel ready, slowly begin to move your focus to different parts of your mandala. As you inhale, let your eyes gently move to a new shape or color. Pause for a few seconds with your eyes on this new spot, and as you exhale, keep gazing at it. Don't look away until you begin to take in your next breath. In this way, you can remain conscious of your breathing while giving your eyes a chance to move gently.

6. Pace yourself as you slowly focus your attention on different aspects of the design.

7. When you feel ready to end your meditation, return your eyes to the center for a moment. Close your eyes and keep them closed as you slowly inhale and exhale. Then take some time to write about your meditation here.

Are You Crazy, or Is It Cell Memories?

A child with an irrational fear of water. A grown man who suddenly can't bring himself to climb ladders. Do these people need therapy?

Maybe a past life regression therapist would be of more help. Because, very often, someone who manifests a sudden aversion or untraceable fear is experiencing cell memories—the intuitive knowledge of a frightening event from a past life.

Here's how Laura has talked about cell memories in her online advice column, "Ask Laura":

> Dear Laura,
> I am 48 years old and have been driving since I was 16. Recently I began to have anxiety, fear, and now terror about driving over bridges. What is going on? Why am I suddenly having such problems with something I've done thousands of times before? Am I losing it?
> —J.M., MA
>
> Dear J.M.,
> This actually is more common than you think, and is likely related to a past life event. Things can be going along just fine until you approach a certain age, and whamo!—it triggers cellular memories of events from another lifetime. Suddenly the woman who's driven over thousands of bridges can't bring herself to drive over one more.
>
> I suggest you seek out professional hypnosis to help you uncover the event that needs releasing. Chances are you'll discover that when you were this age in another lifetime, you had a life-altering event involving a bridge.
>
> You didn't do anything to bring this on. The natural process of aging just reawakened something that was dormant. With professional guidance, you can witness past life events unfold as if watching a movie, and use "reframing" to calm those resurfacing cellular memories. Don't wait much longer to have peace of mind again. And happy safe driving!

The sudden manifestation of cell memories can be a frightening experience, as Laura's correspondent relates. You can't change past cell memories if you have them, but you *can* learn to release them so they no longer haunt your future.

Premonition or Imagination?

You wake up in a cold sweat. You just saw a horrific car accident in a dream. Was it a premonition? Should you take the bus to work for a while? Or did you just fall asleep while the TV news was covering a horrific car accident? Unnerving as such an experience is, take a deep breath before you jump to any conclusions. You may have had a psychic experience. But that's not necessarily the case.

How can you tell the difference? It takes time and experience to know for sure. Premonitions are intuitive blasts that have a basis in reality. They come out of left field and defy all explanation. Imagination, on the other hand, is vulnerable to outside influences and stimuli. Think carefully about everything you saw, read, or even ate in the hours before your dream or vision. Can you spot any obvious influences on your psyche?

Divine Inspiration

Try talking with a sympathetic friend about your experience. Sometimes an outside perspective can really help ("Didn't you see *Gone in 60 Seconds* the night you had this dream?")

Next, write your intuitive experience down on paper. If you've been doing this already, you have at hand a neat record of other such flashes. Compare them. Does this jibe with the experiences you've already had?

If you still can't uncover any obvious triggers of your experience, consider it a symbol or metaphor. Are you in a relationship you fear might "crash and burn," perhaps? In any case, give your complex brain the credit it deserves. Your dream means *something*—but maybe not the obvious thing!

Years ago Laura had a premonition that something was very wrong with Denise, her long-distance landlord. Laura tried to push the premonition aside at first. But the feelings got more persistent as the day went on, and when her then-husband got home that evening she told him about them. After talking it through for over an hour, Laura became deeply convinced that there were no extenuating circumstances to this feeling. She tried to reach Denise by phone, but had no luck. The next day, Laura sent Denise a note by mail saying, "I hope you're okay—I had a funny feeling that something's not right with you, and it seems health-related." A week later, Laura got a letter from Denise. At the same time Laura had her "feeling," Denise had been diagnosed with a virulent form of ovarian cancer. She had spent that week in emergency surgery and undergoing tests.

Taking the time to get to know your mind is just as important as taking the time to get to know your body. Interpreting intuitive messages begins with self-knowing and awareness.

The Least You Need to Know

◆ Meditation is like a workout for your brain.

◆ Walking a labyrinth is a metaphor for dealing with life's problems and a ritual used for thousands of years.

◆ Mandalas are excellent meditation tools, whether you create your own or watch one being made.

◆ Premonitions are intuitive blasts that have a basis in reality.

◆ The better you know yourself, the better you will be able to interpret your own intuitive messages.

Chapter 14

Feelings and Emotions

In This Chapter

- How to identify and name your emotions
- The connection between feelings and physical illness
- Free yourself from emotional blockages
- Planning and following your life path

We know that emotions are based in the connections our brains make deep within them. But feelings never stay there. They emerge and affect every part of us. Sometimes we're aware of those physical manifestations—ever felt as if you were floating on a cloud of happiness, or heavy and weighted with gloom? But most of us have a hard time making the link between mental and physical feelings.

This chapter will help you strengthen those connections, to provide firm grounding for the roots of blossoming spiritual awareness that leads to divine intuition.

Do Your Feelings Help or Hinder?

Emotions can be a tremendous boon in your intuitive life. Your feelings can reliably guide you to your inner self. If you're in touch with your feelings—if you can name them, accept them, and love them (even the difficult ones)—you *can* direct your future intuitively and manifest profound change in your life.

But emotions can also be a huge obstacle that stops your intuitive life cold. Emotions sometimes loom large and out of your control. Because they arise in such a complex process within the mind, they can be sudden, fierce, even frightening. The presence of a powerful emotion, like anger, can make it hard for you to interpret information accurately. If these emotions aren't resolved or acknowledged, they can become manifest, too—in chronic anxiety, depression, or physical illness. The respected World Health Organization estimates that up to 85 percent of illness is caused by unresolved stress.

Identify and Connect with Your Emotions

Of course, before you can do any work with your emotions, you have to know they're there. Naming your feelings, without judgment or shame, is a critical part of the process. And it isn't always as easy as it seems. So many of us were brought up to avoid or minimize volatile emotions like anger and fear, to the point that we may not be able to admit that we even *have* them.

This is where your body can really come to your brain's rescue—because your body knows the truth about your feelings, and it can't lie! Your physical reactions to emotion, honest as they are, can give you clues to the way you're really feeling.

Use this "tuning-in" exercise, either on its own or in conjunction with a specific question or scenario you need help with and can't quite understand. This exercise can also be used with any divinatory reading or meditation to help identify and name your feelings.

1. Sit comfortably, with your legs and arms uncrossed. Inhale and exhale deeply, a minimum of three times, and center yourself.

2. Briefly, focus your attention on your body and each of its parts or regions. Try to get an overall impression of your physical-emotional state right now.

3. With this quick inventory in mind, check off any of the words below that could apply to you right now. Do I feel …

❑ Easy	❑ Light	❑ Simple
❑ Overwhelmed	❑ Drooping	❑ Cranky
❑ Clear	❑ Free	❑ Warm
❑ Exhausted	❑ Heavy	❑ Snappish

❏ Clean   ❏ Critical   ❏ Powerful

❏ Confused   ❏ Mellow   ❏ Depressed

❏ Strong   ❏ Cloudy   ❏ Determined

❏ Achy   ❏ Faith-filled   ❏ Anxious

❏ Lively   ❏ Tense   ❏ Serene

❏ Weak   ❏ Glowing   ❏ Weary

❏ Bright   ❏ Cold

If most of your check marks are in the left column, you are most likely in a state of freedom and alignment. Feelings like happiness, joy, contentment, hopefulness, satisfaction, pleasure, and pride all come into play when we are feeling in sync with life, moving along with the energetic flow.

If most of your check marks are in the right column, you are likely in a state of challenge, energetically. What are the things happening in your life that have your personal energy feeling so challenged? Emotions like sadness, anger, impatience, depression, anxiety, worry, rage, guilt, shame, and fear all loom larger than need be when we are feeling out of sync with the flow of life. In your journal, write about what might be bothering you if your check marks above filled most of the right column.

Intuitive Card Exercise

Naming your emotion is Step One. But now that you know how you're feeling, what are you supposed to *do* about it?

Here's a juncture where divining methods can really help you see the possible outcomes, the "ripple effects," of your reactions. Laura's Ancient Stardust Directional Cards offer a chance to help you understand this and receive potential solutions.

1. Pick one issue noted in the previous lines that you need some assistance in understanding.

2. Sit and quiet yourself. Use a prayer of invocation such as: "Divine Source, please bring about guidance for my highest and best understanding on this issue."

3. Shuffle the Ancient Stardust Directional Cards, keeping all cards face down.

4. When you are ready, select the card that feels different.

5. Turn it over and note which directional category the card is from. Is it a Take Heed, a Take Action, a Resting, or a Releasing card? Refer to Appendix D, or to the booklet that comes packaged with Laura's cards to read more about the category and the actual card you chose. Take notes here or in your journal.

Ancient Stardust Direction and your feelings: _____

_____

Directional card name and your feelings: _____

_____

Aura Reading Exercise

Your aura, that ever-shifting energy field all around you, is exquisitely sensitive to your emotions. So an aura reading can help you understand your emotions better. It can also confirm what you're feeling, if your feelings seem muddled to you, or help you to refine your understanding of how your emotions are affecting your energy flow.

Divine Inspiration _____

Every living thing has an aura, animals and plants included. Plants are good subjects for aura-spotting, as they're relatively stationary. If you have a houseplant nearby, put it in front of a solid dark or white background and look at the area just beyond the edges of its leaves or stem. Can you see a shadow along the outlines of these edges and a subtly glowing light just beyond that? That's your plant's aura!

As we know, it can be tough to get a feel for your own aura when you're inside it. Aura readings work best in partnership with someone else. So first, find a partner!

1. Have your partner lie down on his or her back, with arms relaxed alongside the body. Ask your partner to breathe purposefully for a few moments (teach them the 4-7-8 exercise from Chapter 9, if you like!) and use that time to ground yourself.

2. You're going to be using your hands to sense your partner's aura over each of their chakras. Start at the top of the head, at the crown chakra. Keeping your hands about 6 to 12 inches above the body, and starting at the top of your partner's head, make a gentle patting or smoothing motion with your hands. Keep your fingers straight and together. Try to sense the aura with your hands, not through any other senses (you may want to close your eyes).

3. Focus on the impressions you're getting with your hands. You may feel pressure changes—the aura may feel thin or thick at this position. You may sense temperature, texture, gaps or "holes," and so on. You may be able to get an impression of color. You may also feel nothing, but have a flash of intuitive thought. Keep taking in sensations for one to three minutes. Refrain from talking.

4. Slowly and gently pull your hands away.

5. Take a momentary break to write a few notes about the sensations or intuitive flashes you've experienced.

6. Now go through the same procedure—sensation, break, notes—over the rest of your partner's chakras: the "third eye," the throat, the heart, the navel, the upper abdomen, and the lower abdomen or "root." Don't forget to include the areas over the knees and feet as well. Remain silent throughout. (It might help to have some gentle music or nature sounds playing quietly in the background, especially if you and your partner are accustomed to talking a lot!)

7. When you've gone through all your partner's chakras, gather some overall impressions by re-sensing each part of his or her aura, spending about 10 seconds over each chakra. You might want to "smooth" the aura a bit just before the reading ends; some people find that this feels great. (To do this, use your hands just like you would to smooth a sheet, only 10 times slower and anywhere from 12 to 24 inches above your body.) Before you are done, say a short silent prayer asking for the highest and best blessings for your partner.

8. Ask your partner to sit up, slowly and gently. Now it's time to trade feedback. How did the reading feel to him or her? Did their sensations correspond to any of your notes? If you picked up any images or impressions, how do they relate to your subject's life?

Perhaps your partner will return the favor and do an aura reading on you. You'll get the maximum benefit from this if you approach it like any other intuitive experience, grounding yourself beforehand and journaling afterward. See if you can connect your partner's sense of your aura with your own emotional state. See if you can feel sensations while he or she is over your aura. If you can't help but "peek," are your partner's hands over the same area of your aura where you can feel some sensation?

Take Heed

When you're planning to work with a partner, avoid wearing perfume or cologne, and remove jangling jewelry—anything that could distract you or keep your partner from feeling relaxed and at peace. You want your senses, and your partner's, to remain perfectly clear!

From Your Mind to Your Body: Physical Manifestations

Your body hears everything your mind says, and does what it can to manifest whatever your mind believes. This is Louise Hay's major insight, and a powerful one it is.

Future Focus

Affirmation is a powerful divining aid. An affirmation is a statement that declares or asserts something positively. To be effective, it must be either written or spoken out loud, over and over again. Reading affirmations silently does not have the same effect because the mind cannot distinguish between what you read and all its other constant chatter.

Hay's work is dedicated to the idea that illness is really a manifestation of our powerful, influential minds—and that changing the mind's deepest beliefs will change the body's reactions. In other words, if you tell yourself to be sick, you'll be sick; if you tell yourself to get better, you'll do that, too.

The following table is just a sampling of common ailments, their potential emotional causes, and the *affirmations* that can help overcome them. Of course, the symptoms below can be signs of physical illness that needs to be assessed by a licensed health professional; if so, do not delay in seeking their support while you focus on an affirming movement toward optimal health and wellness.

Problem	Potential Cause	Affirmation
Shallow breathing	Feeling smothered	It is safe to take charge of my own life now.
Heart palpitations	Feeling defeated and unloved, stressed	My life is a joy!
Cough	Barking at the world; seeking attention	I am noticed and appreciated in positive ways.
Earache	Not wanting to hear; closing out turmoil	I listen with love. Harmony surrounds me.
Heartburn	Fear times 10	I am safe. I trust the process of life.
Motion sickness	Fear of not being in control	I am always in control of my thoughts. I am safe.
Neck pain	Stubbornness, inflexibility	I see all sides of anissue.
Sinusitis	Irritation to someone close	I claim peace and harmony at all times. All is well.
Sore throat	Holding in anger and self-expression	I release all restrictions.

Problem	Potential Cause	Affirmation
Stomachache	Frustration and feelings of being "too full," overwhelmed	I am able to see life's simple pleasures.
Back pain	Anger and distress at being overburdened	With my loved ones, we will lift what we can carry, and leave the rest.
Headache	Too much noise	I sing in tune with the celestial music.

You can change your mind's patterns, and changing them will help heal your body! You just have to identify the cause, and tell yourself the new reframed thought of what to believe. With time, practice, and persistence, your brain will actually *believe* the new thought as a fact, and your body will aid in the healing process. Laura calls this "uploading a new program."

Freeing Emotional Energy Blocks

Emotional energy blocks are like a clogged drain in a well-used kitchen sink. When a drain backs up, it's usually because years' worth of potato peelings and soap slivers and dog hair and what-have-you have congealed into a sticky glob in the middle of the pipe. There's nothing wrong with the sink or the drain or the pipe itself; the system just needs to have the gunk cleared out of it to work properly again.

If your intuitive sense is the plumbing, an emotional energy block is the clog. An energy block can shut down the flow of intuition completely, or it can just skew or interfere with your intuitive sense. You know your own stress signals, don't you? If you react to stress by becoming grumpy or anxious or bone-tired, those are the red flags that signal an emotional energy block for you. You might go back to the Bach Flower Essence quiz in Chapter 12 and choose a remedy to help you combat the blockage with better balance.

Another signal: If you've been having trouble with meditation or with journaling or with any of the exercises in this book, an emotional energy block could be at the root of your distress. It might be time to get honest with yourself and take a personal inventory of your body, mind, and spirit.

A personal inventory is a private event. It's about getting real with the highest truths that you know are there, beneath the surface. Because it's personal, we can't exactly walk you through one. Think of it as an energy time-out—a chance to stop and focus on your emotions and their flow at a time when you feel yourself off-balance. For some people, an intensive session with their journal does the trick. For others, it could be a nature walk, a guided meditation, or just some quiet time for doing some intensive looking within. A good talk with a friend, or a consultation with an intuitive professional, could help you resolve what's bothering you and let you move on. Only you know what will get you to the place where you can be completely honest with yourself.

Divine Inspiration

Metaphysically, a time-out can actually arrest the negative energy flow you may be experiencing, giving you a chance to change its direction. Think of your energy as ripples on a pond. Your personal inventory calms the waves; your corrective action is a stone skipped on the waters that changes the energy of the whole system.

Once you have a better idea of what it is that's stopping up your energy pipes, you'll have a better idea of what it will take to clean that blockage out. Identifying the problem is half of finding its solution. These kinds of metaphysical gear shifts can let you regenerate your energy and change its direction so you can manifest the future you desire.

Releasing Anger and Uncomfortable Emotions: Rituals

If you're struggling with long-standing emotional burdens, you may need more than simple nurturing to get past the blockage.

It's hard to feel spiritual while you're struggling under the weight of years of "clogged drains" and negativity. Anger can be an especially challenging emotion to release and diffuse. Rather than dealing with the source of our anger head-on, many of us keep those feelings inside. We may dwell on it unhealthily, replaying the situation over and over. Or it may dog us, like a shadow, refusing to go away.

If bottled-up anger is bringing you down, a personal ritual can help you to let it go, making more room for you to invite goodness and the Divine to manifest in your life. Here are two ways of releasing anger through ritual.

1. Gather your materials together: writing paper, an envelope, a pen or pencil, matches, and a receptacle in which you can safely burn paper. Center yourself with deep breathing and perhaps a grounding exercise.

2. Sit with your thoughts for a few moments. Allow yourself to experience all the emotions you are attaching to this situation.

3. Write out all the details of your feelings. (If your anger is directed at a person, you may want to phrase your writings as a letter to him or her.) Dredge up all

the details that are bothering you, and all the ways your emotions have affected you. Put it all down on paper.

4. Finally, write why you want to release this anger. Write how you feel about all the space this anger has been taking up in your life. Express your forgiveness, if you can, and your willingness to now move forward, releasing this anger that no longer serves you. Express your wish to move forward, anger-free.

5. When your writing is complete, seal it in the envelope. In a fireplace, metal basin, fire ring, or other safe place, burn the sealed paper. Feel and watch as your anger floats away with the fire and smoke. Watch until the anger is consumed and the fire is fully extinguished. (Don't leave a fire burning!)

Visualization is a powerful means of resetting your emotional thermostat. This is a visualization that fights anger with love. This exercise adapts a Buddhist practice called Tonglen, in which the practitioner breathes in pain and difficulty and exhales love and peace, transforming the energy surrounding the situation.

1. Sit in a place where you feel peaceful and safe. Breathe deeply and center yourself thoroughly.

2. Visualize the event, place, situation, person, or thing that is making you angry and pulling your spirit down. Imagine leading the source of your anger to an otherwise empty hut or shed on a deserted beach.

3. Visualize yourself closing the door on the source of your anger.

4. Imagine yourself walking down the beach, away from the source of your anger, uncoiling a long wire as you go.

5. When you are a safe distance from the hut, inhale deeply and imagine connecting your wire to a detonator there on the beach. Exhale deeply and push down on the plunger. Watch the hut, and the source of your pain or your anger, explode. See the flash, hear the sound. Recognize that the force of energy you send to the hut is not the energy of anger, but of love! You have transformed the energy of the situation from negativity to love. Let the cloud of smoke carry off all negativity to the ethers.

6. Visualize yourself, free and lighter, as you turn to an ocean of love and peacefulness that spreads before you, as you realize with confidence that you have the strength and love to resolve your situation in a positive way.

Resonances

Visualization is a powerful tool for healing and affecting the future. When Laura was faced with a cancer challenge over a decade ago, along with listening to healing tapes and meditating, she researched what healthy cells look like, and then created a large painting of vibrant, healthy cells. "Just the process of creating the painting was cathartic for me. I was encased in a dome of healing while I worked. It was a form of moving meditation," she says. She hung the finished artwork in her bathroom, where she couldn't help but "face" those happy, healthy cell images several times a day. To this day, the painting still hangs, and Laura remains cancer-free.

Joyous Movement

With all that negativity out of your mind, your spirit has room to spare! Your body can encourage your spirit to soar when you embrace the idea of joyous movement.

Joyous movement is physical action that embraces your spirit, relaxes your mind, and stretches your soul. It reaps physical dividends, too, as your body and mind mirror and intensify one another's attitudes. The more joyously you move, the better you'll feel; the better you feel, the more joyously you'll move. You may even lose a few pounds!

Yoga for Balance: An Exercise

In yoga, physical balance creates harmony and union between the body's opposing forces. We might say that because the body and the mind are so closely related, physical balance will encourage emotional balance, and vice versa. Either way, yoga has so much to offer us when it comes to healthy movement and healthy focus of the mind and emotions. After all, it takes concentration to hold that yoga pose!

Of the many yoga poses, the warrior pose is especially satisfying for achieving strength, confidence, and emotional clarity in balance. Warrior grounds you in the present moment with the strength to acknowledge your past and divine your future. Stake out your space in the present and reach for your warrior knowing!

1. Begin in the mountain pose (see Chapter 4).

2. Jump your feet a bit more than hip distance apart while extending your arms straight out to the sides, palms facing down to the ground, fingertips reaching outward.

3. Turn your left foot so that the toes point outward as your fingers do. Turn your right foot toward the left as well.

4. Bend your left knee so that it moves in alignment over your calf and ankle. If your knee goes over your toes, you've bent too far! Keep your hips and torso facing forward.

5. Take a moment to ground yourself and check alignment. Your abdominal center, hips and shoulders, and arms and feet should all make a flat plane.

6. Once you are centered, turn your head to the left and look out over your fingertips into your warrior future. Extend through your fingertips, reaching as fully as you can. Grounded powerfully in the present, you access the strength of the past, and reach with strength, intent, and focus to direct your future.

7. Lift your heart as you breathe in, lower and relax your shoulders as you breathe out (keep your arms extended). Continue to breathe deeply and fully from your abdominal center and hold the pose as long as you can, with comfort. You are strong, emotionally confident, spiritually directed, and ready to manifest your future!

Yoga's warrior pose.

Choose to Support the Life Path You Want to Follow

Remember, if you're going to make a change in your life, if you're going to have an effect on the future, you can't just sit by and wait for it all to happen. You have to be willing to do what it takes to help it along. In other words, you have to be willing to do your part. If you want a new job, you'll need to keep your resumé up to date (you *do* know where your resumé is, right?). If you want to embrace better health, you'll need to be willing to move more and make additions to your regime. If love and marriage are your goals, make sure you are doing the work on yourself to be the best possible partner you can be even if you aren't presently in a relationship right now. Keep an eye on your actions, as well as your divinations, and do the things that support your desired outcome, and try not to undermine yourself.

Treasure Map: An Exercise

For any journey, it helps to have a map. The journey of your life is no exception. A map made of symbols and metaphors can help you crystallize the path you plan to travel, and the treasure you'll find where "X" marks the spot.

1. Gather your materials: several old magazines, newspapers, or catalogs; scissors; a piece of large-format art paper; a glue stick; colored pencils or markers.

2. Relax for a few minutes and consider three questions:

   A. How do I feel about my life right now?

   B. What do I want my life to be like?

   C. What do I need to do or change or work on to get from Point A to Point B?

3. Look through your magazines and other materials for pictures or words that reflect how you answered these three questions. Cut them out, making sure to keep the A, B, and C items separated.

4. When you've collected several pictures or words in each category, arrange them on your art paper in a way that you could follow like you'd use a coded pirate map. (For example, you could group all the A pictures on the left-hand side of your paper; group the B pictures on the right-hand side; and string the C pictures along a meandering path linking one group to the other.)

5. Glue each picture down on your paper, then use pencils or markers to add labels and decorations.

You can hang your finished map in an area you see every day—like your bathroom or entrance hall—to keep you focused on where you're going and how you plan to get there. Think of it as something like a business plan—for your life!

The Least You Need to Know

◆ Your feelings can be a help or a hurdle in divining the future; it's all in how you respond to them.

◆ Intuitive techniques offer insight into your emotions.

◆ The mind-body connection is so powerful that your thoughts can make you ill— or make you well.

◆ Releasing anger is the first step toward a healthier emotional life.

Chapter 15

Dreamscapes

In This Chapter

- ◆ Understanding and remembering dreams
- ◆ How dreams help divine the future
- ◆ Dreams as the soul's work
- ◆ Dream interpretation

In our everyday, linear perception, we tend to diminish the dream state. ("It was just a dream, child," says Auntie Em to poor Dorothy, kindly dismissing her life-changing journey to Oz.) We may find dreams interesting and strange, like magic-realist novels; we may see them as a Freudian highway to the unconscious mind. But we don't generally regard them as important work.

In truth, though, the soul never sleeps. When you dream, the soul is at work—sometimes doing simple housekeeping and file management, other times making complex travels and visitations. Energetically, we're a lot like cell phones: If we're not regularly recharged, we won't have the juice to get through the simplest tasks. Sleep is the body's recharge mode, and dreams serve the same function for the soul.

To Sleep, To Dream, To See

"I can't wait to see what I'll dream tonight!" For Laura, who's especially conscious of her soul's journeyings, every night is a new adventure. There are sights to see, insights to make, things to learn, loved ones to visit, oh yes, and even the occasional "chase scene."

You can't preprogram your dreams (though, as we've said, things like television can influence them), but you can use dreams as a form of divination by posing certain questions, and paying attention to what happens.

Most of us can remember snippets or images from our dreams, at least occasionally. If so, you can train yourself to improve your dream recall. If, however, you *never* remember your dreams the next day, it's not because you haven't had any. Everyone dreams, as sleep research has shown. But some of us don't seem to have any access to them. There are many possible reasons for this disconnect, and if this is your experience, you may want to explore it more deeply through a personal inventory process or even with a trained therapist. Or you may just want to try some of the exercises in this chapter to encourage your waking self to get in better touch with your soul's nighttime actions.

Divine Inspiration _____

If you feel yanked, cranky, or rushed out of sleep in the morning by your alarm clock, chances are it's because your dreamwork has been interrupted! Laura doesn't use an alarm clock. She uses a form of Divine programming: You tell yourself what time you want to wake up the next morning, each night before you go to sleep. The Universe will happily assist you in your rising (usually three minutes ahead of the time you requested!).

Sweet Dreams and Nightmares

From earliest childhood, we're conditioned to categorize our dreams as "good" and "bad." When you were young, you can probably remember someone soothing you back to sleep, saying, "There, there, it was just a bad dream." We may wish our loved ones "Pleasant dreams!" when they go to bed; we may complain about the "nightmare traffic" we ran into on the way home from work in our cars.

But in truth, there's no such thing as a good dream or a bad dream. Like emotions, dreams simply *are*. And both the most terrifying nightmare and the most wondrous dream contain messages and opportunities for you—if only you know how to extract them. Dream interpretation can be a powerful source of insight, change, affirmation, and meaning in our lives and our futures.

That's not to say that your natural reaction to a nightmare—fear, stress, anxiety—should be resisted or suppressed. On the contrary: Perhaps these are emotions that your intuition is telling you *need* to be felt in your life right now. What is stressing you? Is there a difficult situation you've been avoiding? Is there a problem in your waking life that you're reluctant to confront?

With a little practice, you can learn to feel safe in your dreams, even when they venture into difficult emotional terrain. Try this: When you go to bed, envision yourself surrounded by a warm light, and tell yourself that you are safe and will always remain safe. You can carry this consciousness of safety with you into your dream state. As you're dreaming, you can learn to remind yourself, "This is a dream"; your bedtime visualization can extend into sleep, allowing you to see yourself enveloped by your light of safety as you dream. This is a first step toward lucid dreaming, a technique we'll explore later in this chapter.

A Ritual for Remembering Your Dreams

I gazed upon the cloudless moon,
And loved her all the night,
Till morning came and radiant noon,
And I forgot her light

—Emily Brontë

Whether they're "good" or "bad," your message-bearing dreams won't do you much good if you can't remember any of them! Most people do dream all through the night, in short sessions that grow progressively longer as morning nears. But because these dream periods are interrupted by periods of deep nondreaming sleep, you usually can only recall the last (and often the longest) dream you had before you woke. And even that final dream tends to fade once you're fully awake.

The classic solution to this dilemma is to keep a notepad and pencil within arm's reach of your bed, and to take notes on your dreams the moment you awaken from them—even if it's still the middle of night and you're barely awake, writing notes in the dark.

Up to this point, all the journaling techniques we've talked about require you to be conscious and aware. Dream journaling is very different. Your very drowsiness is a strength in dream journaling, because as you awaken you may lose your dream's most telling details. So get in the habit of taking notes in the dark. Keep them simple—a face, a name, a phrase, or a message might be all you need to write down—and keep to what stands out in your recollection of the dream's imagery.

> **⚠ CAUTION**
>
> **Take Heed** _____
>
> Keep your dreamwork tools simple—and make sure they work! A clipboard filled with letter-size paper provides room for late-night scrawls and a sturdy backing to lean on. If you use pencils, make sure you have at least two sharpened ones at your bedside. And if you prefer pens, double-check them. Laura will never forget the time she filled pages and pages with imagery from a particularly vivid dream in the middle of the night—only to awaken and find nothing but impressions on the pages. Her pen had been completely out of ink!

The next day, you can merge your midnight notes into your regular journal. Now you can reflect on the dream and its meaning whenever you like, and you have a record to compare with other dreams and intuitive experiences. If you are a visual person, sketch out elements of your imagery and layouts of your dreams in your notes as well. Art can be a powerful tool to help you reconnect with the resonances of your dream energy, and further appreciate its meaning. (Plus, these images are sometimes just beautiful!)

Dreamwork

There are many different kinds of dreams, and each type can appear in multifaceted ways. We'll be talking in this section about only a handful of the most empowering and meaningful kinds of dreams.

Remember, in metaphysical terms every dream is an opportunity for your soul to grow. Sleep research labs all around the world espouse dozens of theories about the role of sleep and dreams in the functioning of the human brain and body. Interesting as these ideas are, that's not what we're focused on. For us, dreams are a way to stretch and strengthen our spiritual selves.

Used properly, dreamwork is an awesome divination tool. You might get more benefit out of your dreamwork than you could from years of therapy! But this is a very personal process—a process that no one can do for you, and a process that can't be rushed.

Dream Visitations—the Sacred Connect

Dream visitations from deceased loved ones are known to be especially powerful and deeply affecting. True dream visitations are sacred, life-changing experiences. Dream visitations are visits that a loved one who's crossed over pays to you in your dreaming state. *Dream visitations are not just dreams about a deceased person.* They are much more. These sacred dreams involve a high degree of energy being transferred and exchanged between dreamer and visitor. There's an intense feeling of the highest form of love as well as telepathy being shared. During a dream visitation, a deceased loved one might come simply to express the immense love they feel for you, and share this love with you through the transfer of energy. No words might ever be spoken in a dream visitation like this one; you will likely wake up with incredible feelings of peace and love—warm and caring energy from your loved one, as well as an extremely vivid recollection of the entire event. This memory is so powerful that you will remember it years later, as if it happened last night.

Sometimes a sacred dream visitation might occur to reassure you about how happy and peaceful things are for that loved one on *The Other Side.* Your sacred visitor might tell you that all is well and he or she is not only at peace, but also filled with bliss, wonder, and joy. This kind of visitation can be a tremendous gift to someone who's still mourning or missing a loved one. It's the gift of knowing that the loved one is not just "okay" on The Other Side, but is feeling fabulous!

Sacred dream visitations like these often have a striking clarity unlike anything we can see with our physical eyes. These experiences can involve all or some of our five senses (touch, taste, sound, sight, smell). Their vivid, living colors and pinpoint focus are to "ordinary" dreams what a plasma TV is to an old portable black-and-white set. There's almost no comparison. Those who've had a sacred dream visitation can often be at a loss for words to fully explain this profound event, and carry the emotional charge of the dream with them for the rest of their lives.

Future Focus

The Other Side is the realm of existence where souls live. It is also known as "the afterlife," "the higher side," "heaven," "home," and so on. The Other Side is not a place that can be defined on earthly maps. It exists simultaneously with us, physically just several inches higher than we are, but experientially in another dimension altogether.

You cannot ask for these sacred visits to happen, or predict when they might occur, as Laura has discussed in her "Ask Laura" column:

> Dear Laura,
> My beloved husband passed away a couple months ago. Although everyone says he will come visit me in my dreams, so far nothing has happened. Another friend of his recently had a dream visit from him. Why would he go to them before he came and visited me?
> —Mrs. E.

Dear Mrs. E.,

I am so glad that you wrote to me. Heartfelt condolences, friend. This is an important question that I often hear from folks like yourself who have lost a loved one. There can be much frustration and confusion from not being able to communicate with the departed in ways that we are used to. It's the same from The Other Side; spirits sometimes feel like no one here is listening or paying attention! All we need to do is be willing to understand and learn that there are new ways to communicate.

Once a soul leaves the corporeal body, it passes through the tunnel of light leading to The Other Side and experiences a life review. Then there is usually a period of re-acclimation. Some souls leave the body, and their Earth lives, more easily than others. Because time does not exist in the spirit world, to them it can seem like five minutes has passed, while to you and I it might be more like five months! Sometimes loved ones will immediately be able to materialize or come in dream visits to let you know they are okay. In other cases, dream visits never happen. Instead, different forms of communication are subtly taking place right before our eyes and we just need to know what to watch for. Which form of contact you get has nothing to do with being good or deserving. Our loved ones are doing the best they can and may even be busy adjusting to their new realm of existence. Whether or not they contact you, it absolutely does not mean that they no longer love you. Love is eternal.

Dream visitations can also be less profound and more periodic, practical, or functional, with an infinite number of nuances. They can involve someone with whom you had a challenging relationship, or who had passed over leaving some unfinished emotional business between you. In these cases a visitation may be intended to heal what was left undone—for example, if the cantankerous uncle who died holding a grudge against you comes to you in a dream and says that he's not angry with *anyone* anymore, leaving you with a feeling of laughter, release, and love. Or dream visitors can give you helpful practical information. Your deceased father might come to tell you about a water leak in your house that is about to cause a lot of damage, or to remind you to pack the bug repellent on your next camping trip. Or perhaps your long-passed favorite aunt might appear in your dreams, holding up the ring that she loved so much and reminding you to keep it with you (and not just in your jewelry box) so that you will feel her closeness. Dream visitations like these may be numerous and ongoing, as opposed to sacred dream visitations that are once-in-a-lifetime life-altering events.

Dream Rituals for Inviting Answers

Other dreams specifically answer questions or work out problems. These are dreams you *can* ask to have, because they're within your influence.

1. Begin your ritual about 20 minutes before you plan to go to bed. Prepare a glass of water with two drops of the Bach Flower Essence called Cerato. This homeopathic preparation is good for strengthening your intuitive sense and helping with dream recollection.

2. Gather your thoughts and center yourself. Focus your concentration on one issue—and only one!—with which you need the help of your dreams tonight. (It could be the presentation you're giving at work next week, or making peace with a friend, or finding a new home—any issue that's worrying you, specific or general.) Formulate the issue as clearly as you can in your mind.

3. Write your issue at the top of your bedside notepaper or in your Progress Journal as a reminder of your request for insight from your dream. (More on the Progress Journal a little later in this chapter.)

4. Turn off the light and forget about your issue. Don't mull it over as you go to sleep; just let the problem go, as gently as you would release a balloon into the sky.

You might wake up with pages of notes on your notepad and a complete dreamed-out plan of action in your head. Or you might not remember a "solution," but just feel a sense of peace about the situation. Or you might feel the need to ask the same question again the next night. That's okay—your answer will come. The Universe won't leave your question hanging! It has to respond—and it will—but in its own time.

Lucid Dreams: Divining Dream Directions

You can watch a dream unfold as a consciously aware spectator, or you can be involved in the action as a conscious participant. In other words, during the dream you know you are asleep and yet you are a participant in the dream, either actively watching the dream events unfold, or able to direct and influence the dream's action, if you choose. Either way, a lucid dream can instruct or influence you on how to act in waking life if you're dreaming lucidly: that is, if you're able to interact with your dream as it's occurring.

If you're aware in your dreams, with a little practice, you can become a highly interactive participant within them. You can turn a peaceful dream's spotlight on a stressful situation and feel better about it; you can face a dreamed fear and ask it, "Why are you here? What do you have to teach me?"

A page from Laura's dream journal.

Dream Healing

Some dreams bring us healing—not just physical healing, but metaphysical healing that affects all aspects of your mind-body-spirit triad. A healing dream imparts specific information, or just an energy impression, that leaves you with a sense of reassurance or calm. The important factor is the sense of peaceful energy you feel after you've awakened. This peaceful feeling is so profound, you have nothing left to worry about—because the "problem" no longer exists, or is literally being handled for you. Talk about clarity!

Some healing dreams can seem confusing at first. We often push away powerful feelings we can't make sense of. But if you make a practice of journaling about your dreams or meditating on them, you can still gain a healing sense of reassurance and peace from a healing dream—even long after you've awakened.

If you feel a need for physical healing that you'd like to address in your dreams, try this exercise to request a healing dream.

1. Before you go to sleep, lie in bed and do three rounds of relaxation breathing.

2. Visualize yourself sitting in front of a great spotlight with four color filters on it: blue, green, gold, and purple. First, let the blue light shine on you. Feel its energy penetrate you and wrap you in warmth and peace. Use the force of your deep breathing to move the blue light from your head to your toes. Feeling it reach your mind, your body, and your spirit.

3. Repeat this process using the green, the gold, and finally the purple spotlight.

4. When you are finished, speak out loud and ask The Great Healers and Unseen Healing forces to come and assist you with your healing need (be sure to state it specifically) while you sleep.

5. As you drift off to sleep, feel yourself surrounded by several loving presences, cocooning you safely while they lift your burdens from you. Feel yourself float off into a calm, restful, and rejuvenating sleep.

Be sure to note any mental, physical, or spiritual changes you feel in your journal the next day.

Your Dream Symbols and Meanings

Everybody knows that if you dream about losing teeth you're really worried about losing power and control—maybe even about dying—and that dreams of water symbolize new life. And of course Freud's famous cigar is never just a cigar if it shows up in a dream, right?

Wrong. Dream imagery often does carry symbolic meaning, it's true. But those meanings are radically different from one person to another, depending on each one's experiences, preferences, passions, filters, and fears. "Dream dictionaries" that assign specific meanings to various images might draw on common cultural traditions and ideas. But they can't possibly keep up with all the variations the human brain can conjure, as Laura told one reader of her "Ask Laura" column:

Dear Laura,

I keep having a dream about a monkey. When I looked it up in dream books, I felt even more confused. What does the monkey mean?

—A friend of Jane Goodall

Dear Friend,

Fear not! Although countless authors feel they have an exclusive handle on dream interpretation, I use a different approach. I believe that elements in dreams mean something uniquely different to each and every person by design. After all, if each of us is as unique as our own fingerprint, then clearly when it comes to dream interpretation, one size doesn't fit all.

Get a pen and paper and write down the answers to the following questions: What does a monkey represent to you (i.e. the circus, childhood, zoo, science)? How do you feel when you see the monkey (i.e. happy, worried, depressed, scared)? How is the monkey behaving (i.e. docile, aggressive, pensive, oblivious)? Does the monkey have human behaviors (i.e. talking, crying, laughing)? What is the setting of the dream (i.e. work, home, outdoors)?

Now look at what you have written and ask yourself if there is something going on in your life that could relate to one of these aspects of the monkey image. (And if that doesn't work, cut out the bananas before bedtime.)

In short, you've just got to figure out your dream's symbols and meanings for yourself! A step-by-step analysis, like the one Laura outlined in her letter to her monkey-dreaming correspondent, can make this process easier.

If you do feel a need for the symbolic suggestions that a dream dictionary offers, look through several of them to make sure that the author's sensibilities mesh with your own. But even if it does, don't expect it to perfectly align with your own personal symbols. Your dreams are your own!

Sometimes a talk with a friend is more valuable than any dream dictionary could be. Joyce was bothered by a dream about ticks. The tiny insects were all around her and all over her body—walking on her arms and legs, embedded in her skin, feeding on her blood. Joyce was completely overrun by them. "What does this mean?" she asked her friend Laura.

Laura only had to say one thing: "The ticks are your life!" And it all clicked for Joyce. She'd been unhappy with her work, feeling that it was "sucking the life out of her." But she'd been resistant to making a change. It took a dream, and a two-sentence conversation, to make Joyce aware of how overrun she was by this problem. She recognized her work as the true energy drain, and started to work on a solution for change.

Free association is a great way to connect your dream imagery with your feelings, but sometimes dream symbolism can throw you for a loop. If you're completely flummoxed by the meaning of a dream, divination tools can come to the rescue. Try drawing just one Ancient Stardust Directional Card to help you classify your mystery image if you're at a total loss. A clue about the symbol's meaning—whether it's a call for action or a warning to take things slowly—might spur your association-making in a new and fruitful direction.

The Relax card, of the Resting category in the Ancient Stardust Directional Cards.

Using the Tarot for Dream Interpretation

Tarot imagery can be very dreamlike; the cards' use of archetypes and symbols dovetails neatly with those of dreams. In this exercise, we focus on the Tarot as a kind of pictorial language to tell the story of a dream.

1. Read your dream notes, or sit for a moment with your memory of the dream in question.

2. Go through your Tarot deck and look at the face of each card. If you have the space, you can spread the entire deck before you, face-up, and examine the cards as a group. Otherwise, go through the deck, card by card.

3. As you examine the cards, pull out the ones whose imagery reflects the energy, feelings, or images of your dream.

4. When you've chosen all the cards that relate to your dream (it could be very many and it could be very few—numbers don't matter in this reading!), arrange them in a "storyboard" format that expresses your dream's important themes or actions.

5. Use the cards' images and their interpretations to meditate on the meanings and resonances they suggest for your dream. Can you see the dream from a new angle now? Have seemingly minor details leaped to the forefront? Note your thoughts here.

_____

_____

_____

Your Dream Journal: Charting Intuitive Patterns

Because dreams so often speak to us in symbols and images, a journal is a crucial tool in dreamwork. But when some people confront a blank journal page, they're at a loss. Where do I begin?

That's why Laura created her own Progress Journal for those who want to document the progress of their spiritual unfolding. The Progress Journal goes beyond traditional journal formats and is a wonderful tool for documenting intuitive development and spiritual progress. Laura's Progress Journal pages are divided into sections and categories that help users make connections between their dreams, their intuitive flashes, and all their other spiritual experiences. It has space for making connections and comments immediately after the exercises. It also has room for afterthoughts—related ideas and thoughts that may come to you weeks or months later! You can use these pages as a model for organizing a notebook of your own choosing. Or you can check the order form at the back of this book for information on how you can get a Progress Journal from Laura.

Date

My Progress Journal™

Exercises

Afterthoughts

Notes

Laura designed the Progress Journal to help those interested in spiritual and intuitive development to better understand and track their progress.

Date

My Progress Journal™

Dreams

Synchronicities

Notes

Gratitude

A Dream Animal Totem Exercise

Dreamwork has always held an honored place in the spiritual practices of many Native American groups. And dreams of animals are especially important in Native tradition, because they're thought to point the dreamer toward his or her animal totem or guide—the animal spirit that has special lessons to teach the individual. You can use Native American insights into nature and dreams to create meaningful dream rituals of your own. Intention is all: Prepare yourself for this ritual with care and fore-thought.

1. Ready a place where you can sleep and receive your dream. Optimally, arrange an outdoor sleeping space, as on a camping trip or simply during a backyard nap. Or you can prepare yourself for an indoor ritual with tapes of shamanic drumming, smudge materials or incense sticks, and Native American blankets or wall hangings.

2. Before settling yourself for sleep, give thanks for the natural world around you. Speaking aloud, state your intention or request for your animal totem or animal guide to visit you in your dreams. Ask for a clear and loving introduction to the spiritual messenger you need in your life now.

3. Make sure you have materials by your side to take notes. Then compose yourself for sleep.

4. Allow yourself to wake from sleep naturally (no alarm clocks today!). Stretch and give thanks for your rest. Then write down all the details you can about your dreams.

5. If you haven't dreamed of your animal guide, don't worry—but do pay attention to all the animals that cross your path or your consciousness during the day. Ask yourself how you feel about each animal and their qualities. Your guide may visit you in the flesh and not in your dreams!

The Soul Never Sleeps

As we've said, sleep is a multifaceted need of ours. Your body uses sleep as its time of rejuvenation and rest. Your soul uses sleep as its time to roll up its metaphorical sleeves and get to work!

The Astral Body and the Silver Cord

You know that floating feeling you can have when you're drifting off to sleep? And how heavy your body seems to feel when you're awakened from sleep suddenly?

These aren't just physical quirks of the sleep state. Chalk them up to your astral body.

Future Focus

The **silver cord** is like an umbilical cord of energy, connecting the spirit to the mind and body.

The *astral body* is an energy extension of yourself, similar to your aura. Unlike the aura, though, the astral body doesn't have to stay with your physical body. It can move independently wherever it wants to go whenever you are sleeping (or in a direction of your choosing when you are meditating), thanks to the *silver cord*.

The silver cord connects the spirit to the mind and body, no matter where the spirit may astrally travel. What we know as death is metaphysically just the breaking of the silver cord, the separation of the spirit, which is eternal, from the impermanent physical body.

In dreams (and sometimes in conscious meditative states), the soul, via the astral body, leaves the physical body to gather information, resolve conflict, or travel—to do its work, in other words. But wherever it goes, no matter how far, the soul is connected to the body by the silver cord, until death severs that connection. Your nonsleeping soul is an accomplished traveler. It journeys far and wide in dreams, and it can go anywhere—even to The Other Side. Loved ones can come to visit us in our dreams, but we can go to see them there, as well.

Dream journeys can take you anywhere in the world we know, as well as into the world beyond. No wonder you can wake up knowing something without being able to define how you know it, and feeling released from things that had been driving you bonkers. Your soul divined the problem and sought its resolution in your dreams.

The Least You Need to Know

- In dreams, your soul does its work.

- Dream imagery is as unique as you are; only you can interpret a dream's symbolic meaning.

- In dreams, your soul can travel anywhere via your astral body.

- You can receive profound dream visitations from deceased loved ones on The Other Side.

Chapter 16

Intuition with a Capital "I"

In This Chapter

- ◆ Intuition in daily life
- ◆ Why intense experiences heighten intuition
- ◆ Toning up your intuitive skills
- ◆ Intuition for the higher good

By now, you've had a chance to practice intuitive techniques and (we hope!) experience aspects of your own intuition firsthand. Everyone has intuition, to some degree. Tools can help you access it; so can your dreams. But to make intuition a real force in your life, you need to start getting in the habit of paying attention and remembering to use it—and use it often!

In this chapter we're going to revisit the whole concept of intuition and enhance what we already know about it the only way we can: Practice, practice, practice.

Intuition Is Knowing

As you know, intuition is knowing something without knowing *how* you know it. And it's not just any kind of knowledge—it's a feeling of irrefutable certainty, something you know from the soles of your feet, as Laura likes to say (not just "from your gut," but even more deeply). Rational arguments can't talk you out of intuitive knowledge. And it's insistent: it will gnaw at you until you pay sufficient attention.

Not only that, the more you do pay attention to your intuitive sense, the more it will increase. If you've been marking your progress with a journal, now would be a great time to go back over your entries with a highlighter. Can you see the connections and patterns emerging that illustrate your own intuitive knowledge?

If not, don't be discouraged. Learning how to work with your intuition is like learning a foreign language. It goes so slowly at first, as you laboriously memorize letters, words, and sounds you've never known before. But at some point it all finally starts to gel in your mind and on your tongue—and before you know it, you're not only speaking a few basic sentences, you are understanding a few, as well! Give your body, mind, and soul all the time they need to learn this new language of intuition.

Activating Your Psychic Senses

There are many reasons why people do the work of learning this intuitive language:

- For protection and safety
- To help in their business or career
- To help them make better choices in general
- To enhance physical health
- To improve self-esteem
- To be of service to themselves or to others
- To increase their trust and faith in the Universe or the God of their understanding
- To control stress
- To improve personal relationships
- To better "ease into the flow" of life
- To seek inner peace
- To find spiritual guidance
- To use as a tool in crisis situations
- To increase the level of flow in everyday life

Some people are born with innate intuitive strengths. Most of us aren't quite so gifted, but we all have some intuitive capacity. Practice does make perfect, to some degree; the more you use your intuition, the more your intuition will make itself known to you. It's like when you first begin to exercise: Your muscles may initially seem weak or unresponsive, but with time, they begin to perform. And so, too, can your intuitive muscle.

Divine Inspiration

A near-death experience, or NDE, occurs when the physical body experiences a clinical death—the heart stops beating, the brain ceases its functions. During this time, the spirit leaves the body and begins to travel to The Other Side. (Almost universally, this involves a moving through some sort of tunnel that bears the soul toward a place of shining Light.) When life returns to the physical body, the spirit returns as well.

But apart from that, there are certain intense life experiences that do tend to heighten your intuitive ability. Falling in love is one of them. So is having your heart broken. Abuse and trauma can also have the positive side effect of deepening one's intuitive skills. A near-death experience (NDE) almost universally leads a person into a more intuitively sensitive life. Why is this? It seems that extreme tests of emotion or intense spiritual events can awaken your intuitive energies.

NDEs are life-changing events that often spur wholesale energetic reordering. People who've "come back" have been reunited with a conscious memory of what's beyond this world. That memory lights up the intuitive centers in a whole new way, and forever changes their perspective on who they are in the here and now. Few can see a glimpse of the afterlife and not feel profoundly changed.

Dannion Brinkley was an angry, mean, out-of-control young man. Then he had a near-death experience after he was struck by lightning, and he began to have a profound sense of precognition. Yet he was unable to make peace with this newly found understanding, and he fell into a *dark night of the soul*. It took a second NDE (yet another lightning strike—defying all earthly odds!) for him to come to terms with his intuitive abilities. Dannion Brinkley is now a world-famous speaker, author, and advocate who

Resonances

Short of seeking out life-changing drama or a dark night of the soul, Laura encourages her students to create rituals that open the mind to greater insight and understanding. These include prayer, affirmation, meditation, visualization, journaling, or use of the Bach Flower Essence, Cerato. Using a ritual is like having the key to the front door of a house—it's so much easier than trying to climb in through a window!

assists people in the final stage of their life journey: death. His dedication to this cause takes him around the world, where he trains others in how to comfort and support the terminally ill and the elderly in the last steps of their sacred transition from this life to the next.

A dark night of the soul is one name for a spiritual crisis of larger capacity. It can be brought on by sudden or by known events, such as heartbreak or loss, health challenges, and yes, even by depression. It often involves a test of your innate faith and strong questioning of previously deep-seated concepts or values. Although they can be painful and frustrating periods, dark nights of the soul often lead to increased understanding and a spiritual elevation of some sort, once the mind is able to "put the questions to bed" and go on with the business of living.

Sometimes, though, intuitive work can be frustrating. If you ever get the desperate feeling that your intuition is just not there, take a step back, and don't force the issue. Relax, and ask yourself whether something in your heart is blocking information, stopping it from getting through to your consciousness. Or perhaps you're asking about something that the Universe just cannot have you know at this time. Be open to the possibility that the answers you seek might be coming to you later—but not just now.

Using the Intuitive Arts to Enhance Knowing

By its very nature, intuitive knowledge is a slippery thing. Because you don't know how you know it, it's easy to doubt an intuitive feeling, especially when you're just beginning to explore this aspect of your own energy.

When you question yourself, and you can't verify your intuition with factual "proof," it's time to pump up the intuitive volume with a divining method. A Tarot reading or astrology chart, or whatever method makes you most comfortable, gives you a new viewpoint on the matter in question. It could verify the information in your mind, or it could tell you, instead, that your doubts are valid in this case. With the help of a divinatory reading, you can break through to the truth that's already within you.

Imagine the Possibilities!

You've only taken the first few steps on a lifelong journey of intuitive understanding, and already you've learned a lot. But there is so much more to see and experience! Each encounter with your own intuition can teach you more about yourself, and about the energies at work all around you. Each level of deeper understanding opens your eyes to yet another wondrous level ahead.

When it comes to true intuition, always remember to go with your first thoughts, your first intuition. Resist the urge to rationalize and overthink your intuitive vibes! You can use a series of divining methods to help support your initial impressions and instincts and get in the habit of trusting them.

Palmistry offers an intuitive check-up for you. If you examined your hand back in Chapter 8, now is a great time to study your palm once again. Reexamine your hand and compare it to your previous observations. Can you see any evidence of an intuitive shift reflected in your palm?

If you haven't tried palmistry yet, then now's the perfect time to do an "inking" that you can refer to months from now. You will need ink, paper, and a roller. Ink your palm completely, press it firmly down on the paper, then carefully peel the paper off your hand. Wash your hands, then repeat with your other hand. You now have an irrefutable record of your hand's lines, mounds, phalanges, and so on that you can refer back to later.

To do further and deeper intuitive exploration, you have to be well prepared on all levels—body, mind, and spirit. Meditation, affirmation, and divining traditions can get you ready for all the adventures to come.

Meditation to Improve Intuitive Focus: An Exercise

We call this the "alignment meditation." It's a simple visualization that straightens out your energy, allowing it to flow freely.

1. Picture a large stack of staggered bricks, standing about six feet tall, in a pattern like this.

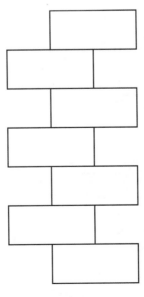

2. Hold this image in your mind as you settle your body and ground yourself for meditation.

3. Now picture your seven chakras superimposed on the bricks. Let them *become* the bricks in your mind. Your root chakra is the bottom brick; your pelvic chakra is the next brick up; and so on, all the way up to your crown chakra at the very top of the stack.

4. Slowly, very slowly, holding the root chakra brick firm at the base, visualize pushing the upper bricks over so that the second brick is aligned with the first. You don't want to topple the whole stack! So imagine pushing slowly, firmly, and gently. Remember these are large blocks, and the tower is quite high. Easy does it! No rushing and risking toppling the tower! It's a slow and deliberate process to get them aligned. When you're done, imagine that your chakra bricks look like this.

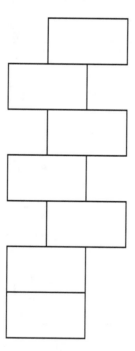

5. Brick by brick, repeat the process until you can visualize your blocks as a straight, perfectly aligned tower, like this.

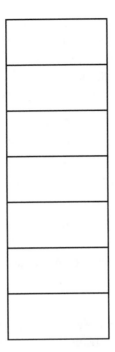

6. When the last block is in place, step back and watch as the tower lights up from within. You've completed all the energetic connections! Admire the beauty of the work you've done.

"Cleaning Out the Closets": An Exercise

The tidal forces of everyday life drag a lot of detritus along with them. Every home gets cluttered up sometimes with all that unnecessary stuff—old newspapers, mismatched socks, stray pet toys, holiday decorations, broken parts, you name it. That's when it's time to roll up the sleeves and do a good spring cleaning (no matter what season it happens to be).

Your psyche is just the same. Life goes on, thoughts and feelings sweep through, and after a while your mental junk builds up. Just as a cluttered room can make you feel disoriented or claustrophobic or just plain grumpy, a cluttered mind can really get in your way.

This divination exercise's combination of physical activity with verbal affirmation is a great way to change your existing energy patterns when you need some mental "spring cleaning" and to make room for something new (like more intuition!) to come into your life. And as a side benefit, it completes a household chore at the same time!

This exercise can bring about a major change in attitude. So please remember that doing it should be a labor of love, not one of drudgery. It's not the same as receiving an ultimatum to "clean your room or else." Only attempt this exercise with the clear intention to feel lighthearted and mentally free. Done properly, this exercise scenario will leave your mind and spirit feeling lighter, happier, and more at peace.

1. Choose *one* small area of your home that really needs to be cleaned and decluttered. A single closet, drawer, or cabinet would be perfect.

2. Pause in this physical space and ground yourself. Say out loud, "I'm cleaning out the closet of my mind" (or "the desk drawer of my mind" or whatever it is you're cleaning).

3. Give this closet the most thorough cleaning and reorganization it's ever had. Take everything out and set items aside for the trash or to give away. Wipe down the shelves, clean out the cobwebs, sweep up the dust. Every few minutes throughout the process, say out loud once again, "I'm cleaning out the closet of my mind."

4. When the closet is clean, now it's time to reorganize. Put back into the closet only those things you have positively chosen to keep. Don't just shove all the old clutter back in—throw things out or give things away so that you retain *only* the items you really want or need. Now that there's less to put in, it's a perfect time to rearrange the manner in which you are stacking and organizing your closet's contents. Rotate, switch, and adjust as you put the remaining items back, affirming out loud, "I'm cleaning out the closet of my mind."

5. Step back, survey your work, and say what you've done: "I've cleaned out the closet of my mind!"

We're not trying to make you feel silly in this exercise, by the way. An affirmation like this only works if you say it out loud! That's how your brain knows to pay attention to it; otherwise, it's "just another thought." Saying an affirmation is like skipping a stone on the energy pond. Watch those ripples go out as the energy changes course!

Numbers Can Be Intuitive: A Numerology Exercise

We often think of numbers as precise and logical—in short, scientific. But numbers have other connotations, as well: intuitive ones. To numerologists, numbers can be read as an intuitive language carrying meanings and messages.

A great way to give numerology a try is by figuring your Personal Year Number. Numerologists believe that for each one of us, every year holds its own theme and lesson. These themes rotate on a nine-year cycle. You can access your theme for this (or any) year by performing a simple calculation. The formula is:

month of birth + day of birth + current calendar year = Personal Year Number

An important principle in numerology is that of *reduction*. Generally, it's the single-digit numbers, 1 through 9, that have meaning to numerologists. To get down to single digits, you just keep adding. The number 14 equals 1 + 4, or 5. The number 29 equals 2 + 9, or 11; because 11 is a two-digit number, you need to add the digits again, giving you a final number of (1 + 1 =) 2.

Knowing all that, let's find the Personal Year Number for Maggie, a student. Maggie's birthday is October 14. She wanted to find her Personal Year Number for 2004. Here's her calculation:

10 (month) + 14 (day) + 2004 (current year) =

1 (month reduced) + 5 (day reduced) + 6 (year reduced) =

12 =

3

So 2004 will be a 3 year for Maggie, an active year full of creativity and self-expression. Maybe this is her year to finally take an art class, learn piano, or audition for the community theater.

Ready to do a little math? Fill in the following spaces to figure your own Personal Year Number.

1. Your month of birth: _____ (reduce if necessary) = ___ = ___

2. Your day of birth: _____ (reduce if necessary) = ___ = ___

3. Current year: _____ (reduce this number) = ___ = ___

   (*Note:* Use the full year, not the last two digits!)

4. Add together the final numbers from steps 1, 2, and 3: ___ + ___ + ___ = ___

   (If this final number is more than one digit, add them together: _____ + _____ = _____. You may have to repeat this step until you come to a single-digit number.)

The final number in step 4 is your Personal Year Number. Now consult the following table to better understand where you are in the nine-year cycle.

Personal Year Number	Meaning
1	New beginnings, planting seeds—an active year
2	Emphasis on cooperation, relationships—a slow year
3	Creative ideas, speaking your truth, self-expression—an active year
4	Hard work, discipline, laying foundation for the ideas of the 3 Year; a productive year, if you persevere
5	Change, unpredictability, risk, freedom—an active year
6	Family ties, domestic affairs, nurturing others; constant effort and home-centered activity
7	Spirituality, contemplation, turning inward; study, reading, time alone; outwardly, a quiet year
8	Business and finance, administration, achievement, recognition—an active year
9	Completion, forgiveness, transformation, release, rest—a quiet year, possibly busy in the first half

Now, take a moment to reflect on what the numbers tell you about this year. What resonates with you? What rings true? Use your journal to explore these thoughts.

As always, the numbers won't predict what will or will not happen to you during this year. Free will is too strong for that. But the numbers *will* point out the forces that are at work in your life at this time. Are you working in the flow of the year, or are you fighting its currents?

Due Caution: Interpreting Intuitive Messages

Exploring your intuition is a deeply personal experience. But through it all, you need to stay detached, as well, if you're going to interpret your messages properly. It's easy to get too close, to become so wrapped up in the particulars of a reading that you forget about its place in the big picture of your life.

The goal of the intuitive arts is to help you become grounded and centered enough that you'll be able to turn your energies outward, brightening and enriching the world around you. But go easy. That doesn't mean inserting yourself or your divination opinions into the lives of those around you without their prior request or permission. Always maintain a balance.

Is It Literal or Symbolic?

Sometimes intuitive messages can be confusing. You have to be in a state of detachment—from the situation, and from your own emotions—to understand them. You can reach that state of detachment through journaling, dialogue, and focused meditation. Only regular self-examination can give you the skills you need to understand what your intuition is trying to tell you.

Take the case of the postmenopausal woman who came to Laura confused about her recurring dreams of pregnancy. The details of her dreams were so realistic—right down to the woman's feeling that she needed to eat well and get enough rest to prepare for the imminent birth. She was perplexed. "I *can't* have a baby, but these dreams are so real!" she exclaimed.

She was too close to her own situation to see that her dream was symbolic, not literal. This woman was on the verge of launching a new business—"giving birth" to a new chapter in her life. Her pregnancy dream had been recurring all through the venture's gestation period (yes, for about nine months!).

So don't get caught up in the obvious and jump to quick conclusions! Take the time to write it out, talk it out, and work out alternative possibilities before you assign meaning to a divinatory experience.

Intuition with Intent—What Are You Looking For?

As you may have already seen, divination in any form can be fun, affirming, exciting, and life changing. But our discussion would be remiss without a few reminders about intent.

Your intention is your aim, goal, or purpose for knowing something. Without proper intention, information can be wielded clumsily, awkwardly, and even harmfully. Remember, at their best, intuition and divination are ways of connecting with your mind, body, and spirit. They help make life easier. More specifically, they make *your* life easier. And while you are here on Earth, the first rule is: *You can only control yourself.*

Respecting Personal Boundaries

If divination can bring you such great personal benefits, wouldn't it be wonderful to use your intuitive skills to help your family and friends? Even your neighborhood, your town, the world as a whole?

Careful—we're on dangerous ground here. This is where well-intentioned people, out of the goodness of their hearts, can inadvertently do some real damage. That's why the next most important rule is: *Thou shalt respect the boundaries of others.*

It's not right to ask for divinatory messages on behalf of someone who hasn't asked you for that help. First, it's trespassing! Others have the right to keep their private thoughts and emotions, well, private. No matter how intuitively skilled you are, it's wrong to pry. Second, it's rude. Who wants to be the recipient of unsolicited advice?

Still, it's easy to fall into this trap, as Laura has discussed in her "Ask Laura" column:

> Dear Laura,
> Why do people get offended at someone wanting to offer something that may better their life?
> —Just trying to help

> Dear Just Trying,
> Because they didn't ask for your help. And who are you to say that one life is better than another? There's nothing worse than unsolicited advice pointing out how silly, stupid, foolish, unwise, unlucky, unproductive, unhealthy, etc., that someone thinks you are. Your intentions, however good, are completely inappropriate. It's time for you to learn more about boundaries. Your job as a soul is to work on you and you alone. A desire to tell everyone around you to "fix this" and "change that" is really a statement about you yourself being out of balance and unhappy.

> The deal is: You can only work on you. You'll find that when done properly, it's a 24/7 job that leaves you no time to work on anyone else!

Before you turn your intuitive attention to others, take a moment to check your intentions and to think. Ask yourself: What's the point? How will I use this information? Do I need to know it for the good of my relationship with this person? Am I just idly curious, or acting out of anger or another strong emotion? Am I doing this for the higher good—or just to make myself look good? All of these are important questions that can skew your results!

Remember to check yourself using multiple divination sources before pushing any panic buttons or breaking any hearts. And, when in doubt, *don't*. Be careful how you wield your intuitive insights on others. Remember that they, too, have their own free will. You can always invite further insight in through meditation or dream requesting. That should help bring you clarity if you are feeling compelled to act.

It is *never* appropriate to use divination to hurt or control someone. Even if you mean well, your intuitive knowledge about another person can do more harm than good if your personal filters have skewed the information, or if your interpretation is incorrect. A good rule of thumb: Use your intuition only to seek information about yourself and your reactions to those around you. Some things are just none of your business!

Sharing Information

You can't always help it, though—when you open yourself to the Universe's energy, you open yourself to all kinds of information. What do you do with intuitive knowledge about others that just comes to you?

Information is power. And intuitive ability does not give you the right to wield power over others.

When you receive important information about another person in your life, take a deep breath and look hard at yourself. How did you receive this information? Were you well grounded when you received it? Can you confirm it with another divinatory method? Can you think of alternate symbolism or other meanings for the message you have received?

> **Take Heed**
>
> Act according to the physician's maxim: First, do no harm. Don't run out in a panic and tell somebody, "Get to the hospital! I just know you've got cancer!" When you receive intuitive information about others, ground yourself and look inward carefully before proceeding.

If, after careful consideration, you believe that your information is valid, think about how you would feel if you were on the receiving end of this kind of news. Then speak to the person accordingly. A simple, kind conversation-starter is often the way to go. Try this: "You've been on my mind lately. How have you been? Are you okay?"

Be especially cautious if your intuition leads you to conclusions about a person you don't know at all, or about events in the news. The Universe is pretty logical, all things considered, and it knows how to get information to those who *really* need to know it. Is it likely that you're the only person who knows about a plot for a presidential assassination or the location of a missing child? No. The Universe works regularly with those who "need to know," such as law enforcement officials, the FBI, and the skilled intuitive professionals who assist in this work. Check your own filters carefully before you act on your intuitive knowledge! It takes many factors, many decisions, and many choices to determine the course of world events.

Acting on Intuition

If you have been opening up (or unfolding, as Laura likes to call it) and practicing along with us so far, then intuitively speaking you're probably getting excited about using your newfound intuitive muscles to peek at those around you. Please remember that it's important to always respect people's boundaries and to get their permission beforehand. The Universe does have rules of ethics you know. Don't be so excited to share that you trample another person's feelings or boundaries. Go slowly, and work on your delivery skills and understanding of intuitive metaphors and messages. Be sure to check your intention, and don't meddle where you haven't been asked. Your friends and family will thank you (and so do we!).

If you are receiving scary messages about a person or a situation, don't panic—and don't jump to any conclusions. Take care to check your feeling with several divining methods. Be open to consulting a professional for help in interpreting your information. After all, even trained psychotherapists report to more senior therapists to discuss and evaluate their work. And stay positive: there's a reason why you're knowing what you know. Act, at all times, for the higher good.

It all goes back to the golden rule: *Treat others the way you'd like to be treated yourself.*

The Least You Need to Know

- Intuition is knowing something with irrefutable certainty, but without knowing *how* you know it.

- Divining techniques and methods can "pump up" the intuitive volume.

- Personal work, like meditation and affirmation, can prepare you for new intuitive possibilities.

- Respect the boundaries of other people when you use your intuition.

- Your intention can help you to better understand an intuitive message about the future.

Part 5

Reading the Spirit

Spiritual energy is the force of the soul, and it's tied most closely to our intuition. In this part, you'll learn how to understand your soul's larger journey, how to access the guides who help us along the way, and why there's no such thing as coincidence. We'll see how all our energies—body, mind, and spirit—can work in harmony. And when mind, body, and spirit do come together, you can slip right into the Universe's flow.

Chapter 17

Understanding Spirit Energy

In This Chapter

- ◆ Mind, body, and spirit harmony
- ◆ Analyzing your personal energy
- ◆ Communicating with spiritual energy beings
- ◆ Understanding your journey and life lessons

In terms of energy, you are one entity with three parts: body, mind, and spirit. These parts are different in nature but closely linked, interrelated in all that they (all that *you*) do. To be balanced and feel whole, to be able to divine and intuit the future, you need to be aware of your three energy systems and be willing to work with all of them. We might call it union—a feeling of inner harmony that allows your energy to flow freely.

When you're in a state of inner union, you're able to join the outer world in a balanced way, and balance is a worthy goal. Without this balance, the future will always seem murky and uncertain, as you struggle to know what to do is the right thing. When you live within balance, you may still not have all the answers, but you *will* know where, and how, to look to find them.

In Union: Body, Mind, and Spirit

You can see and feel your physical body. You can experience the workings of your mind. But the spirit is more of a mystery. Your spirit is housed within your body (for now, at least), but it is not *of* your body. Unlike your mind, your spirit isn't housed in a particular spot within your physical self. And your spirit works closely with your mind and your body, but it's also connected to a much bigger system: the Universal energy as a whole.

It's unhealthy to have any one of your energy systems be too dominant, but all of us have had times in our lives when we've allowed that to happen—when we're ruled by our emotions, or obsessed with our health. At these times it is hard to see our path through the present, much less the future. Visualization can help put things back into perspective.

Laura calls this the "Three Gingerbread Men" exercise. It is a combination of meditation, visualization, and positive programming.

1. Begin by sitting with your back straight and your feet flat on the floor, using a round of three centering breaths to ground and still yourself.

2. Close your eyes and visualize a large indigo screen. Floating in front of the screen are three large silhouettes of shimmering white (each about six feet tall) in the image of standing gingerbread men. (Think of a cookie cutter in the land of the Jolly Green Giant!)

3. See yourself guiding one of the giant shimmering silhouette images, gently and carefully, over so that it sits perfectly on top of the center image. Take a moment to align the outlines exactly. What were three are now two.

4. Now take the remaining single silhouette and guide it, gently and carefully, over to the stack of two, repeating the precise alignment process. What was before two piles is now one neatly stacked pile of three—three perfectly aligned layers that now equal one solid, unified "cookie."

5. Because of their shimmering nature, when all three images are aligned into one, the "cookie" now glows—even hums—with beautiful hues of sparkly color within what was once just white. Take a moment to enjoy your work.

6. When you are ready, and you feel satisfied with your handiwork, slowly open your eyes and affirm out loud, "My mind, body, and spirit are now functioning as one."

This meditation involves several principles to promote wellness. The images of the gingerbread men represent mind, body, and spirit. By combining them deliberately, you end up with a simple and effective equation: unity + harmony = momentum. Momentum makes daily living easier, and is the catalyst that moves you confidently into the future with your intuitive pump primed and ready to fuel your journey!

Once you're familiar with this meditation and its imagery, you can recall it easily and quickly put it in place to harmonize and align yourself whenever you feel the need by applying a simple *Neuro-Linguistic Programming (NLP)* principle. As you feel your energies combine in harmony, a spoken affirmation seals the deal: *My mind, my body, and my spirit are now functioning as one.*

Future Focus

Neuro-Linguistic Programming (NLP) is the use of a predetermined signal or symbol to reset the mind's inner program and effect a desired result.

Your Personal Energy Profile

When you experience those vague feelings of unhappiness, or discontent, or anxiety that everyone goes through sometimes, chances are your spirit is out of alignment. Often, it's because you're not doing what you're supposed to be doing at this point in your journey. You feel uncomfortable because you know something isn't right … and you don't have any idea what that might be. At these times, you naturally find yourself turning to divinatory methods to help get your life back on track.

It's time to do a thorough intuitive inventory of your life—everything from your work to your relationships to your living space to your leisure activities—to uncover the source of your problem. It may not be what you expect it to be!

That's because things change as life goes on, and the things you wanted and needed during one part of your life's journey are not what you want or need on another stretch of the road. That's not fickleness; it's reality. After all, the shoes you wore at age 7 didn't fit you at age 10, or age 15, or today. It's natural to outgrow things in our lives. We leave them aside and find something that feels like a better fit. If it's okay to outgrow your shoes, it's just as normal to outgrow jobs, or ideas, or habits.

When you're in alignment, "in the flow," there's no such thing as a dead end. You always find the energy you need to manifest your future. Roadblocks become challenges; choices become opportunities. Really, the only way to grasp essential joy is through balance and alignment, by *doing what you're supposed to be doing*. The price of being out of balance is indeed high: depression, anger, despair. It doesn't have to be that way. If we look within to find the source of unbalance, and if we have the courage to embrace change, harmony is always within our reach.

Communication from the Higher Side

The spiritual energy within us is what links and unites us to the plane of pure energy, what's often called the higher or The Other Side. Its inhabitants are pure spirit, pure energy. We have many names for them—loved ones, ancestors, angels, guides. These beings have different qualities, but they have one thing in common: They are pure energy, and so energy is their means of communicating with us.

Guidance from Loved Ones

Besides visiting in dreams, your loved ones (and your angels and guides, as well) can also communicate to you through the manipulation of energy. Because they exist in the realm of pure energy, this is often the easiest way for them to reach out to us. One of the more common contacts is through tapping or clicking. If you hear a tapping on the windowpane when nothing is "there" to explain it, or you get a clicking sound on the phone line when you are using it, you could be experiencing an energetic visitation. The sense of smell, which is so subtle and yet so powerful, is another way that your loved one might get in touch with you. You might smell a hint of their aftershave or perfume in the air, or the distinctive scent of their favorite brand of tobacco. Or the visitation might be purely intuitive: You might experience the sensation of someone sitting on your bed at night, or be filled with a sense of knowing that you are being helped through something or that a situation was made easier for you. The more you notice and appreciate these subtle communications, the more you will draw in your loved one's energy.

But when you're in the depths of grief and mourning for someone who has passed, you can miss the signs that are all around you. It's important to remember that the love doesn't change, only the language does—and our loved ones always find ways to reach out to us. There's no such thing as a "coincidence" when the energy of our loved ones is at work!

Wise Counsel from Spirit Guides

Often, after someone close to you dies, you feel at some point a desperate need for that person's presence: "I wish my dad were here! He's the only person who could possibly help me; he'd know what to do." As real as the feeling may be, the thought isn't quite true. Your loved one would be able to give you advice and help, certainly. All of it, though, would be subject to his or her own soul nature, experiences (both on the earth plane and the spirit plane), and filter system.

But there *are* those who can help you without bias or preconceptions—energy beings whose job it is to support you through your life's journey, beginning to end. These are your spirit guides.

Your guides have access to your Akashic records; they can see everything about you, past, present, and future. Unlike humans, they don't have filters that might prejudice their answers. (Something our deceased relatives might have!) Their information is direct and unbiased. But still, they don't spoon-feed you or act for you— they're not meant to live your life, make your choices, dictate your future, or learn your lessons. They're your support system, your spiritual back-office operation, as you do your own important life work.

> **Divine Inspiration**
>
> Spirit guides are our ever-present energetic supporters and mentors from The Other Side. We each have one main guide, as well as others who help us episodically. Our deceased loved ones are *not* our spirit guides. We choose our spirit guides before we incarnate, so they are with us during the time prior to our birth.

Many people have experienced dreams in which they're accompanied by people who seem familiar, but whom they can't actually "see," recognize, or name. When that happens, your soul may be meeting with your Guides, people you "know and don't know how you know" in the manner of intuitive experiences.

If you ask your guides for help, they *will* respond. They have to; it's one of the basic rules of the road. When and how they get back to you isn't quite so easy to predict. Somehow, some way, at some point, they will provide an answer, if you ask.

But you do have to ask. How? Well, you could just flip through the pages of this book and use the first tool or method you see. Yes, we communicate with our guides through intuition. A divinatory reading, a prayer, a dream, a meditation, a yoga session, a journal entry—anything that gets intuition flowing is a pathway for us to access our guides, and for our guides to reach us.

Greetings, Guides: A Meditation

Ready to meet your guides? This beautiful guided meditation from Laura can help bring you face to face.

Guided meditation is a deep meditative experience that includes elements of visualization to lead you through a series of steps, a thought journey. This particular guided meditation also uses affirmations to give you positive reinforcement along the way.

Read the meditation all the way through before you settle down to "walk" its path. You might want to tape yourself reading it aloud (if you do, pace yourself—read it very slowly!). Or you could ask a partner to read it to you, so that you don't have to keep breaking your concentration to find your place on a page. (You can also order a taped version of this meditation in Laura's own voice via the order form in the back of this book or through her website: www.ancientstardust.com.)

Before you begin, please sit straight up with your legs and arms uncrossed (to avoid blocked energy) and your feet flat on floor. Take off your shoes if that will make you feel more comfortable.

Remain aware of your breathing throughout the meditation. Deep breathing can restore us, help us to relax, and help us to nourish ourselves by slowing us down. If you focus on your breath, particularly in parts 1 and 2 of this meditation, it will alter your state of consciousness and allow you to enter a deeper state of trance.

Our meditation experience begins here. Close your eyes, and begin by taking some deep breaths in and out (three times). Please note that affirmations are shown in **bold type.** Read them with special emphasis.

Part 1 is our grounding meditation.

Starting at the top of your head, breathe in deeply from the belly and relax. Release your hair and scalp as you exhale, knowing **all is well and you are safe.** Breathe in deeply again, relaxing your face, forehead, ears, and neck as you exhale. Another deep breath in, and feel the relaxation continue down through your throat, your jaw, and into the tops of the shoulders.

Breathe in deeply once again, and let go of all the stuff you don't need to carry with you anymore today. Feel your shoulders let go, and sink deeper into relaxation.

Breathe in deeply again, letting go of all the tension in your upper torso, feeling the wave of relaxation moving to your heart, your lungs, and into your stomach as you exhale. Breathe in again and move all that calmness down into your stomach area, relaxing those muscles that have been held so tightly. Feel the warm wave of kindness move down through your pelvis. Breathe in deeply and let go, feeling waves of calmness move down into your upper legs, down through your knees; breathe in once again and relax your calves as you exhale, knowing that **all is well,** and that **you are safe.** Feel the relaxation move down through your feet, which carry you all day long.

Now take another deep breath in, and as you exhale visualize attached to the soles of your feet a beautiful gold thread that leads to an intricate system of roots that intertwine down through the floor and down into the earth. Take another deep breath in, and as you exhale, extend these roots down deeper, deeper, and deeper into the earth, breathing in and relaxing and knowing that you are now connected with the center of the earth. Anything you don't need to carry is now moving down through your beautiful roots, down deeper and deeper into the earth, and being released there. **You are**

safe and perfectly grounded now as energy moves all the way through you and into the earth.

Part 2 is a clearing meditation.

Take a nice, easy, deep breath in and visualize above your head a brilliant white orb of exquisite light, a circular, transparent cloud that begins to move slowly down to the top of your head. As you breathe in it sweeps over your head and relaxes any lingering tension that is left there. Down through your face the beautiful, warm white light moves, moving down with each rhythmic breath. As you exhale, this light is further relaxing those jaw muscles, moving down through your neck. Breathe in again as the healing light moves down through your shoulders and into your torso; breathe in as it reaches your stomach and you feel that area let go to the warmth; breathe in and move this magical light down into your pelvis, relaxing your hips, down through your thighs; breathe in and let this warm light move through your knees, down through your lower legs, relaxing them, and down through your toes, knowing that **all is cleared off** and now moves down through your wonderful roots and into the earth so that **all tension is now let go.** Just take a moment and thank your body for carrying you along on your life journey, feeling this sparkling, wonderful light moving all through you now, knowing that **all is well,** that **all is working for good in your life,** and that **you are safe.** Smile inwardly as you feel how special you are, and how magical your body is. **You are absolutely unique!**

In Part 3, we'll take a walk to meet your spirit guide.

Imagine you're outdoors on a beautiful, warm summer day, and you are standing at the end of a footpath. You are wearing a comfortable loose white gown, and begin to move by floating along, hovering above the ground ever so slightly, noticing the stones and how love-worn the path is. Take a nice deep breath, feeling how light and free you are as you progress on the path, floating up a gentle slope, feeling the warm, loving sunlight surrounding you.

To your left on the path is a beautiful evergreen tree. Move closer to this tree, feeling safe, knowing **all is well,** breathing in deeply. You can feel its energy as you begin softly touching its branches, smelling its fresh, clean scent. As you look up, there sits a beautiful, tiny angel on top of this evergreen.

Looking closer at the angel's face, you see that the angel is starting to speak. It wants to tell you something. It could be a few words, it could be a picture, it may just be a loving smile to let you know **you are loved** and how special you are. Take a moment to receive this message and thank the angel as you move back toward the path and continue on your journey.

The path begins a gentle climb now, and it starts to curve. As we round this curve there's a clearing to your right, and in this clearing is another of God's creatures, an animal friend who wants to greet you. It might be a bird, or an animal, or even an insect. Perhaps it's peeking out at you from behind a tree, or standing in full view. Ask this creature what it wants to tell you. It may be a word, a phrase, a feeling, or an image. Maybe the animal just came to notice the day with you. Receive its message, and thank it for its presence, then move your attention back to the path.

Take a deep breath in, and continue moving effortlessly, up, up, up the pathway. Up … up until you reach the top and there is a beautiful, brilliant temple. The pathway leads right to the temple door, and you move up the steps and inside. Your eyes focus on a room filled with lovely artwork and bubbling fountains. **It's a safe place,** and as you move through the room, you notice a corridor leading to a center room. You move through this corridor until you reach this inner sanctuary room. It's a circular room with a large comfy chair in the center that is facing another doorway across from you. You go to this beautiful chair and sit in it. You understand that you are here to meet your guide. **It is a sacred place, and you are safe here.**

In the corridor across from you, you can see a white mist. Slowly, a shape starts to emerge from the mist. It steps forward toward you. It is your spirit guide, who has come to meet with you and offer you a message. Don't worry if you cannot see the guide clearly. Ask your guide if he or she has a message or something that you need to know right now. It may be a single word, it may be a picture, or it may be an emotion you sense. Receive your message and know that **you are not alone on your journey.** No one is. You may be filled with a sense of connectedness and love. Take a moment to enjoy this beautiful, tranquil place. Thank your guide for all he or she does to help you on your journey. Thank your guide for coming today.

It's time to leave the inner sanctuary room now, so see yourself slowly and gently getting up from the chair. Begin to move back through the corridor, and into the outer room with its art, fountains, and plants. Take a quick look around at the magnificent treasures displayed here before stepping back out into the daylight. You may return again another time, but for now we must go back down the hill, down this well-worn path, down, down, down, breathing in the fresh air, knowing that **you are good, strong, and deserving of all good things in your life;** that **everything in your life is working for good now.**

> **Take Heed**
>
> There's no need to jettison your religious tradition or beliefs to meditate or work with spirit guides. Many faiths already incorporate these concepts in their regular practices. Mysticism and prayer are closely related to meditation and visualization; patron saints and guardian angels can correlate to spirit guides. If it makes you feel more comfortable, substitute *archangel* or *patron saint* for all references to *spirit guide* in this meditation.

As you reach the bottom of the hill, realize it's time to return to your physical body. Feel yourself sitting in your own chair, feeling the clothes you are wearing today, hearing the sounds in the room around you. Come back slowly, moving your feet a bit, squeezing your toes, taking your time before opening your eyes. Feel yourself come back into your body, back into your room, and just take a few moments for yourself, taking nice deep breaths, feeling renewed and restored and knowing that **all is well.**

The Station of This Physical Life

This life is one leg of a longer, greater journey. Your spirit lives on beyond the lifetime you're experiencing now. But while you're here, in this life and in this physical body, you have to deal with the situations that life presents to you, because dealing with them is the reason you're here.

If the same issue keeps coming up again and again in your life—be it abandonment, control, health, or any of a host of recurring challenges—it's a good bet that part of your life's mission has to do with this. In the next chapter, we'll talk more about identifying and understanding these patterns.

Why Are You Here?

We live our lives so that we can learn from them—so that we can deepen our understanding of the Universal truths that link us all.

More specifically, you're here in this lifetime to do the work at hand! Your experiences in this life help your spirit grow. Your tests and challenges on this part of your journey prepare you for future lessons. You can't "skip a grade" in this process; your soul has to have experience of life to learn about it, and your soul has to learn about life if it's going to grow. Developing your intuitive nature will help you see your soul's work with greater clarity and move you toward manifesting your best future and your best self.

All of us experiencing life at any one time are at different levels on the larger journey. All of us are learning our own lessons—often through the actions and choices of one another. Our interactions with others present us with the challenges and experiences we need to move forward. We need each other, whatever road each of us is on!

What Is Your Journey?

Just as you are as unique as your own DNA, your journey is unlike anyone else's. Your mom was right—never compare yourself to anybody else, because nobody else is walking the same path that you are! We're each here to experience our own life lessons.

Divining methods can help you see your journey for what it is. They can help you make the choices and changes that are right for you and keep you on your path. Divination sheds light on the road before you so you can travel where you need to go.

Resonances

Very often, we can grasp the contours of our life path at a very young age. For example, one elementary-school teacher has her students write a letter to themselves about what they want to be doing when they grow up. She then saves the papers and mails them to her charges after they've become adults. She's found that 75 percent of the time, the children's career plans actually come to be! Talk about the soul knowing what it's supposed to be doing!

Astrology: Sowing and Reaping

Astrology offers many methods to analyze the ways that the planets and stars interact with us all through our lives. Your birth chart can easily tell you if this is a "sowing" or a "reaping" lifetime for you.

1. If you had your birth chart done back when we discussed astrology in Chapter 5, pull it out again now. If not, have your birth chart done (either local or online sources can create a chart for you quickly).

2. Study the chart itself, a wheel divided into the 12 houses of the zodiac. Notice how the houses form two halves of the wheel. Houses ten through three should be on the left half of your chart. We call this the eastern half. The western half of your chart is formed by houses four through nine on the right side of the wheel.

3. Looking within the spokes of your chart's wheel, count up the number of planet symbols that appear in the eastern half. Then count the number of planet symbols in the western half of your chart. Write your totals here.

Eastern planets _____

Western planets _____

Which half of your chart has most of your planetary influences?

4. If most of your planet symbols are on the eastern side of your chart, we say you're in a sowing lifetime. That is, you are mainly planting seeds now that will bear fruit for your soul in the future. You have lots of opportunity to chart your own course, but success won't ever "arrive on a silver platter." You'll have to expend a lot of energy and work consistently for your achievements.

5. If most of your planet symbols are in the western half of your chart, you're in reaping mode this time around. You're harvesting the seeds you've planted before, collecting the rewards of the plans your soul has previously put in motion. You're likely to have mentors to guide you as your life almost effortlessly falls into place. Your choices are fewer than they are in a sowing lifetime, but your successes are likely to come more easily.

In general, astrological methods of gauging your life path will assume that this lifetime is one of many your soul will experience. If you believe we each get a single lifetime, though, this analysis still offers insight: a sowing lifetime means that you'll be making your own way and blazing your own path through life; a reaping lifetime is filled with gifts and graces from outside sources.

If you look back at Gandhi's birth chart in Chapter 6 and count the symbols for the planets in the eastern and western halves of his chart, you'll find that Gandhi's planets are pretty evenly divided between the two. For Gandhi, his was a lifetime of reaping *and* sowing.

Biofeedback: Guiding the Flow of Your Personal Energy

It's time to come back to the here-and-now. You'll be much better equipped to deal with your life lessons if your energies are in harmony. (Remember, the body hears everything the mind says!) But did you know that your spirit has powers over the physical body and mind even when they are deep under general anesthesia?

When surgeon Dr. Bernie Siegel was practicing in the 1980s, he found that he could get patients to lower their blood pressure readings while they were fully anesthetized on the operating table—without drugs or any other physical intervention. How? He simply asked them to do it! He'd lean down to the anesthetized patient and say gently, "I need you to lower your blood pressure now." And sure enough, eight times out of ten, the patient would do just that: The blood pressure reading would drop. What a powerful witness to the power of the energetic connections between body, mind, and spirit! While the body was clinically "under," the spirit gladly obliged the request.

And what a testimony to the effects of affirmation in even the most trying circumstances.

The phenomena we described is called *biofeedback*. This is just one of the areas researchers are looking into as they explore the mind/body/spirit communion in health. With practice, concentrated focus, and conscious intent, it is possible to direct basic physiological processes that were previously thought to be involuntary, such as blood pressure, muscle tension, and brain wave activity.

Divine Inspiration

Biofeedback is a guided meditation technique that uses visual or spoken instructions and affirmations to both consciously and subconsciously affect involuntary physiological processes. Biofeedback is used with success as a complementary health approach to treat conditions such as hypertension and migraine.

If biofeedback can help us control our heart rate, breathing, blood pressure, and other body processes, then it is only one step beyond to consider how much we are capable of knowing and doing with conscious intuitive intent. This is why more and more often we hear of folks who "leave their body" during near-death experiences or routine surgeries, and can later recount to the astonished medical staff what they were doing or discussing during the entire event!

When it comes to managing your own personal energy, ask yourself questions to periodically "take your energetic pulse," such as those in the intuitive health scan exercise in Chapter 11. Then make whatever conscious shifts you need to make so that you feel more at peace in the flow.

As the spoon-bending boy in the film *The Matrix* counseled Keanu Reeves' character, Neo, "It's not about the spoon." To reach the essence of all things, you must see its energy. Or as Bruce Springsteen sings in "You're Missing" from his CD *The Rising*, "everything is everything." Find yourself in the flow of Universal energy, and you will find your future!

The Least You Need to Know

- When your energies are in alignment, you feel inner harmony and peace and your mind, body, and spirit come into balance.

- Loved ones and spirit guides communicate with us through energy.

- Meditation and visualization can get you in touch with your spirit guides.

- Your life journey is uniquely designed to help your soul learn and grow.

Chapter 18

Past, Present, and Future Lives

In This Chapter

♦ The many lives of the soul

♦ All about the Akashic record

♦ Karma chameleons: change and patterns

♦ Exploring your past lives

Your soul is eternal. And in many faith traditions, it's thought that your soul lives on the earth not once, but many times—not in one single lifetime, but in many. Through them all, your soul is your own, and it continues on a larger journey before and beyond your current existence.

The idea that each soul is part of a continuum far beyond the span of a single lifetime goes back a long way. The Egyptians scrupulously prepared their dead for the afterlife, right down to the food, clothing, and possessions they'd need on the long journey (and even games to keep themselves entertained!). That's how certain they were that life would continue. We see the same belief in continuation of the soul in many other cultures and faiths, although expressed differently. In Hinduism and Buddhism, the lifeless body, no longer a vessel for the soul, instead of being scrupulously preserved, is cremated.

The Continuum of Existence: One Soul, Many Lives

Souls come to live lives on the earth plane for one reason: to learn. Here, in our human lifetimes, we have the free will to make choices and overcome challenges. Ever hear that "We learn through our mistakes"? That's true of your soul as well. You can't stub your toe in Nirvana—so soul work and learning there is of a different nature and purpose! Here, in human incarnations, souls find their proving ground.

And so many of us have had lots and lots of "repeat performances"—but not because we're forced to make them. Your soul *wants* to be on this journey. Every step taken and every lesson learned brings it closer to perfection—closer to Universal harmony and truth. To the Universal sound, Om. To God, in a word (and by this, we mean, of course, the God of your understanding).

The Sanskrit symbol for Om, the universal sound. Raise the Om energy of the Universe by performing the Om mudra in your meditation sessions, uniting your soul with divine energy.

Every person around you is another soul on the journey, young souls and old souls alike. The age of your soul has nothing to do with your chronological age, of course. Young souls are taking their very first steps on the road to perfection. Old souls have learned so many lessons that the ultimate goal of perfect Union is in sight. (Although it may not seem that way to the old soul grappling with those lessons!)

Soul Lessons

Here in our physical bodies on the earth plane, we're in the realm of free will. It's an imperfect place, but it's our learning ground. Here, we are tried and tested, over and over again.

Coming to the earth plane is far from a "punishment," and we encourage you to release the negative energy of this view. We *choose* to come into a physical body, knowing that tests and trials will be part of the package. We even choose the lessons we come to learn! You decide what aspects you'll be working on in your lifetime. (So don't blame anybody else when things seem to go wrong in your life. You asked for it—literally!)

You're here, then, so that your soul can do its best to learn and grow as much as it possibly can. You have free will at your disposal—and the free will of *other* souls affecting you at every turn. We're all in it together, sometimes traveling together to learn lessons over many lifetimes of shared experience, but each of us *is* working on our *own* set of lessons—lessons that are uniquely ours.

> **Take Heed**
>
> Remember, each of us has our own chart containing the lessons and issues we chose to put in it. For example, souls can choose to be part of events that change others' lives, or for their exits to be part of a greater change that impacts humankind (such as the September 11 terrorist attacks). But by contract, none of us can consciously remember this.

What about pets, you ask? Do they travel with us on our soul's learning journeys as well? Could your Chihuahua be the reincarnation of your Great Aunt Nellie?

> Dear Laura,
> Could my deceased loved ones reincarnate as my next pet or do people always reincarnate as people and dogs as dogs, etc.?
> —Going Around and Around

> Dear Going Around,
> My experience is that people reincarnate as people and not as animals. (One exception is dolphins, highly evolved mammals who fall under a different set of energetic theories.) Animals are not working as closely on soul growth as we are, and don't come in with a lot of "stuff" to work out. They are here to help us learn about unconditional love and about ourselves. Humans reincarnate to keep working on their issues. But animals don't have anything like that to work on. Don't worry, though; your pets are on The Other Side and will greet you in the tunnel and beyond.

Our soul lessons are what links all the events and experiences of our lives. All the good things and bad things that come your way are part of your soul's syllabus. As Laura teaches each one of her clients, life isn't happening *to* you—it is happening *for* you, so that your soul can make progress. Once you know that, you can approach each day, even the most difficult day, as a new opportunity for growth. When you can get in the habit of asking yourself "What can I learn from this?" as soon as a challenge confronts you, you're on the right track!

This Life, Other Lives

If you're a young soul in this lifetime, you'll be a young soul all through this lifetime, even if you live to be 103. It takes more than one lifetime for a soul to "age"—for it to mature or make real progress. If you're an older soul, you may already know that your lessons have gotten more advanced as your lives have progressed.

Young souls and old souls have much to teach one another; often our lessons come through other people. But they're on such different wavelengths that they can drive each other a bit crazy. Young souls can feel confused, threatened, or frustrated by older ones, and it can take every ounce of an older soul's patience to live with younger ones. Wouldn't it be so much easier if we could consciously remember all our souls' other travels? Or if we could see the lessons and travels waiting for us in this or future lives? Sure, but then again, we can't learn our lessons *this time around* if we don't *fully* experience this life we are given now.

Did you see the movie *Groundhog Day?* At first its time-traveling hero knew he'd lived this day before but seemed only dimly aware, if aware at all, of why this phenomena occurred and what he needed to do. And instead of harnessing the power of his experience, he panics! As days pass, though, Bill Murray's character "gets used" to living this day over and over again and begins to use its energy to learn. With every repeat day, his lessons grow more complex and compassionate as his soul evolves in fast-forward fashion—over days instead of lifetimes! But the lesson of each day is unique and unknown—you need to get to tomorrow to discover and explore it.

Cell memories, recurring dreams, even birthmarks can be reminders of your soul's experiences in other lifetimes. Use your intuition and your tools to look deeply into these signs, and to resolve them if they're holding you back from doing the soul work now at hand for you.

Because you're part of this grand repeating cycle, you may work on the same issue in many lives. For sure, you're working on an interrelated set of issues in *this* life. That's why it's important to see the pattern of your repeating lessons in the life you're living now—and perhaps even in the lives you've had before. Then you can decide to make energy shifts and changes, to take charge of your life in a way that gives you more control over what comes next.

Understanding Your Past, Shaping Your Future

As we aren't ordinarily conscious of our souls' larger existence, we tend to blame ourselves far too much for our problems and difficulties in life. We forget that at any moment we can use our free will to reinvent ourselves. You can't change the past, but with a deeper understanding, awareness, or consciousness of your soul's work you *can* make adjustments that will alter the future.

If you have a good understanding of your past (in this or in previous lifetimes), you have a handle on who you are, how you work, what makes you tick. Know your patterns, and you'll know what in your life needs to change, and what's working well and should be kept. Your choices expand and your decision-making ability improves. You'll also be better able to deal with other people if you can discern *their* patterns and learn how the lessons they are working on might affect you.

 **Divine Inspiration** _____

Divining methods can really challenge your understanding of the energy currents and patterns at work in your life. An intuitive exercise might tell you to move forward, but your fears might be holding you back. If you ask the same question with different methods and get the same answer each time, you'll begin to learn more about the patterns that are keeping you from doing what you're meant to do.

Your patterns shape the course of your life's journey, but they don't doom you. You always have the power of free will at your disposal. Your choices make all the difference!

Your Akashic Record

As you've learned in previous chapters, your Akashic record is the record of your soul's journey across all its lifetimes on the earth plane and beyond, and through all its time spent on The Other Side. An Akashic record can be holographic, multidimensional, and all-encompassing. It includes all the details of all your lives—your incarnations, your experiences, and the soul lessons you've worked through.

Your soul may carry resonances and ripple effects through many of its lifetimes. Deep-seated fears, like phobias or a fear of abandonment, and uncontrollable emotional responses, such as rage, can often be linked to issues of past lifetimes. Whatever form your issues take, the Universe will test your responses to them throughout your life, in all kinds of scenarios. It's up to you—and you alone—to explore these issues and work on them to the best of your ability, so your soul can learn and grow.

Akashic records are available for each and every one of us, and because every detail of your soul's existence is included there, each record is huge beyond our human understanding. The linear human mind simply can't grasp its vastness.

But spirit guides can, and through them we can gain additional access to Akashic record information that we may need. If you're struggling with trials and testing—if the same problems keep coming up over and over again in your life—your Akashic record can help you understand what's happening. Knowledge of your record can support you as you learn whatever lesson your soul needs to learn.

Karmic Resonances

Karma is the law of cause and effect in Eastern philosophical tradition. Everything you say, do, and even think has an immediate effect on the Universe that comes back to you, one way or another. It's not unlike the Golden Rule of Christian philosophy: "Do unto others as you would have them do unto you."

Future Focus

Karma is the effect of one's actions on future events. It is traditionally associated with Eastern philosophy, particularly Hinduism and Buddhism.

Some people take the concept of karma to an extreme, becoming fatalists about life. They hold the gloomy notion that if something is going wrong, it's because they *deserve* it—because of some "bad" thing done in another life (or in this one) that's cause for punishment.

As a metaphysician, Laura emphatically resists this idea. She often finds that when her clients attribute all their suffering to "bad karma," they move away from a state of empowerment, and quickly move into a state of martyrdom or victimhood. She encourages them to go back to the central point that we're on the earth plane to learn, and she challenges her clients to find something positive to learn from every experience or lesson. We have rich opportunities to learn in times of adversity or conflict. And, because your soul comes to the earth plane expressly to learn, problems and difficulties *have* to happen for your soul to get a chance to do its work.

That's not to say that karma, the law of cause and effect, isn't real. Past actions *do* have an effect on you. But free will is always here in the present moment: The path of the past's effects can be changed by your conscious effort to understand and heal them.

Soul Work and the *I Ching*

The subtle nuances of the *I Ching* find their match in the subtle nuances of soul work—especially when we bring the notion of karma into the mix. When you consult the hexagrams to cast a sharp spotlight on the issues and lessons of this lifetime, you can also use them to illuminate the past patterns that might be hindering or helping you as you do your soul's work.

1. Breathe deeply and center yourself. Focus your attention on the question, "What is the lesson I am meant to learn in this lifetime?" Ask the question aloud for full effect.

2. Use your coins to cast, one by one, the six lines of the primary hexagram. (Refer to the chart in Chapter 13 for the value of each coin toss.) Draw them in the following primary hexagon box. Consult your *I Ching* source to assign a number to your primary hexagram.

3. Create a relating hexagram, if you wish, by transforming all of the "changing" lines into their opposite. Draw the relating hexagram in the following box.

"What is the lesson I am meant to learn in this lifetime?"

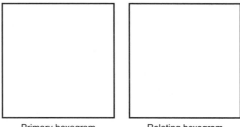

Primary hexagram   Relating hexagram

4. Now shift your focus to a new question: "What patterns from a past lifetime (or, if you prefer, your past history in this life) are impeding my soul's progress?"

5. Repeat the procedure in steps 2 and 3 above to create a new set of primary and relating hexagrams. Draw them, line by line, in the following boxes.

"What patterns from the past are impeding my soul's progress?"

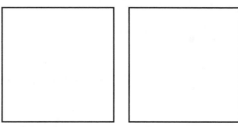

Primary hexagram   Relating hexagram

6. Consult the *I Ching* edition of interpretations you prefer from the many books available, and read its commentary on the first two hexagrams, starting with the primary hexagram, for insight into the issues your soul is meant to master in this lifetime. The relating hexagram can cast further light on the matter. And if you

do have any "changing" lines, read your *I Ching*'s commentaries on those particular lines for even more depth.

7. Read the primary, relating, and changing-line commentaries for your second
hexagram. Pay special attention to any shared images or common themes in
your two hexagrams. Can you discern a cause-and-effect relationship in your
life's patterns? Do the *I Ching*'s insights ring true for you?

Major Arcana: Destiny in the Tarot Cards

As you've learned, the Tarot's Major Arcana are concerned with life's Big Picture:
They speak in terms of archetypes, themes, mythology, and dreams. So these 22 cards
are particularly apt tools when you're looking into the deeper meaning of your own
life's path. Lay out the Major Arcana cards in order from 0, the Fool, to 21, the
World. Within this progression you'll see the archetypical soul path from innocence,
through the world, to enlightenment. After you've meditated on the cards in order,
choose three cards that answer this question: *What is the lesson I am meant to learn in
this lifetime?*

Putting It All Together

Now that you've asked the same question of two different divining methods, you can
put a lot of information together in a new and exciting way. As you did in comparing
your two hexagrams above, look in both your Tarot and your *I Ching* results for
shared images, descriptions, warnings, or ideas. Don't be too surprised when you find
them—after all, there's no such thing as a coincidence! (As we'll discuss further in
Chapter 19.) Pay special attention to the commonalities you find in your readings,
and notice how they amplify one another to deliver a soul message.

Looking Back: Lives That Were

It can be fun and interesting to learn about the times and places and personages you
inhabited in a past life. But for it to be anything more than an idle parlor game—to
get anything useful out of it—you need to look back with *intention*.

For example, if you're stuck on something in your life, if there's a pattern that you
just can't understand or get around, it makes sense to seek deeper understanding and
find out why that is. Past life exploration can give you insight into why your patterns
exist, and can offer an opportunity to release you from them if that's what you need to
do to move more freely on your life path.

Resonances

In the movie *Defending Your Life*, each soul must defend the actions and choices of its most recent lifetime to advance—or not. In one scene, the two main characters (played by Albert Brooks and Meryl Streep) visit the "past lives pavilion" to learn about their other incarnations. Brooks' fear-filled character has a million excuses in the defense of his life. True to form, he views a series of humiliating (and humorous) past lives in which he repeatedly runs for his life in terror. Streep's character is defending a particularly heroic life. She finds that her past lives had been just as noble! It's a wonderful illustration of how we can work on aspects of the same issue over and over again in our lives.

Past life analysis can be a very intense, deeply emotional process. So we don't recommend that you explore your past alone. For your health and safety, you need the support of a certified or licensed professional, whether a skilled medium or a psychologist trained in hypnotherapy, with whom you feel comfortable and protected.

Past Life Reading

When Laura looks into a client's past incarnations in the course of a reading, it's always in terms of seeing connections between past experiences and current struggles. She feels that while it can be fun and entertaining to have someone tell you about your past lives, without a reason for making this discovery, it's often just idle information of little practical relevance. If you consult a reputable medium or licensed psychologist for a past life reading, be sure to make the most of your opportunity and ask to work only with lives and information that will help you with what you are dealing with in the here and now.

Knowledge is power. When you know why your patterns are the way they are, you can choose to be less reactive in fraught situations, giving you a chance to work on your life's issues with a lot less agony and a whole lot more power. Information alone can release the anxiety, fear, and other blockages left over from past lives and give you the freedom to move on.

Laura had a client who couldn't bring herself to commit to making a life with her boyfriend, even though he was a trustworthy man and she loved him. Laura's access to the woman's Akashic record put it all into perspective. In a past life, she had been a frontier wife, married to an impractical man who took her West without doing any proper preparation. Her trust in him was destroyed in their first harsh winter, when—isolated in the mountains—he starved to death and she barely survived. A similar pattern of threats to her well-being emerged in other past lives they discussed, as well.

No wonder Laura's client was so reluctant to entrust her future to a man! When she understood the roots of her fears, she was free to make new and healthy choices and change her pattern.

Past Life Regression

Past life regression is a hypnotherapy technique in which a licensed hypnotist guides you into a deep meditative or trance state. There, the therapist helps you gently uncover the deeply held memories and emotions you've held from past incarnations.

This is decidedly not something you should do out of simple curiosity. Please, avoid carnival-hypnotist types if you intend to explore your past lives. If you undertake past life regression for a purpose, it will have real meaning for you and help to remove the burdens that plague you.

Choose a hypnotherapist the way you'd choose any intuitive practitioner, with a few caveats:

♦ Look for a practitioner who is licensed in past life regression.

♦ If part of your purpose is to seek physical healing, consider working with a psychotherapist who uses hypnotherapy in conjunction with his or her practice; psychotherapists are trained to make medical connections.

♦ Make sure the therapist is willing to record your session so you can listen to it later.

♦ The therapist's voice should be soothing, calming, or pleasing to you—you'll be following it closely during your session and listening to it on tape afterward.

♦ If you're working on a particular issue or with a firm focus, make sure the regressionist knows this and will concentrate on it, as well as insert some new programming to help you heal from whatever is revealed.

Using your intuition as you choose your practitioner will help you be a partner in the process, not just a passenger. And the more actively you participate, the more fruitful your session is likely to be.

In most hypnotherapy sessions, you'll sit or lie down on a couch or reclined chair in the therapist's office. You'll close your eyes and the therapist will gently lead you into an altered meditative state. When you're there, feeling relaxed and "floaty," the therapist might use guided visualization to explore aspects of past lives. You might, for example, be taken visually into a corridor of doors and asked to open the most recent door, or the door that relates to the issue at hand. Then the therapist will ask you to describe what you see, feel, and experience there. The emotions that pour can run the gamut, from terror to hilarity. It takes a skilled practitioner to keep you feeling safe through all this feeling.

At the end of regression, a good practitioner will help you put your recollections in perspective, help you process the experience, and give you all the support you need. You might not

Divine Inspiration

A past life regression is a great opportunity to heal residual anger and other toxic emotions. A good regressionist can help you heal these emotional scars by delving into the "closet of your psyche" and cleaning out all the strong feelings that were left over from past experiences and cluttering up your emotions today.

remember anything you saw or said during the regression (though of course you can hear it all on tape); you might only recall bits and pieces, as if from a dream. No matter what you can remember, you can still resolve difficult issues through regression. A skilled practitioner will help you leave the experience feeling safe and grounded. And even if you don't remember every bit of your session, that doesn't mean that healing hasn't taken place! A trained professional will guide you and implant whatever healing energy thoughts you request from them before you leave that meditative state—and remember, your spirit will hear these thoughts, even if you consciously don't!

Looking Ahead

It all comes down to this: If you understand your past experiences (of this or other lifetimes), you can illuminate your present—and you can even cast light on your future.

The simplicity and clarity of angel cards offer positive, direct messages as you contemplate this well-informed future.

1. Breathe deeply, center yourself, and settle into a peaceful place in your mind. Shuffle your angel cards and ask aloud, "What is my five-year outlook or theme, based on all that I've learned about my past, my patterns, and my soul's lessons?"

2. When you feel ready, stop shuffling. Draw out the one card that feels right to you. (As always with angel cards, if an extra card or two seems to "stick" to your chosen card, pay attention to them as well!)

3. Lay your card down and contemplate its message and meaning. Use this space to jot down some notes.

_____

_____

_____

Don't forget to thank your angels for your message when you're done!

Free Will Is the Only Destiny

Just a reminder: The past does not control you—unless you let it. Free will is the key. It's what puts you in the driver's seat of this and every lifetime. If you choose, you can use your free will to work with your themes and patterns, not fight and flail against them or submit meekly to them. It's your life, and it's your soul's work. It's all up to you!

The Least You Need to Know

- ◆ Your soul comes to the earth plane to learn, and it learns through adversity.

- ◆ You may experience repeating patterns in your life as your soul works through its lessons.

- ◆ Karma is the law of cause and effect, but it's not the reason why bad things happen.

- ◆ You can explore your past lives, but do it with care and purpose for your own protection.

Chapter 19

The Divine Around You

In This Chapter

- ◆ How the Universe intervenes in our lives
- ◆ Why nothing is random
- ◆ Seeing synchronicity all around you
- ◆ Giving credit where credit's due

Laura and her former husband once had to attend an important meeting in a city they didn't know well. They set off for the meeting in separate cars, at different times and from different places. As Laura neared the office building, she stopped at a traffic light, not sure which way to turn. Suddenly she heard a car horn. It was her husband, who had arrived at the same stoplight at the same moment! He motioned for Laura to follow him, and they went straight to their destination.

Weird, huh? Funny how life is.

No, no, a thousand times no! It isn't weird at all that two people on two entirely independent paths should meet so perfectly. It's meant to be. It's synchronicity: real help from beyond our understanding.

Synchronicity

Synchronicity is the miraculous arrangement of events beyond our understanding, comprehension, or control. Guess what? *There is no such thing as a coincidence.* Banish the very word from your vocabulary! Every time we call something a coincidence we are doing a disservice to the many unseen benefactors tirelessly working for us.

Even if we spent our every waking hour trying to arrange or explain away a "coincidental" event, we would never come close to being able to replicate one. That's because they aren't from *our* realm at all. They are from The Other Side.

Future Focus

Synchronicity is the union of events happening at the same time and occurring exactly together where the events seem to have no apparent causal relationship. But we know better! The Divine in the Universe is at work in our lives when synchronicity occurs.

Why do those on The Other Side go to so much trouble to arrange synchronous occurrences for us? Partly because it's their job to help us learn our soul lessons, and synchronicity gives them a way to point us in the right direction. But mainly it's to open us up to the presence of the Divine in our lives, to the reality of miracles. It's like panning for gold: Finding a few precious pebbles here and there gives you the encouragement you need to keep going. When you recognize synchronicity in your life, you open yourself more and more to the gift of the Divine that's available to us all.

Everything Happens with Intent

No matter how linear your thinking and how random life's events may seem, there's a reason for everything. Nothing is random in this delicately ordered Universe of ours—not even its seeming chaos. There's a rhyme and a reason to it all, a divine order that's always at work. We don't force the earth to spin or the moon to rotate, do we? And yet they do, in a delicate dance sophisticated mathematics strives to understand. That's divine order.

We may not comprehend this order, of course. That's because we can only see a small part of the whole, and a disjointed part at that. The Universe is like a gorgeous, complex tapestry, but the only view we have of it is from the back—where all we can see is a patternless array of threads and knots. It takes a lot of trust to believe that with distance and with time you'll see the front of the tapestry in all its glory. (But you *will!*)

There's No Such Thing as a Coincidence

Divine order and intent mean that one thing's for sure: Coincidence simply isn't possible. Not only that, it's an incredibly arrogant concept! It completely discounts the efforts of our guides and angels, who work so hard to set synchronicities up for us. (And how would *you* like to work for someone who didn't even *acknowledge* your accomplishments—let alone ever said "thank you"?)

Resonances
Much as you might want to, you can't force synchronicity—not even if you're a famous rock band. When The Police made their album *Synchronicity*, they wanted the cover to be a demonstration of the concept. So the band members had their photos taken separately, in hopes that linked images or themes would emerge. And they did! (Unfortunately, most people dismissed the similarities because the record company arranged for each photo to be taken by the same photographer.)

Here's an example of how uncannily synchronicity can operate, even over long spans of time. Almost two decades ago, when Laura was just out of college, she and several coworkers attended a function at a hotel. The hotel was handing out complimentary matchbooks, and Laura took one.

Fast-forward 13 years. Laura and a friend had spent the day sailing, and as they anchored for the night in a distant harbor, a beautiful boat coming up really caught her eye. The very sight of it seemed to cap off an exhilarating and spectacular day. It was a particular style of sailboat that Laura hadn't seen in any of her sailing adventures. Excitedly, she asked her friend what kind of boat it was. "That's a J-boat," her knowledgeable friend explained. "Now how are we going to light the grill for dinner? The butane lighter is out." Automatically, Laura reached into her bag and pulled out some matches. "I never pack matches," she said, "but something told me we might need them." With that, she tossed a matchbook to her friend. He lit the grill, then came back to return the matches to her. "You're freaking me out," he said. "How do you have this matchbook and not know about J-boats?"

Laura looked down at his hand. The matchbook that had come from her bag said "The Magnificent J's," and pictured a silhouette of the very boat that had just swept so seamlessly past their mooring. A warm tingly chill went down her back. Incredible! How did that matchbook make its way into that exact moment? It had survived several moves, and *many* random drawings from the miscellaneous matchbook bowl, to arrive exactly on time at that particular moment of that particular day.

In Laura's journal, she later wrote, "The power of that synchronistic series of events changed the outlook I had for the entire summer. Those sailing adventures were some of the most spiritual moments of my life, at a juncture where I was questioning every-thing and beginning to find my place on the path as a practicing psychic and channel. Having synchronicity sneak up on me in such a big way left me feeling content and at peace. I felt that things would be all right, no matter what, because I could see and feel the power of the Universe."

Pay Attention!

Signs and wonders are all around you. They can be clearly miraculous, or seemingly everyday. Sometimes they come when you're genuinely wrenched about a decision you have to make. Sometimes they're just a little "pat on the back" when you really need one. You'll see them. Just open your eyes.

Once Laura went shopping with a friend who needed a new bed frame. Her friend found a beautiful frame, but there was one problem: She thought it was too expensive. She walked out of the store without buying the bed frame, but felt worried as she and Laura drove away. As they were driving, she weighed her decision aloud: "It was per-fect … just what I wanted … but still, so much money … I don't know …" As they stopped at the next traffic light, a car pulled up in the lane beside them. "…Do you think I should buy it?" she asked. For answer, Laura pointed at the car's license plate: "BUY IT." They shrieked in laughter and excitement. In less than three seconds the light for the other car's lane changed and the car drove off. If they hadn't been paying attention, they would have missed this message entirely. Her friend promptly decided to go back and buy the bed frame! (And she got a discount to boot!)

Do spirit guides really set up such signs to help solve seemingly minor problems like this one? Yes, they do—because to your guides, there's *nothing* minor about your stress and suffering. When you're in pain, no matter how slight, your guides can take the opportunity to get involved (unless, of course, learning to deal with such a situa-tion is an integral part of your life's lesson). But when you're "in the flow" enough to recognize synchronicity in your life, life gets much, much easier.

Let's try listening for synchronicity. In this exercise, you'll be paying special attention to the sounds around you—music, television, radio, strangers' conversation—for pat-terns of threes.

1. Settle yourself into a focused meditative state. When you feel ready, ask aloud for some help on one particular issue or situation.

2. Once you have stated your needs, let go of that energy. Imagine that you have written your request on a slip of paper and attached the slip to a large helium balloon. Release the balloon, mentally, to the ethers. Then go on about your day.

3. As you do what needs to be done in your normal daily life (keeping your notepad with you at all times), pay particular attention to what you hear on the TV or radio, or in conversation. If the morning radio chatter contains a word or phrase that speaks to you, catches your ear, or tickles you, jot it down. This might be anything from an obscure reference—"swinging like a monkey" or "looking like a cowgirl," for example—to an unusual word.

4. Keep your ears open for the same words or similar references. Listen for three such references, usually within three days. Then sit and consider the energetic links you can make between the references and the issue you'd asked for help with.

Or try this brief exercise, which sets up an opportunity for synchronicity. (It doesn't make synchronicity happen—you can't force it, you know!)

1. Gather together three of the instruction manuals that came with your divining methods. Your *I Ching* book, your Tarot guide, and your angel cards booklet, for example, would do fine.

2. Take a few moments to breathe deeply and get centered. Tell your spirit guides that you're open to receiving a message, if they wish to send one.

3. Take one of your books in hand, close your eyes, and flip through the pages until it feels right to stop. Keeping your eyes closed, put the opened book face down. Then repeat the procedure with the other two books.

4. When all three books are face down, and still without looking at the opened pages, use your intuition to arrange them in order of importance.

5. Now read the pages you opened to. Do you see any relationships here? That's synchronicity!

You can open your eyes and your mind to synchronicity, but remember, you can't force it. Indeed, if you look too hard you can swamp the very signs you want to see, as one of Laura's correspondents found.

> Dear Laura,
> My father died about a year ago. I look for signs that he is around me, but I don't see or feel his presence. Am I doing something wrong?
> —Mary Ann

> Dear Mary Ann,
> I hear this question a lot. We are wired here on earth with very linear minds. The signs can be all around us and we dismiss them for lack of certainty or "proof." Relax and let go of the idea of connecting with him. Trying too hard can shut down the flow.

Instead, have faith that your father is indeed near you, and then watch for synchronistic signs. Affirm that, "Despite appearances, everything in my life is working for good." Our loved ones are doing the best they can. The language they use to talk with us has changed, that's all. Love is eternal.

Every Day I Write the Book: A Journal Exercise

You'll need your journal for this next exercise. (A Progress Journal is ideal, because it already has space for recording synchronicities included!)

Remember, we can't force synchronicity to happen. We observe it and receive. We welcome it like we'd welcome any gift. That's why journaling can really help bring clarity and understanding of your progress, as well as preserve evidence of the accumulating signs all around you. This is one exercise that can be done on the fly, throughout any day.

1. Keep your journal or a small notepad with you at all times: on the seat of the car, or in your pocket or purse.

2. Put yourself in the role of observer and recorder of events. Give yourself permission to quickly jot things down as they happen.

3. Repeat!

Divine Inspiration

Synchronicity happens quickly—before you have time to second-guess it, it's gone. If you wait until the end of each day to record your recollections of synchronistic events, you might not remember them. That's why you need to remain aware as your day unfolds, and quickly jot down whatever uncanny things might occur. Only practice will get you tuned in to the subtle powers of synchronicity. And journaling does it!

Some synchronicities are straightforward and clear right there in the moment; others gain meaning and momentum after a series of supporting events, or with the passage of time. Either way, the record of your journal will keep them real to you, and available for later reflection.

Written on the Subway Walls ... and All Around You

Once you start paying attention to the subtle energies of synchronicity, you'll see the wisdom of the prophets (as Simon & Garfunkel called them in the song, "Sounds of

Silence") everywhere. You'll begin to feel energized by life's everyday challenges, not bogged down by them, when you know that you've got willing helpers on your side.

But don't forget that synchronicity can be a very momentary thing, and you have to be paying attention or you'll miss it.

Here's a quick quiz on everyday synchronicities. Check off any of the situations that have happened to you, or any that remind you of a similar experience in your own life.

❑ You prepare more food than you need for a meal, only to be joined by unexpected guests.

❑ You buy something on impulse, not knowing why, only to reach for that precise item days, weeks, months, or even years later, grateful you had on hand exactly what you needed!

❑ You run into someone in a place away from home, far off the beaten path where neither of you ordinarily goes, only to learn that they have something that can help you (be it a job connection, a medical lead, some form of information).

❑ When you're thinking about something, strangers or acquaintances keep bringing up the issue in passing conversation.

❑ You spontaneously adopt a new pet. Later that night, a neighbor (not knowing about the adoption) calls you and asks if you know anyone who can use any pet supplies.

❑ You've been invited to a party at a friend's home, but you forget to bring the directions. When you get to their neighborhood, you decide on impulse to follow someone you see on the street. Sure enough, they lead you right to your friend's block, and turn out to be attending the same party.

❑ You never wear a watch, but whenever you look up to check the time, you do so at the moment when the numbers on the clock align (1:11, 2:22, 5:55, and so on) or repeat (12:12, 3:13).

❑ When you start up your car, the lyrics of the song playing on the radio hold the perfect answer to something you have been asking for help with.

❑ The image of your animal totem appears in the most unlikely places.

Jot down some notes in your journal about some synchronicities you once chalked up to "coincidence."

Don't Spend Your Time Looking for Burning Bushes!

Even major Divine interventions can look like very small, personal occurrences. Moses may have gotten a burning, talking bush—a sign that, you've got to admit, is pretty hard to ignore—but most of our synchronicities, although they may be very meaningful and even life-changing, aren't quite so spectacular.

When Mary Kay was considering her move from full-time worker to full-time mom/part-time writer, she worried about everything from family finances to her own identity. She found herself praying about it one day: "If only I could know for sure that this is the right thing to do!" Just then, she felt a tap on her shoulder. It was an absolute stranger, a balding older man with smiling eyes. He spread out his hand toward Mary Kay's children, who were with her, and said, "I just wanted to tell you—these are the most precious years of your life." Mary Kay smiled back and watched the man walk away. It took her a few minutes before she realized she'd gotten the sign she'd been asking for.

During a dark night of the soul in Laura's life when she was starting over on several levels, she was starting to recognize synchronicities around her and called on her guides in faith. "I just want to feel a little bit normal again," she said. "If I could just have the money to rent a movie and order a pizza, things wouldn't seem so bad." She left her house to walk down the hill and check her mailbox. When she got there, there in the middle of the road was a $10 bill—just enough for a small pizza and a movie rental! She could hardly believe this money was meant for her; she looked all around for anyone who might have dropped it and agonized over whether someone else might need it more. But in the end, she did the only thing she could do: She accepted the money as a gift, and joyously thanked her guides for their help and concern before heading off to pick up that pizza and movie.

See the Signs, Get the Message: Points of Empowerment

On the other hand, you shouldn't see *everything* as a sign! That's why it's so important to be well grounded as you work with intuition. Solid grounding will help you see Divine gifts for what they are—and will keep you poised, calm, and clear-headed enough to know when there's no real sign to be seen.

Sometimes we grasp at straws when we're fighting change or resisting a new experience. So if you're in a troubled relationship that your intuition tells you must end, don't go searching for signs that you should stay together. "But our first date was on a night with a full moon, and I was born on a night with a full moon—isn't that a sign?" Probably not. You need to look within yourself to validate a sign with what you know in your heart. Don't squint to turn it into something else.

Take Heed

Synchronicities are all around you, but you shouldn't have to strain to see them. When you're getting assistance from The Other Side, usually you just know it in your gut. You might even get goose bumps, or the hair might stand up on the back of your neck. By paying attention to your body's physical signals, you can avoid talking yourself into believing in messages that aren't really there.

Synchronicity and Nature

The Universe often uses messengers to help orchestrate synchronicity. These messengers can be human, animal, or insect. So for example, if a spider appears out of the blue in your clean cabinet when you are reaching for a mug, take note! In animal totemry, spiders symbolize creativity and the ability to weave the web of the life you want to live. Spiders are messengers from the Divine who tell you that you can create your own destiny. On its side, a spider has the geometric form of the figure eight, which is also the symbol for infinity.

Spiders remind us that everything we do now weaves the pattern of what we will encounter in the future. The Wheel of Fortune card in the Tarot deck deals with rise and fall, flow and flux, and the sensitivities necessary to place ourselves within the rhythm of nature. Meditating on this card will help expand your understanding if the spider is your totem.

Synergy

When you weave together synchronicity and life's circumstances, that's *synergy*—the combination of Divine signals with inner knowing and intellectual understanding to make choices and shape emotions. Synergy adds momentum to your life, as well.

Signs are given to us all the time, but you may not be seeing them. The gifts of synergy and synchronicity aren't ours to bestow. Recognizing them, though, is within our power. Are you seeing little signals for what they are and understanding their messages? Or do you ignore or brush off your signs? You make the choice. Creating synergy can be as easy as a decision to accept your signals as they come, now that you know what to look for.

Future Focus

Synergy is when the combination of efforts and contributions produces a result greater than any individual effort or contribution could produce alone.

Gratitude

Synchronicity isn't something you can force or induce. And it's wrong to try to test your guides and the Universe with it ("If synchronicity is true, then make a red bird fly past my window right now!"). No, synchronicity is more like receiving a birthday gift. Open it, admire it, ooh and aah—and then say, "Thank you!"

The more your guides and deceased loved ones know you're receiving and understanding the synchronicities they work so hard to achieve, the more the energy in your relationship increases. So please don't forget to be appreciative. Thank the Universe or the God of your understanding for synchronicity and synergistic energy in your life. Be grateful for your messages of encouragement and help.

When you do invite guides and helpers into your life, don't micromanage them. Let them work, and be open to receiving their results—even if the answer isn't quite what you expected. Remember, when you ask your guides for help, they *must* respond. That's their mission, after all!

In Love and Light

When you're in the metaphysical flow, you accept the reality of intuition, synchronicity, and the Divine in your life and in the lives of all those around you. It changes how you pray, how you manifest, how you meditate. It changes you, too—for the better. It brings peace, serenity, and love into your life—true love, that is, not merely romantic love (though that can be a beautiful manifestation), but Universal love. And a soul in love with the Universe is a joy to behold. We wish such joy for you.

The Least You Need to Know

- Synchronicity is the miraculous arrangement of events beyond our understanding or control.

- There is no such thing as a coincidence.

- Synchronicity is all around you if you open yourself to it.

- Be grateful for your guides' interventions in your life in the form of synchronicity.

- The Universe often uses nature to reach us.

Part 6

Endless Possibilities: You Choose!

And now we put it all together! The divining methods and techniques we've practiced all through this book bring us to this threshold: contemplation of what you want your life to be, and the first steps toward making that vision a reality. Free will is at your disposal, and your intuition is, too. What will you do with them? It's up to you!

Chapter 20

Go with Your Gut, Suspend Your Mind

In This Chapter

- Leaving behind limited, linear thinking
- Opening yourself to limitlessness
- Sharpening your intuitive skills
- Being kind to yourself and to others

We hope the full force and scope of intuition and the Divine in your life is starting to all come together for you. Like a jigsaw puzzle, these are things that you comprehend piece by piece—a corner here, an outline there—until, slowly, it all becomes clear. Small sections of "understanding" begin to emerge.

Now you've learned all the basics. So in these next few chapters we're going to encourage you to keep stretching those intuitive muscles. Don't stop "working out" if you've started to see your intuition in action. Keep up the good work, and you'll grow even stronger, as the direction you divine for your future grows ever clearer!

If you've come this far with us and you haven't felt your intuition working, please don't be discouraged. After all, each time you meditate or work with any divining method you open yourself to a new and different message. Why not go back to a previous chapter and try a card reading or a visualization exercise again?

Limitlessness

Everyone knows Shel Silverstein's classic children's book, *Where the Sidewalk Ends*. In one of the book's poems, Silverstein tells the innocent child to listen to the "musn'ts," "don'ts," "shouldn'ts," "impossibles," "won'ts," and "never haves" people will throw at him or her in life—but then Silverstein goes on to advise the youngster that anything can manifest itself, can happen or be. We believe Silverstein's book and poem beautifully illustrate the Universal concept of limitlessness.

Future Focus

Limitlessness is an understanding that things are without bounds, restriction, or continuance. In metaphysics, we use it to describe anything endless, immeasurable, innumerable, and infinite.

When you're contemplating the enormity of the Universe and all its energies, our logical, cause-effect, point-A-to-point-B human thought processes only get in the way. *Limitlessness*, on the other hand, opens up your consciousness to the kind of thinking you usually only access in dreams. When you're dreaming, you simply accept whatever twists and characters that come along. We can accept the illogic in dreams, which is one of the reasons why they have so much to teach us. In our waking lives, we aren't nearly so open.

Children are unrestrained thinkers—until we adults, all too often, squeeze the limitlessness out of them. With the best of intentions, of course! If a little girl told you, "When I grow up, I want to be a ballerina *and* a doctor *and* a mommy *and* a paleontologist," how would you respond? Would you say—quite logically—"Honey, those are all great things to be, but you'll really have to concentrate on just one"? Or would you say, "Sure! Why not?"

It doesn't have to be that way. J. K. Rowling is one adult who seems to have escaped childhood with her imagination intact. Her *Harry Potter* books are a great example of the limitless potential of human thought. In Rowling's stories, she conjures a complete parallel world of wizards and magic that exists just beyond the perception of us "muggles" (nonmagical people). Readers happily follow along as she takes us for rides in flying cars, teaches us to tame basilisks and three-headed dogs, and challenges us to games played on flying broomsticks. The very limitlessness of Rowling's ideas is what has attracted millions of children and adults, all around the world, to her tales.

Resonances
Before Laura took her seven- and eight-year-old nephews to the beach for the first time, she talked with them about the ocean and its vastness. Because the boys were from the city and had never seen the sea, they innocently struggled to understand what water "as far as your eyes can see" could possibly look like. Their only reference points were swimming pools and bathtubs—*contained* water. Their earnest concerns about being able to "splash the sea dry" quickly faded when they arrived on the beach and stared in shock and dismay. But it took mere seconds for them to take it all in and begin to whoop out loud in extreme delight! Now, if adults could accept limitlessness so easily …

Technology is another example of limitlessness in practice. Who could have believed, 20 years ago, that anyone could be reached at any time on his or her mobile phone? Or that we'd no longer be "dialing" at all? That people around the world could meet and communicate instantaneously via computer? That hybrid electric cars would exist? Or that anyone could microwave entire meals in seconds? Or be able to travel at the speed of sound? Who can imagine what gadgets will be available to us 20 years from now? Anything is possible!

Remember, these technological advances exist today only because someone dared to think outside the box all those years ago and begin the process of proving everyone else wrong.

Limitlessness asks us to wrap our minds around the incomprehensible hugeness of the Universe itself and stretch our understanding beyond the limitations of our linear minds. And intuition helps us to do this by its very nature.

You Can't Analyze Intuition

Intuition is beyond our understanding, but not beyond our experience. By definition, it's "knowing something without knowing how you know it." The very fact that you can't grasp the reasons for your knowledge is the hallmark of intuition.

Let Linear Thinking Rest

Now try and wrap your linear, logical mind around those last two sentences and you'll find yourself in quite the mental thicket. "If I know it but I don't know how I know it, then do I really know it? How do I know that I even know it if I don't know how I know it?" Yes, and who's on first, what's on second …

Relax. We'll say it again: Relax. Much as we love our human logic, sometimes it doesn't serve us well. In matters of the soul, logic only gets in the way. Somewhere along the line, we have to admit that we don't—we *can't*—understand everything. Linearity has to give way to faith. (Logically speaking, could Noah really have gathered up two of *every* animal and built a sailable boat that could hold, house, and feed them all? Not in terms of linear thinking. But within the realm of faith and limitlessness, he could.)

> Dear Laura,
> Why are some people psychic and others not?
> —The Morning Walking Club

> Dear MWC,
> The answer is simple: Balance. We need all kinds of folks on all different levels to help make the world go round. We are all born with intuition, but as we age, the veil slips down more firmly for some than others. Without regular practice, the intuitive "muscles" atrophy as we leave childhood behind. Some psychics require little to no practice, because they are naturals; others require regular exercises and formal studies. Find what you are naturally good at and be proud.

Understanding the Nuances of Limitlessness

Now here's the first important nuance when it comes to asking the Universe, your guides, angels, or the God of your understanding for help. First of all, don't assume that they will just automatically fix whatever it is that's bothering you—and that they should just go ahead and do it before you even think of asking for help or trying to work it out for yourself. There are rules at play. You are here to learn, after all. So you're going to have to learn how to ask! And the more specific your request, the better. (Remember the story in Chapter 4, about the woman who accidentally manifested a puppy instead of a romantic partner?) Name it to claim it!

Now, here's the second important nuance: Be reasonable. Asking for help from the Universe is a little like winning the Golden Ticket to get inside Willy Wonka's Chocolate Factory. We all remember where greed, gluttony, and dishonesty led kids like Veruca Salt and Violet Beauregard. You don't want to end up as a giant blueberry, do you? No, Charlie is our role model there. His sincerity, honesty, and integrity were what helped him realize his wildest dreams.

Of course, the Universe has millions of prayers, requests, pleas, and affirmations rolling in around the clock. If owning a Lamborghini, a Rolex, and a Malibu beach house are on your list of requests, just wanting them isn't enough—you have to be willing to do the work to earn them. You can use affirmations to raise your awareness, but then you've got to be there when life calls for you to do your part! Guides, angels, and master teachers do not exist merely to do our idle bidding. They support and encourage us on the journey, but the journey is *always* studded with our own choices, the results of our free will. Guides aren't magical wish-granters and fairy godmothers. They respond to all our requests, but that doesn't mean they always give us the "responses" we had in mind. They use synchronicity to get our attention, to point out things that will be helpful as we make our choices, and to remind us that we are not going through our journey alone.

The final all-important caveat: Acknowledge your limitations when you ask for help so that the limitless answers of the Universe can unfold for you. If you are desperate to retire your worn-out bicycle and acquire a car for commuting, ask for help. A Lamborghini is not a reasonable request here. You might ask simply for a car that runs, but remember to leave room for the Universe to go one better. You can do that like this:

> "Universe, bring me (a car that I can commute in—state whatever it is you're specifically asking for)—*or something even better!*"

Because, when it comes right down to it, you *don't* know it all. And why limit or pigeonhole such a gift when something even better could delight, amaze, and tickle you instead? Maybe your used-car workhorse will be replaced with a good, reliable, fuel-efficient new car instead!

Be patient and full of faith as you wait for the parts to come together. The Universe has its own concept of time. With that in mind, here's a homework project for affirming and manifesting without limits.

1. Get a blank piece of paper and write at the top *This Is What I Want.* Then write out a clear description of what you would like to have in your life right now. Take as much space and time as you need. Use lots of details! When you're done with your description, write boldly at the bottom of the paper "*This or something even better is now coming to me.*"

2. Every day, for the next 30 days, read this entire sheet out loud each morning. Speak slowly and clearly, with conviction in your voice.

3. Use your journal (or Progress Journal) to make a record of the time and manner in which any of the items on your list come through.

4. In your journal, describe any synchronistic events related to this exercise that you might notice. (See Chapter 19 for more on synchronicity.)

5. As the 30 days pass, pay attention to your own energies. Record any physical, emotional, or spiritual changes in yourself. Have you noticed any shifts in your attitude? How does your body energy feel? Did you notice that some days you believed in yourself as you read your list aloud, and that other days you had doubts? Did your linear mind argue with you as you tried to read your statement? As things began to manifest, did you feel happy, overwhelmed, or confused? Did you want to adjust or fine-tune that list as the days of reading it aloud unfolded, because your intuition and needs were shifting? (And if you actually did change your list, that's great!)

6. Don't forget to record your "gratitude attitude" as items on your list come to fruition and you get to cross them off.

Expanding Your Intuitive Skills

Here's a personal research challenge. It's time to do a little self-evaluation. Take a few minutes now to go back through the notes you've jotted down in this book, or in your intuitive Progress Journal. Can you see yourself becoming more and more aware of the energies at work around you? Could you only write one or two thoughts at first, but find that your notes now are packed with detail? Or has the quality of your observations increased dramatically?

The more aware you are, the more you will actually be able to see the future.

Seeing with Your Inner Vision: An Intuition Exercise

We're going to go back to basics now, armed as we are with our deeper intuitive understanding, and do a free-writing exercise. Get out those pens and pencils!

1. Start with a few deep breaths to calm yourself, and be sure you're well grounded. Now close your eyes and picture a white screen in your mind's eye.

2. Hold in your mind a conflict that's in your life right now. It could be a coming confrontation with someone that's got you under stress, or any interpersonal scenario you're anxious about.

3. Ask the Universe or your guides, "Please give me insight and information of the highest and the best on what I need to know about this situation." Meditate on this for several minutes. (Don't *think* about it; just hold it in your mind.)

4. Now ask, "Can I see this situation from another point of view?" On the blank, white screen in your mind's eye, watch the conflict play out from a different vantage point or perspective as if you're seeing it unfold on stage.

5. Reflect on this for a few moments, then open your eyes and, without any analysis, write down how the scene played out from your new perspective.

_____

_____

_____

6. Whenever you feel you've lost the flow, know that you can always go back to your blank screen, then "hit the play button" and have the scene play out again. The goal here is to use your new vantage point to help you see new possibilities without your own blocks and filters—to do an end run around your ordinary reactions. This will stretch the bounds of your limited thinking.

7. If you feel you need more information, go back to step 4 and ask to see the scene from another _person's_ point of view. (That is, if you're dreading a confrontation with your boss, ask to see the situation from that vantage point.) You might be surprised to find how different the view from their vantage point is from yours!

Reading the Energy Around You: An Aura Reading Exercise

If you've already practiced sensing auras, you're ready for a new challenge: picking up on auras by intuition alone. This is a "portable" exercise you can do anywhere. It actually works best when you're in a public place surrounded by strangers—at a bookstore, an airport, or a doctor's waiting room.

1. Look at the people around you and try to pick up on or get a sense of their energy. (Be subtle about it—don't stare!)

2. In a notepad or your journal, write down the _first_ impression of the energy around each person you see. Resist the input of your linear mind! Discard all its observations on physical appearance, style of dress, age, gender, and facial expression. Don't be distracted if a person resembles someone you know. Instead, go for an energetic interpretation of each person. Does their energy feel light? Cloudy? Clear? Jagged? Just one or two words per person is all you need.

3. Now compare and contrast your subjects to one another. What do the "cloudy" people have in common? Are there different kinds of cloudiness?

4. You might want to choose one person (make it someone at a distance from you so you aren't obtrusive) and see if you can spot his or her etheric double. (An etheric double is like an energy shadow of your physical body. It often appears as

a sort of white shadow with a dark edge one to two inches all the way around the outside of your body.) Squinting can help as you look at your subject's "edges"—the boundary area just beyond the clothing the person wears.

5. Say a prayer asking for all good things on behalf of the people you've scanned.

Open Yourself to the Possibilities

Think back to your childhood. If you're like most of us, your skills and talents were probably neatly boxed and labeled as soon as you hit elementary school. "You'd be a great librarian someday!" "What a talker—we've got a future lawyer on our hands." "Look at that throw! Keep that up, and you could be a major league ballplayer."

But kids don't limit themselves this way. The whole world is open to them. They genuinely do believe that they can be ballerinas/doctors/parents/paleontologists. Only later—as we adults hammer home the message that a choice must be made, and the earlier the better—do children lose their limitless perspective on life.

Divine Inspiration

How can you recapture some of that wonderful, freeing limitlessness of childhood? One word: PLAY! Joyous movement, unguarded laughter, and unlimited imagination open you to the Universe's energy and to the gift of synchronicity. If you have a child in your life—your own, a young relative, or a neighbor or friend—get down on the floor and let him or her show you how it's done. If you don't know any children, well, no one can stop you from skipping to the bus stop, singing in the rain, or playing a game of fetch with your pet!

The funny thing is, the limited mind is what cripples us later on, in career matters and in everything else besides. Studies show that most of us make a major career change at least once during our working lives, and that in today's society even more frequent change is becoming the norm! The average person now changes jobs every two to five years. Rare is the person whose working life relates to those our parents may have had, doing one particular job for one particular company for 30 or 40 years.

In the long run, the messages of our limited minds—"I can't …"; "But I'm almost vested in the pension plan"; "The mortgage!"—are nothing but roadblocks that we have to overcome when we must make necessary changes. Sometimes, before we can work up the courage to make a change ourselves, the Universe does it for us! Pink slips, mergers, layoffs, downsizing … all of these things, as traumatic as they are, can also be a way for the Universe to offer you an invitation to do something else, somewhere else. Who knows, maybe you'll find a little more peace and happiness in the process!

What do *you* believe? Take a moment to think about the limiting messages you have been told or have come to believe about yourself and record them here or in your Progress Journal. It's a powerful way to connect with the self, and to identify any outdated ideas that are no longer serving you.

_____

_____

_____

_____

If You Could Do Anything, Be Anything, What Would It Be?

We do mean "anything," in a totally limitless way! After all, no one will tell a motivated 12-year-old that he'll never go to college, if that's what he wants to do. But we might say that to an 80-year-old.

Why? Because they're too old to do anything with that degree? Because there's nothing more to learn? Hogwash. You can still learn every day of your life—and since when is education only about career training? Laura's Great Granny, for example, was mentally active and learning right up to her passing at the ripe *young* age of ... 102! Somewhere in her 70s she walked away from a lifetime of crafting and took up a new hobby: shooting pool. Eight Ball was her game, and she played well into her 90s, until her eyesight began to leave her. Great Granny was known to have beaten more than one tournament winner, to their utter dismay!

So forget the timetables we lock ourselves into. Suspend the limitations of age or gender or finances or past choices. Plant a foot outside your comfort zone and write it here: If I could do or be anything, I'd ...

_____

_____

_____

Limitlessness in Action: A Faerie Card Exercise

If you've been staring at those blank lines above (or if you filled them with something banal like "go out for a nice sandwich"), maybe you need a little help getting over the hump of limited thinking.

That's okay—it's divining methods to the rescue! Now would be a great time to enter the realm of limitlessness with the help of faerie energy. Angels and faeries have different sets of focus when it comes to helping people. Angels tend to be concerned with helping us remember our Divine purpose and giving us support and the courage to fulfill it. Faeries are more involved with helping us to "lighten up" so we can have more fun. They teach us to manifest what it is we want, and enlist our support and assistance in helping everyone on the planet, including members of the animal kingdom.

When it comes to divining methods, faerie cards are great at giving detailed messages and helping with discernment. Faeries are the nature angels. They help us remember to play, and not to take things so seriously. The faeries in Laura's garden and woods are very clear about how they would like the word to be properly pronounced: It's *FAY-reez*, with the emphasis on the first syllable. They often intervene to help her ground and release any earthly worries about her clients or life itself.

If you want to see the faeries in your own life, you'd best be outdoors, surrounded by some form of nature. State your intentions—ask to see them. Then listen for them giggling and appearing just beyond your peripheral vision. Remember, these magical pixies are tiny! Let your intuition feel and sense them there, even if your earthly eyes can't. Think limitlessness!

There are some beautiful divining methods involving faerie energy. Choose the one that speaks to you with its energy, artwork, or design. Before you begin, carefully choose your setting. If you're indoors, have a potted plant or fresh flowers close by, or sit beside a window to bring nature closer to you during the exercise. Or you might picture a nature scene, like the beach or a garden, and hold that image in your mind before shuffling the cards and beginning the exercise. If you can do the exercise outdoors, that's even better! Finally, remember to stay relaxed; enjoy the process. When it comes to faerie readings, you cannot do a spread wrong!

1. Get yourself settled in to whatever location you've selected. Take a few nice breaths, and quiet the mind. Use a grounding mechanism to root yourself, and a prayer or invocation to help remove any filters that might get in the way.

2. Ask the faeries to help you focus on what you want, not what you don't want.

3. Shuffle the cards and keep them artwork side down. Using your intuition, begin to lay out cards from left to right, choosing a minimum of three cards, and stopping when you feel there are enough. Turn the cards over, being careful to let the picture remain upside down or right side up, just as it naturally is chosen from the deck.

4. Each upside down card represents an area where you need some additional attention (also known as a "block"). Remember, everyone has blocks of some sort or another. Faeries are wonderful at helping you to heal them; just go outside and ask!

The first card represents your immediate past concerning the topic you've asked about.

The second card shows your present situation.

The third card (and each card you draw and continue to place to the right of the third card) shows your future in three-month increments. If you have a fourth card, for example, it indicates the future six months from now.

5. Use the booklet that came with your cards, as well as your intuition, to identify each of your card's messages. Then use your journal to help understand and reflect on the card messages. If the artwork resonates with you, meditate on it further for highest insights.

What Keeps You from Following Your Life Path?

Now, we hope you have a better idea of a goal to reach for on your life path. Whatever it is—no matter how over-the-top outrageous it may seem to you—know that you can make it happen, or make aspects of it happen, if you want to.

You have to let go of your fears: fear of failure, of disappointing others, of following an unknown path. You have to let go of your stereotypes, the idea that any external factor could disqualify you from achieving this dream. You have to let go of your all-or-nothing attitudes: the thought that you're going to be the next Alicia Keys, or you won't play piano at all.

Instead, you'll have to embrace *all* the possibilities, opening yourself to "this *or something better*." If playing piano is your dream, you can achieve it—and get great joy—by playing piano for your friends, for the clients at the local senior center, for the community theater, or just for yourself. When you focus on doing the thing you love, you can find your own way to do it.

Now, contemplate the wide-open, limitless goals you wrote earlier or you identified in your card exercise. Ask yourself, "Is there a way in the here and now that I could bring aspects of that into my life?" How about through further reading? Volunteering? Researching? Push yourself to look beyond your knee-jerk "no" reaction and challenge yourself to think limitlessly, creatively. Write your ideas on the following lines. Don't censor them! Just write!

_____

_____

_____

Change What You Can

There's no such thing as failure—because any failure is an experience you can learn from. If you pick yourself up, dust yourself off, and learn the lesson, you haven't failed at all! In the words of silent movie star Mary Pickford, "If you have made mistakes, even serious ones, there is always another chance for you. What we call failure is not the falling down, but the staying down." Remember, we're here to learn, so your failures are your teachers.

Change can be frightening, so we resist changing unless we absolutely have to. But sometimes we really do have to.

The Limits of Circumstances

Now, we're not encouraging you to abandon your commitments, or to jeopardize anyone's health or safety. When you embrace limitlessness and follow your heart to new goals, you still have to consider the realities of the life you've built thus far. Debts, health insurance, and putting food on the table have to remain as genuine considerations.

What we're saying is, whatever your dream might be, you can find a way to achieve it if you free yourself of limitations. If you burn to teach, paint, write a novel, or wrestle alligators, anything at all, you can do it, without breaking your other commitments—if you're willing to embrace "this _or something better_," to let alternative pathways emerge that will help you toward your goal.

Perspective Has No Limits

It's possible to get so caught up in achieving the end result that you pay no attention at all to the process that carries you there. When that happens, you miss out on all the learning opportunities along the way.

But when you have a balanced perspective on your life, you know that the journey is just as important as the destination, and that you can't quantify happiness—you can only experience it. What brings more joy: Publishing a best-selling novel, or completing and self-publishing a novel that pleases you? Who can say? (Both sound pretty good to us!)

Life is ever-changing. You can't step in the same river twice, because it's a different river every moment. As you live your life, sure, opportunities slip past you. But new possibilities are always floating down from around the bend.

Be Kind to Yourself

As you open yourself to intuition and divination, bear in mind that it's a process—and like any process, it has its ups and downs. Gentleness is key. It takes time to unfold: Even when spring flowers seem to just burst into bloom, in reality it's taken weeks and months of growth and preparation to reach that crowning moment. You can't force intuition, and you can't control the actions of other people. Sometimes, kindness to yourself is simply knowing when you have to take baby steps toward your goal. (After all, even baby steps will get you *somewhere!*)

If you've been working through this book with us, you've made real progress even if you've "only" taught yourself to meditate, or learned how to use a certain divining method. Subtle shifts can yield big results, given enough time and freedom to work.

If you do start to feel down on yourself—that your goals are completely out of reach, or you'll never get to where you want to go—look back to our balance exercise in Chapter 18 to get your energies back in alignment.

Be Kind to Others

Kindness to others means doing whatever you can to understand their point of view. Mind you, you don't have to agree with their vision or adopt it as your own. But empathy will go a long way toward improving communication and even fostering positive change in your relationships with other people. Divination is not a license to direct and trod on others. It is an aid to support life, first and foremost—your own.

In the Swing: A Pendulum Exercise

You might try working with pendulums to gain new information about your relationships. The book *The Practical Pendulum* is filled with useful charts that are appropriate for any kind of question. Choose the chart you need and a weighted string or chain, and you're ready to go. You can use a pendulum to examine the past, present, and future aspects of any situation: Just repeat the exercise, each time stating your intended focus.

Before you begin—you guessed it!—you need to do some grounding and filtering. A few minutes of meditation will go a long way in adding conviction and sincerity to your readings.

1. Sit with your elbows supported on a desk, table, or other surface, and take a few deep breaths to get centered and focused on the question.

2. Draw a half-circle divided into eight equal sections, like pie slices. The sections are labeled with various things that might be standing in the way of happiness in your life: health, sociability, finances, and so on. Write in whatever eight obstacles might lay in the path to your best future.

Take Heed

When you feel your energies in alignment and your life in balance, it can be all too easy to feel "above" others—especially if they start to notice how serene, peaceful, positive, and energized you're becoming. Resist the temptation to preach about all you've been learning and the benefits of increased intuition. Leading by example is much more powerful than your words could ever be!

3. Ease your pendulum off the center baseline. Remember to keep breathing evenly, and in a relaxed way allow the pendulum to swing of its own free will. (Crystal rainbow-catchers or a favorite necklace on a chain make great pendulums.) Watch for motion in any direction, either straight, back-and-forth, or elliptical patterns. Notice the motion's strength, distance, and swing as it increases or decreases.

4. Keep your eyes on the pendulum's point, barely looking at the chart data until you note a well-defined swing. This is so you don't influence the swing to go in the direction of your desired outcome. Remain unbiased and learn from the energy that moves through the pendulum.

See the Potential of Your Life in New Ways

There are many, many ways to do what you love. The paths you could follow to find your own kind of happiness are truly limitless. And when you believe in the wide-open potential of your life, you can adjust and set your own course. Maybe you *can* be a ballerina/doctor/parent/paleontologist after all—who but you is to say you can't?

The Least You Need to Know

- Leave linearity and logic behind and embrace a limitlessness future.

- When you're asking for help from the Universe, request what you want "… or something better."

- Intuitive exercises can strengthen your skills and expand your perspectives.

- Faeries have a lot to offer us in divination; they remind us to lighten up.

Chapter 21

Understanding, Mindfulness, and Self-Knowing

In This Chapter

- ◆ "Taking the wheel" in the journey of life
- ◆ Divining methods to look within and look ahead
- ◆ Why the past is a nice place to visit—but …
- ◆ Physical, spiritual, and emotional energy meld

It's time to look within, time to put the whole package together. The better you know yourself, the better you can know your future.

Now you've got the divining methods and intuitive aids you need to go deep, to understand yourself and your life's path in a whole new way. With a sense of reflection, you can look back at where you've been and take hold of the present so that the future—your life—can go in any direction you choose.

Are You a Passenger in Your Own Life?

Clients often come to Laura for help when they're feeling that their lives are out of their control. If life is like a car being driven down the highway, it's as if they're being dragged along behind it. And not only are they feeling battered and bruised by the experience, they're also feeling completely at the mercy of the unseen forces behind the wheel.

One of Laura's goals is to help these clients pull themselves back into the car and get firmly planted in the driver's seat. Because, in reality, you're *not* a passenger in your life—not ever. No matter *how* in or out of control you may feel. You have free will, and that means you steer that car wherever you want it to go.

And sometimes we do *feel* out of control, so much so that we feel we have no impact or say in anything that happens to us. On your life journey, there can be some nasty surprises, saddening setbacks, and times of fear or grief. But as we've said before, none of these things, no matter how painful, are happening *to* you. They're happening *for* you, so your soul can learn and grow.

When you can put all this together, when you're aware of your soul's lessons as they're happening and can keep on driving, that's when you can "peek ahead" to your best ability. That's when you can be a co-creator of your future.

When you are feeling your most vulnerable is when you also need to be the most careful in consulting a psychic, medium, or intuitive professional. Certainly, a reputable and truly gifted intuitive can give you invaluable insights in periods of confusion or sadness. But there are unscrupulous people who might try to take advantage of your situation.

> Dear Laura,
> A woman says she is a healer and can cure my terrible shyness if I give her $300. She prays and attends church, so maybe I can trust her. What do you think?
> —HG

> Dear HG,
> Do not give this person your money. Good practitioners have references. They have set fees and schedules for sessions. They do not tell you they can "cure" you. Only you and God have the power to do that. If you feel you are having numerous problems and need to talk, a reputable intuitive professional will help you find answers, tools and clues. The good ones will even tell you when they can't help you rather than waste your time or money. Find an established practitioner who will treat you with the dignity and respect you deserve. There are no shortcuts.

One of the most useful characteristics of divining methods is that they give you an alternate perspective on your own life. Exploring the circumstances surrounding your situation, either on your own or with a good professional intuitive, you can get a clear, dispassionate picture of the forces that seem to be driving you.

Understanding the Path of Your Natal Chart

You can use your astrological birth chart to illuminate your own life's path. Let's look again at the birth chart for one of history's greatest humanitarians and explorers of essential human nature, Mahatma Gandhi. "Mahatma" means great-souled. You can see Gandhi's birth chart in Chapter 5.

Gandhi's Sun, the planet of personal identity, resides in the mystical twelfth house of the spiritual self. His Sun is in harmonious Libra, shaping a life path of spiritual growth through justice and equality. His Moon, the planet of inner self, resides in courageous and determined Leo in the tenth house of service and career, supporting Gandhi's drive to pursue his life's mission through service to others. And Uranus, the planet of innovation and change for the masses, resides in sensitive, nurturing Cancer in the ninth house of beliefs and truth to foster this spiritual leader's ability to encourage others to follow the course of liberation from oppression and prejudice.

> **Take Heed**
>
> Remember, your astrological birth chart can reveal much about your past lives, present life, and even your future potential, but it does not tell you how you must act or who you will be. How you manifest the potential you see in your birth chart is the essence of your free will journey through life. You, not the stars, create your life path!

What does *your* astrological birth chart reveal about your unique life path and destiny?

The Messages of Your Dreams

Dreams, especially repetitive dreams, often carry special messages about your life path. Stress can dredge up unpleasantly familiar images and situations from the past that then make an appearance in a dream. Usually, these dreams mimic or amplify the emotions you're going through in your waking life, but in terms of the past. For example ...

◆ You dream that you're back in high school. You're late to class and can't remember your locker combination.

- You dream that you're returning from a trip, but the home you're coming back to isn't your own but a house where you lived as a child.

- You dream of a former workplace, filled with all your old colleagues—none of whom recognize you.

- You dream you are trying to keep an eye on your children, but every time you round up one, you lose sight of two others.

Some people experience repetitive dreams night after night; others find they crop up every now and then. Some people find that it isn't the complete dream that recurs, but a theme (like falling) or an image (like a certain animal) that comes back to them frequently. Whatever your pattern, most of us find repetitive dreams to be very memorable—and, often, somewhat disturbing.

Interestingly, though, it usually isn't the dream itself that's bothersome. What's nagging at you are the factors in your waking life that are *triggering* the dreams! An intense dream analysis isn't going to be of much help in these situations. What you need to do is focus your intuition on the possible stress factors that bring those images back to you. Maybe that looming deadline gives you the same feeling that being late to class once did—so here comes that locker dream again! As always, when you recognize these dreams for what they are, you receive the inner message that you're sending to yourself. Only then can you deal with the situation in waking life that's making you so uncomfortable.

Here's a simple way to examine the factors that trigger your own recurring dreams and dream images.

1. Breathe deeply and center yourself.

2. In your journal, write down a few dream themes, dream images, or complete dreams that you've experienced several times.

3. Looking at the first dream on your list, pose a question to your guides: "What factors in my life give rise to this dream [or image or theme]?"

4. Letting your brain be your scribe, write in your journal whatever answers come to you intuitively.

Destination Fixation

If you want to have a clear picture of where your life path is going, you need to understand where it has been. The intuitive arts offer many different divining methods to gain this deeper understanding of your own past.

Seeing the Writing on the Wall: A Graphology Exercise

We first looked at the art of handwriting analysis, called graphology, in Chapter 9. Your handwriting offers fascinating insights into both personality and life's influences on your emotional well-being. You can learn a lot about yourself by examining how your handwriting changes over time, because in its loops and lines you can see how your goals, hopes, stresses, and preoccupations have changed.

1. Go back into your old papers and find several samples of your own handwriting. Old passports or driver's licenses would be terrific. Or perhaps you have journals or diaries stretching over time, or school or work papers from various years. The important thing is to have a number of samples from various points over a broad span of time, and to have a definite date attached to each sample.

2. Arrange at least three samples before you in chronological order. It would be best if each sample could use exactly the same words—your signature, for example. Otherwise, pick out the letters and words that your samples do share. (Common letters like E, M, and S can be very revealing!)

3. Focus your attention on these common words and letters. For each time period, note your letters' size, legibility, the openness or tightness of loops, the direction of their slant, and any flourishes you may have added.

4. Different graphologists assign certain meanings to these elements (and their work is definitely worth your study if you're interested in the subject), but you're going to use your blossoming intuition to analyze your samples. Now that you've picked out the major characteristics of your handwriting at different times, center yourself. Open your senses to the insights of your intuition. What does it tell you about the person who made these writings? Use the following lines to make a few notes on how your handwriting reflects how you have changed over time.

Childhood writings: _____

_____

*Teenage writings:*_____

_____

Adult writings: _____

_____

Of course, the most intimate piece of writing you create is your signature. How you sign your name says a lot about how you present your identity to the world. Your signature is actually a piece of art, a kind of self-portrait. Of course, you don't think about your signature this way—as a work of art—when you make it, and that's all the more reason to explore its full import. To see what intuitive meaning your signature reveals, gather examples from significant documents or letters that carry importance for you, such as a marriage license, mortgage papers, the first anniversary card you gave to your spouse, or that Mother's Day card you gave your mother as a kid that she kept forever and that you found in with old family photos when she passed away.

Examine the signatures under a magnifying glass, if you have one. Like a detective, what can you deduce about the person who wrote this name in this particular way? Is the signature patient, measured, large, small, decisive, neat, illegible, flowery, spare, inside the lines, or outside the lines (or over the lines!)? Beyond the appearance of the words, what emotional significance does the manner of the signature tell you about that time in your life when you signed your name to paper? What do you remember about that day, and how do you feel about it now?

Resonances

Buddhist monk Thich Nhat Hahn speaks of mindful living as a work of art in his lovely book, *Peace Is Every Step*: "When we do not trouble ourselves about whether or not something is a work of art, if we just act in each moment with composure and mindfulness, each minute of our life is a work of art. Even when we are not painting or writing, we are still creating. We are pregnant with beauty, joy, and peace, and we are making life more beautiful for many people."

Where You've Been, Where You're Going: A Body Wisdom Exercise

The physical energy that animates your body has a wisdom all its own—and its own kind of memory, too. This exercise helps you access your body's wisdom about events in your life and your feelings about them. Have some paper and a pen or pencil handy as you begin.

1. Sit peacefully and breathe deeply for several moments to center yourself.

2. Close your eyes and picture the whole of your life, up to now, as a long colored ribbon. Let your inner vision travel back along the ribbon to its first section—the first decade of your life.

3. As you focus on this part of your life's ribbon—your specific memories and the general feelings you associate with this time—notice how your body energy changes. Do your shoulders hunch? Does your back straighten? Do your hands clench? Or your toes? Do you get a bad taste in your mouth? Or do you feel light and free?

4. After you've noted all these reactions, take a moment to write them down.

   The patterns of energy I see, feel, and sense from my first decade are: _____

   _____

5. Repeat the process for each successive decade of your life. (If you like, you can use the exercise to look more deeply into longer or shorter stretches of time, or even particular events, in your life.)

6. Now look back over your notes. What does your body tell you about how it has experienced your life?

For example, if nostalgia keeps you living in the past—always longing for a remembered time of your life, rather than enjoying the present or contemplating the future—your body's reactions can help you identify what it is you love about that period. Once you know that, you can take steps to re-create those good feelings in the here and now. Your body's information can help you redefine and reset your goals so that you're driving that car—not belted into the back seat by your memories of another time.

Life Lives in the Present!

Yesterday is history
Tomorrow's a mystery:
Today is a gift, and that's why we call it the present!

—Anonymous

Okay, so it's a sentiment you're likely to see embroidered on a pillow. We grab truth wherever we can find it! And this is very true. The whole reason for our existence here is to live, and learn from, our lives. We do need to take every moment of our lives and live each one to the fullest—and not just the joyous, exciting, and exhilarating times, but even the hard times, frightening times, times of grief or sadness.

When the present moment seems too hard or too stressful to bear, it's natural to want to reach back to a happier or more peaceful time. But living in the past is also a refusal to move forward. And the present is the only time over which your free will can exert any influence! One of the Bach flower remedies (see Chapter 12), Honeysuckle, restores your balance if you're having a hard time living in the present. After all, you can't undo the past. Acknowledge it, understand it, incorporate it—and then *move on*.

Similarly, if life's reversals have you feeling like a victim, the idea of exerting your free will to affect the present might sound absurd. And as Laura tells her clients, it's the victim mentality that makes you feel like you're merely a passenger in your life, never the driver. That kind of disempowerment can be incredibly damaging to the spirit. With your eyes downcast, you simply can't look ahead. You can't live in the present, or take hold of your future, if your past problems make you feel so powerless. Try saying an affirmation: "Everything in my life is working for good, in spite of all appearances." When you believe that truth, your focus can shift into a healthier place.

When you accept the fact that every moment just *is*—that it's neither good nor bad—then you're in a state of empowerment. Then you can affect the present moment to weave the future you want for yourself.

Divine Inspiration

In Driver's Ed class, we're taught never to look at the car's hood while we're driving. Its appearance, in relation to the reality of the road itself, is very deceptive. A driver should always look *beyond* the front of his or her own car, fixing the gaze at *the road ahead*. By doing that, the driver just naturally steers the car so that it's aligned in the center of the lane. It's the same in life. Look *ahead* and you'll stay on a straight course! (And you might even be able to swerve in time to avoid a few potholes!)

You can't change the past. You can't change others. You *can* take hold of yourself and your future, as Laura assured one correspondent.

> Dear Laura,
> I am a 62-year-old grandma having a terrible time forgiving my mother and sister for some awful things that happened to us in the past, including sexual abuse. They continue to dismiss my attempts to discuss things and bring them out into the open. Contact with them is full of barbs, denial, and pain. I have done a lot of work on myself to heal and understand, and yet this last piece with my family is still very hurtful. How can I ever get peace and move on?
> —JW

Dear JW,

You have made a lot of progress on yourself and seem ready to approach this from a different angle. Imagine your mother and sister as little children at the playground trying to play on the monkey bars, but not being able to because they aren't mature enough yet. They're too small to even reach the bars, and there is nothing that they can do to "speed up" the growth process.

In this image, you might feel a bit sorry for your mother and sister because they are so ill equipped. Let it stir up new feelings of understanding and compassion within yourself—the feelings you'd have watching any child in that predicament. This is an analogy of soul development: The monkey bars represent a form of growth. Remember, just because we are of a certain number of Earth years, it doesn't necessarily mean we are equipped to understand and use the "monkey bars" on the playground of life. The monkey bars are not better or worse than the swings or the slides or the see-saws. They are simply different, and they require different skills.

Your family members are not yet ready to use this particular piece of equipment. And they may never be ready in this lifetime. You, on the other hand, have a talent for the monkey bars. You're comfortable enough up there to have time to look around and notice who isn't so adept.

You could choose to spend all your time attempting to speed up the development of your family members, but because they don't believe they need your help, don't want your help, can't understand your help ... why try?

Your only job is to work on you. Divine design says that each of us can only change ourselves. Take this newfound awareness and move along, grateful that you are able to see this painful situation from a new point of view. Know and trust that everything is part of the divine order, despite appearances, and that all is well.

Developing Mindfulness

Mindfulness is the practice of being aware. It's an awareness of, and sensitivity to, the energies at work within and without oneself at all times and at all levels—physical, emotional, and spiritual. Mindfulness is like having peripheral vision to the Nth degree. It's an understanding of all your own feelings and energies, and those of others, as well, beyond just the surface level.

In practice, mindfulness helps you see all that's really going on in a situation—knowledge that enables you to intervene and even to affect its outcome.

If your synchronicity meter has been on full alert since Chapter 20, use the following chart to learn what nature's creatures might be trying to tell you when you are mindful enough to notice them. Connecting with a living creature serendipitously during waking hours can be different than those you meet up with in your dreams, making them subject to different interpretations.

Animal Speak by Ted Andrews is a great book for learning more about animal messengers. Here are just a few of its many insights.

Bird Totem	Represents
Turkey	Shared blessings and harvest
Robin	Spread of new growth
Penguin	Astral projection and lucid dreaming
Owl	The mystery of magic, silent wisdom, omens, and night visions
Mockingbird	Finding your soul purpose and acknowledging your innate abilities
Hummingbird	Tireless joy and the sweet nectar of life
Hawk	Guardianship and visionary power
Dove	Peace, maternity, prophecy
Blue jay	Proper use of power, higher knowledge that can be used
Peacock	Resurrection, wise vision, reminder to laugh at life

Divine Inspiration

Peacocks represent resurrection and wise vision, or watchfulness. The peacock is a powerful and protective bird. Its raucous call is reminiscent of laughter and is thought to be a reminder to laugh at life. For all their refinement, peacocks have ugly feet. One story goes that peacocks screech every time they catch sight of them. Their feathers appear to have "eyes" on them, which have been associated with wisdom and intuitive vision (like the image of a third eye sometimes drawn on mystics' foreheads where the third eye would actually be, if it could be seen).

Creating Union: A Yoga Exercise

As we know, the only way to reach a place where inner focus can operate is to be in balance and alignment within yourself. It's a state that requires regular upkeep and repetition to maintain. Yoga practice is great for the care and feeding of your inner alignment. And the Sun Salutation is the classic set of balance-enhancing poses. It endures because it's simple, it's straightforward, and it works!

Sun Salutation is one of Yoga's *vinyasas*, or moving sequence of postures. You can do Sun Salutation slowly and with deep intent to relax and concentrate mind and body with purposeful, flexible motion. Or you can do Sun Salutation with vigorous, rapid joy that boosts your heart rate, strengthens your muscle tone, and lifts your spirits. However you choose to do yoga's Sun Salutation, here are some hints to enhance your practice:

- Take the time to center yourself in Mountain Pose before beginning the sequence of postures. Lift your heart, center and ground your body. Breathe deeply and purposefully from your abdomen.

- Raise your hands to prayer pose, close your eyes, and repeat an affirmation of your choosing to deepen your experience, such as *Om, shanti, shanti*, which means "the Universe is peace."

- Begin the Sun Salutation sequence of postures with purposeful intent.

- Inhale as you move into any back-bending posture.

- Exhale as you move into forward-bending postures.

- Hold each pose only as long as you can with comfort.

- Always do two rounds of Sun Salutation, one bringing your left leg back, as shown in the illustration, and the second bringing your right leg back.

- As you reach to the sky, give thanks to the sun. As you lower yourself to the ground, give thanks to the earth.

- Feel your body, mind, and spirit creating an energetic connection to the earth and sun.

- Remember, you are divine!

Yoga's Sun Salutation sequence of postures in motion.

The Least You Need to Know

◆ Don't just ride along through life—get in the driver's seat!

◆ Learn to look beyond appearances and see with your intuition.

◆ Birds and other animals send us messages with great precision.

◆ Yoga's Sun Salutation is a journey of balance, strength, and self-knowing.

Chapter 22

Your Future Is in Your Hands

In This Chapter

- ◆ Free will and fate: You have the power
- ◆ Using divining methods to make choices
- ◆ Taking action to make your future happen
- ◆ Change the world!

So now you've learned, you've practiced, you've looked within, and (we hope) you've seen synchronicity, synergy, and intuition at its divine work around you. Now the real adventure begins.

It's time to strap on your divination tool belt and head off to build a connected, aligned, tuned-in-with-the-Universe future!

Fate Is What You Make It

One meets one's destiny often in the road one takes to avoid it.

—French proverb

In Greek mythology, the Three Fates are the goddesses of destiny who are said to welcome you into the world. They are thought to be present at the time of birth. The imagery associated with them has to do with the ancient arts of spinning and measuring. Clotho, the first fate, would draw the thread of life for that individual from her spindle. Her sister Lachesis would measure the thread and determine how long that life would be. Atropos, the third sister, would cut the thread, thus determining the person's hour of death. Some people believe that the Fates complete their process of spinning, measuring, and cutting at the moment of birth. Others believe that the spinning and measuring process go on throughout a person's life, and life ends when the thread is finally cut. The Fates dole out portions of life in the form of thread, but they do not say what each life is to contain. Only you can do that. And that's called free will.

It's Not Whether You Win or Lose, It's How You Play the Game

One of Laura's clients found out the hard way that *fate* isn't the whole story. C, a former health-care administrator for an HMO, wanted to start a medical consulting business. Although the pathway was clear, and all the signs that both he and Laura could see pointed his plan forward, external forces—economic recession and shifting government policies in regard to this new industry—came into play. C chose to put all his efforts into a single event to launch the new business. Even though thousands of invitations were sent out, the first event drew an unbelievable response of 1. Everything had pointed to success, but overnight, C's goal of imminent prosperity seemed to melt away.

> **Future Focus**
>
> **Fate** is thought to be the ultimate power by which the order of things is prescribed. It is often misconstrued as a prophetic declaration of what must be. For some, that may even mean death or ruin. A true fatalist might use the concept of fate as a license to not try.

Shaken, C struggled to see that he actually could choose to be empowered by the experience, rather than choose to be forever scarred by it. But sadly, C turned away from the new business venture.

Was C's business setback a matter of fate? Was it destiny? Was is a cruel punishment for something done previously ("bad" karma)? Was his own intuition that far off, and Laura's as well? Absolutely not. Any number of choices along the way could have changed the outcome. In fact, the external forces that hurt C's business launch shifted significantly a few months later; had he chosen to hang on a little while longer and regroup, he would likely have manifested the desired outcome of a successful medical consulting business.

> **Take Heed**
>
> Experience is a hard teacher because she gives the test first and the lesson afterwards.
>
> —Vern Law (1930–), baseball player

The moral of this story is this: *When you lose, don't lose the lesson.* The lesson may be the sole reason for the "loss." Your future isn't ruled by fate. Destiny is real, but you move toward it in a continuous state of evolution that you affect with your own free will. If you're mindful of that fact, you can make positive, conscious choices with your free will's power. You'll be on a life path of limitless possibility.

Henry Ford, Ted Turner, Donald Trump, and Tony Robbins are all highly successful businesspeople who had the tremendous good fortune to fail miserably more than once. But they used those failures to learn and grow so that next time they tried, they stood better positioned for success. Even though they may have "lost" in one respect, they never lost the lesson—and therefore, they won! Remember, life's reversals don't happen *to* us. They happen *for* us. Life is what you make it.

Turns out, C was not being challenged merely with starting a new consulting business. He was being supremely tested in his faith skills and his perseverance *as a soul.* Limited thinking is just that: limited!

Probabilities and Possibilities: A Tarot Card Exercise

Now that you've worked through this book with us, you've got all the background you need to do the classic Tarot spread, generally known as the Celtic Cross. This is a spread of great depth and power, and because of that it can be easy to imagine that your Celtic Cross Spread itself defines your future. It doesn't, of course: Free will can always come into play. But a Celtic Cross *does* show you multiple facets of a situation, including the approaching outcome of events that you've already set in motion.

1. Take your Tarot deck of choice in hand and center yourself for a moment. Consider the situation or problem you'd like to focus on in your reading. Then slowly look through the cards, one by one, to choose one that represents yourself in the situation at hand. This is your querent card. Place this card upright in the center of the table.

2. Now shuffle the remaining cards thoroughly. When the time feels right, stop shuffling and divide the cards into three piles. Choose whichever pile seems to draw your attention and discard the other two.

3. Take the first card off the top of your chosen pile and place it atop your querent card, at a right angle to it. This is your cover card.

4. Now deal out the next eight cards in your pile in this pattern.

5. Grab your favorite Tarot reference—or just use your own intuition—to interpret the spread, card by card.

Tarot's Celtic Cross Spread.

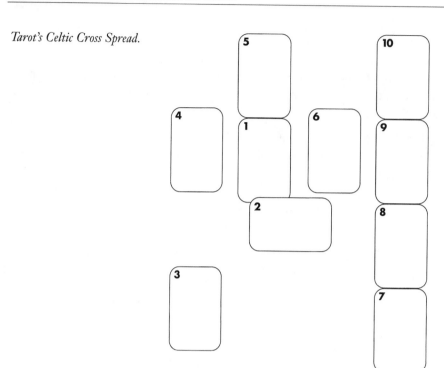

Here's a quick key to the meaning of the card in each position:

- ◆ Card 1, the querent card, represents you in this particular situation. (If you didn't have a situation in mind when you started, the querent card you choose always points to the question in your heart!)

- ◆ Card 2, the cover card, always interpreted as an upright card, reveals the forces that are opposing you—or the energies that are supporting you—in this situation.

- ◆ Card 3 shows the foundation of the question, and tells you why it's an issue for you in the first place.

- ◆ Card 4 is your past experience in regard to the situation. Remember, this is your *past* experience. It might be affecting your feelings and therefore your choices, but that's up to you.

- ◆ Card 5 shows the energy around you now. This is subject to the action of your free will: You can manifest this energy, or not.

- ◆ Card 6 is what's before you in regard to the situation. It shows energies that are already in progress, but not yet manifest. This card shows what *will happen* in the immediate future.

- Card 7 reveals your fears in regard to your question—whether or not you know you have them!

- Card 8 shows how other people feel about you in regard to your situation. Only you can say whose opinions this card represents—and if they matter.

- Card 9 tells you what you still must do or go through to resolve your situation.

- Card 10 represents the situation's ultimate outcome. Like card 6, this result has to do with the energies that are already in motion, so it does reveal something about the immediate future. You may learn something about the timing of this outcome here!

Record the cards and their possible interpretations here:

Card 1 *(you)*: _____

Card 2 *(opposing or supporting energy)*: _____

Card 3 *(foundation of your question)*: _____

Card 4 *(your past experience)*: _____

Card 5 *(energy around you now)*: _____

Card 6 *(what's before you)*: _____

Card 7 *(your fears)*: _____

Card 8 *(what other people feel)*: _____

Card 9 *(what you must do)*: _____

Card 10 *(the outcome)*: _____

Free Will Reigns—the Future Is in the Moment

We'd like to take this opportunity to remind you that the future doesn't control you. Your destiny doesn't control you. The intuitive professional who reads your Tarot cards doesn't control you. You're the one in control. *You decide.*

You can get great information from all your divining methods. You can learn about yourself—body, mind, and spirit—through yoga, meditation, and chakra work, for example. But you've still got to put your divining revelations to work for you as you walk the everyday world, if you're going to get anywhere. You might do a pendulum reading that tells you you're destined to be the next Norah Jones. But if you never get up and *sing*, it's just not gonna happen!

And if you quit after the first audition, how will you ever know how great you could be? Any would-be novelist, artist, actress, or scientist knows that there is an important connection between perseverance and success. Just ask J. K. Rowling and Stephen King if you can see their sheaves of publishers' rejection letters.

Divine Inspiration

Athletes stretch before they take the field. Scholars study before they take a test. Scientists examine data and work out ways to test and integrate their theories. And yes, even you have to take action for your life to unfold. It's simple cause and effect. After all, if you want clean clothes, you've got to do the laundry! And if one detergent doesn't work, you try another …

More than just persistence, though, they recognize the power of synchronicity. Stephen King wrote this in his memoir, *On Writing:* "Let's get one thing clear right now, shall we? There is no Idea Dump, no Story Central, no Island of the Buried Bestsellers; good story ideas seem to come quite literally from nowhere, sailing at you right out of the empty sky: Two previously unrelated ideas come together and make something new under the sun. Your job isn't to find these ideas but to recognize them when they show up." We couldn't think of a better way to describe artistic synchronicity!

But you've got to stay in the moment to see the possibilities of the future. Give up, give in, or turn your attention away, and you'll miss out.

Free Will in Action

Figuring out what free will means in any specific situation is exactly the purpose of the Ancient Stardust Directional Cards. If you're wondering, for example, if now is the time to leap from your secure job into your own business, or if you should buy that house or take on a new volunteer commitment, the Ancient Stardust Directional Cards offer guidance that cuts right to the heart of the matter.

1. Sit quietly for a few moments and center yourself. Use one of the meditations you've learned to align your energies. Ask for support from the highest and the best.

2. Focus your attention on the decision at hand—not thinking about it logically, but rather holding it in your mind. Ask aloud for guidance as you choose how to exercise your free will in this situation.

3. Shuffle the Ancient Stardust Directional Cards, keeping all cards face down.

4. When you are ready, fan the cards out, still keeping them face down. Select the card that draws your hand or feels different to you.

5. Turn the card over and note which category it comes from. Is it a Take Heed, Take Action, Resting, or Releasing card? Refer to the booklet to read more about the category and the actual card you chose. What does the card and its category tell you about your decision?

Category/notes: _____

_____

Card/notes: _____

_____

If you feel a need to peek further ahead, return the first card back to the deck and reshuffle. Before you draw a second card, ask for help and insight for an upcoming timeframe (specify a period of time, such as two weeks or three months). You can repeat this process as many times as you like, each time returning the previously selected card back to the deck and reshuffling. Be sure to document your results, noting both the category and card message itself. This can take you beyond the immediate situation and help you to understand the plan of action and pattern of energy at work in your life.

Nothing Is Carved in Stone: A Runes Exercise

The graphic simplicity of rune symbols stand for some complex messages. You can use those ideas to create a cause/effect reading that's great to use when you're pondering how to exercise your free will. *If I choose this course, what will happen?*

1. Sit quietly, get centered, and frame your question: *What will be the result if I choose …?*

2. Move your fingers gently through your rune stones until one seems to "stick." Choose seven stones in this way and arrange them in the following pattern.

3. Analyze your pattern with the help of the rune reference guide you're comfortable using. Now you have more information with which to make your choice. (But please remember that the choice remains up to you!)

Charting your course with runes.

Rune
7
Outcome

Rune
5
Rune
6
Your Actions

Rune
3
Rune
4
Outer Influences

Rune
1
Rune
2
Situation

Information = Possibilities

Working through this book has been like a journey. At every stop along the way, we've presented divining methods to try and techniques to test. Not every tool or method resonates for every person. Now you might have a better idea of what works best for you.

Just like we've emphasized the benefits of an integrated approach to healthcare, we'd like to remind you that an integrated approach to divination is the best way to work the intuitive arts into your life. Divination is a way to expand and better understand the choices that await each of us in any given situation. It can support and enhance your existing beliefs, or lead you to wonderful new possibilities.

Think back over all your experiments with the divining methods we've introduced you to, as you answer the questions in the following quiz. (Don't worry, it's not a test—there are no wrong answers here!) Then check off the boxes next to any of the answers that are right for you.

While on vacation you lose your wallet and your passport. Your heart begins to race. You …

- ❏ Panic.

- ❏ Do some deep breathing.

- ❏ Blame someone else for the loss.

- ❏ Visualize a peaceful place.

- ❏ Take a few drops of Bach Rescue Remedy.

- ❏ Wish you had never taken the trip.

- ❏ Say an affirmation aloud: "I am safe. Despite appearances, everything in my life is working for good now."

- ❏ Seek out and befriend some kind-hearted locals who might take you under their wing and help you get situated.

You've met someone with whom you seem to have an instant rapport. To understand the meaning of the energy between you, you …

- ❏ Consult the *I Ching*.

- ❏ Go by what your friends say about the person, and disregard your own intuition.

- ❏ Ask your guides for a dream message about the person.

- ❏ Dive in feet first and have a fling that turns out to be a big mistake.

- ❏ Meditate about the relationship.

- ❏ Ask for their birth date so you can check your astrological and numerological affinities.

- ❏ Assume they are available for romantic pursuit—but they aren't.

- ❏ Talk with a past life regressionist to see how you might have known this person in another life.

- ❏ Ignore the energy and miss what could have been a great opportunity.

You've been feeling run-down lately, but your doctor can't find anything wrong. You …

- ❏ Secretly worry that you are dying.

- ❏ Consult a trained health intuitive for help.

❏ Do nothing, because the doctor always knows best.

❏ Try to discern an emotional basis for your symptoms.

❏ Take out your frustrations on your family.

❏ Have an acupuncture treatment.

❏ Do a meditation to align your energy centers and ask for information.

❏ Research your symptoms online.

❏ Get a second opinion, and a third if need be.

Rumors of layoffs are flying about your workplace, and your job is one of those in jeopardy. You …

❏ Update your resumé.

❏ Check your astrological birth chart.

❏ Plan to sabotage a co-worker to make yourself look better.

❏ Examine your palm's destiny and life lines.

❏ Suck up to your bosses even though you hate them *and* your job.

❏ Visualize possible new jobs.

❏ Complain to your co-workers that you deserve to stay.

❏ Ask your guides for "job security … or something better!"

❏ Contact a professional psychic for a new take on the situation.

Now look over the responses you've checked off. You may find some common threads running through your answers—that divining methods really speak to you, perhaps, or that you should keep on exploring body-wisdom techniques. Or you may find that you have changed, either subtly (as in the nuances of your palms) or outwardly. The knee-jerk reactions you might once have made by habit might now be integrated with some powerful divination concepts. And if that's true, then your number of options has just increased tenfold!

Learn, Understand, Evolve

We do not grow absolutely, chronologically. We grow sometimes in one dimension, and not in another, unevenly. We grow partially. We are relative. We are mature in one realm, childish in another. The past, present, and future mingle and pull us backward, forward, or fix us in the present. We are made up of layers, cells, constellations.

—Anaïs Nin, *The Diary of Anaïs Nin*

For most of us, learning is the first step in the process of integrating the intuitive arts into our lives. Our linear-thinking culture has, up to now, not fully valued intuition, so we don't grow up with it as a part of our everyday lives. Those with natural intuitive gifts might take them for granted. But for most of us, after "the veil slips down" in childhood, intuition is something we think we no longer experience. (Or perhaps more accurately, it's something that we can't name or easily accept whenever we *do* experience it.)

Once you do begin to learn about intuitive practices, though, you just can't resist the chance to try them. When used appropriately, they are empowering—and even fun! And with that experience come the first glimmers of understanding. It might take many attempts to find the right methods and tools for any one individual and their various changing moods. And certainly, once you've identified the divining methods that resonate with you, it takes a lot of practice before you can truly master them.

If we've done our job, this book has served you well in your learning process, and it's helped you take the first few steps toward understanding. Now it's up to you to take your future in your hands and run with it. Go beyond the boundaries of this book and evolve! There are so many resources to explore. Read more deeply about the divining methods and techniques that appeal to you. Take a class. Attend a retreat (Laura leads a couple each year—see the order form at the back of this book), get hold of a visualization tape, find an intuitive practitioner to work with. The possibilities for future growth are, well, limitless!

You Can Change the World

What kind of world would you like to live in? Maybe a world of peace and tranquil harmony, or one of boundless adventure. The perfect world for you might be one that values spiritual energies, or one that holds learning and wisdom in high esteem.

Whatever your vision, you *can* help make our world more like the one you want most to live in. Remember, we are all part of the energy that animates us and connects us. We simultaneously influence that energy and are influenced by it. Each one of us has that power. It all begins with you. Or as the Dalai Lama has said, "Although attempting to bring about world peace through the internal transformation of individuals is difficult, it is the only way."

Start with Yourself and Anything Becomes Possible

Or "Think globally, act locally!"

As Glinda the Good Witch tells Dorothy at the end of *The Wizard of Oz*, "The power is within you; you've had it all along." You can marshal your energies and use your powers for good! You do have power, you know. Free will is on your side, and even small changes can lead to big results for the future.

At every moment of every day, you make an infinite number of soul choices to use—or to *not* use—the energy of your body, mind, and spirit in an endless number of ways. The Universe's infinity is reflected, in microcosm, in *you*.

Your Destiny Is Humanity's Destiny

To the world you're just one person. But to one person, you might be the world. You really can't tell how you might affect another person's journey. Your choices—even your very presence—can have a ripple effect on others. And not just on the people who are close to you, those you know well; your life can matter a great deal to people whom you encounter only tangentially. Synchronicity regularly defies the mind and links people across great divides with adept nuances.

Resonances
Years ago, as Laura was chatting with a new co-worker, he suddenly told her that he already knew her to be most honorable. He explained that, several years prior, Laura had helped his girlfriend when she came to work at the company and was having a hard time. "You sent my girlfriend a personal note at one of her darkest hours," he said. "What you wrote really helped her, and she still counts you as one of the influential people in her life." But Laura herself could barely remember what she had written—or what had possessed her to send that letter at that time.

The Universe sends you an invitation, each day, to simply show up and do the best you can. You may feel impotent and unimportant all on your own, especially in the face of global problems or intractable crises. But never forget that each one of us has power—and when we band together, that power is *huge*. Limitless.

Build Your Own Future

It's great to know that you can begin to build the new realities of your own future, and that of the world, as well. One little question, though: *how*?

Trust Your Intuition

Intuition is your first, gut, visceral reaction to something. It comes to you before your brain can interfere with it—before your brain has any chance to argue about it, analyze it, or tear it down. Have faith in it, just the way it comes to you, and you'll make your hoped-for future happen.

That's why journaling in the moment is so very important: When you journal as intuition happens, you have a record of whatever you felt. The very act of writing validates your intuition on paper, in black and white (or any color you like!). Later you can let your brain tear it all down, if you want to. But if you don't write it, you've lost it.

And if you stop to think about it while you're writing about your intuitive experience, you'll lose it just as surely! Intuition is quick, rapid, instant, and subtle. That's just how its energy works. It's not to be discussed—it just *is*. And you have to be able to recognize and name it, right as it happens, to have it.

Divining methods are a steppingstone, a springboard, to intuition. They set up a specific time and circumstance and "language" in which intuition can come through. And the writing and recording of a reading done with divination is as important as writing and recording your dreams and synchronicities as they happen. Even if you don't understand a reading at the time, later on you might be able to go back and see its relevance.

Stay Grounded, Use Your Filters

Remember, divination and intuition are powerful. Be sure to wield your power responsibly. *Always* take the time to get yourself properly grounded. Center yourself with the source of your understanding. We can't overstate this. Grounding is important!

You can visualize, meditate, invoke, pray — whatever floats your boat. But do it. You'll have much more peace and confidence in your endeavors when you do. Always ask for the highest and the best information to come to you. If you're meant to know it, you will.

Integrate the principles along with the techniques. As you understand the principles, you can develop your own techniques. We all have the power within us!

Trust the Answers Within You

The best practical effects of intuition are to be found in your everyday life. You may not always have time for a guided meditation or a formal reading, but you can always use intuition simply to make your life flow more smoothly. When all the lights are green, when you can smile at a synchronicity, when you speak gently to someone because you just know they're having a bad day … these aren't little things at all. They're *huge!* There's such peace, such comfort, such an exuberant love of life that comes of being in the flow. And once you've sensed that flow, it only leads to more of it!

We'd like to leave you with a thought that seems especially apt here at the end of our journey—and the beginning of yours. All the things you've learned have had an effect on you. You've already begun to change—maybe a little, maybe a lot. Continue to explore your soul work and the world around you, and the Universe to infinity and beyond. In the words of Eleanor Roosevelt: "I think, at a child's birth, if a mother could ask a fairy godmother to endow it with the most useful gift, that gift should be curiosity."

One person at a time, may our curiosity and intuition move us, inexorably, toward humanity's best destiny. May you divine and manifest a future filled with joy, peace, and delight.

The Least You Need to Know

- ◆ Free will gives you the power to change the future—and the world.
- ◆ Divination tools and techniques can inform your free will, but they never control it.
- ◆ When you lose, don't lose the lesson.
- ◆ Grounding and filtering are your friends.
- ◆ Integrate the principles in this book, and develop your own techniques, to keep yourself centered.
- ◆ You can manifest a future filled with joy, peace, and delight.

Ancient Stardust Directional Cards

Laura Scott designed the Ancient Stardust Directional Cards as a divination tool to help people receive guidance as they make life decisions—big or small. Readings with the cards give deeper understanding into the energy surrounding the querent's question and situation. The very simplicity of the Ancient Stardust Directional Cards is their power.

Sometimes the best way to proceed when you are unclear or stuck on what to do is to ground yourself, look inward, and consult the cards for the energy that will release the situation and help you gain needed clarity. With 16 cards in 4 categories (Take Heed, Take Action, Resting, and Releasing), you can call on the healing messages and images contained on the cards to help focus and direct you toward the energy that is "the right thing to do."

You'll find exercises using Laura's Ancient Stardust Directional Cards throughout this book. In addition to these exercises, you can create your own readings using the cards and their lovely reassuring images to spark your intuition and deeper knowing. You can also get Laura's cards, reproduced in beautiful, calming color and packaged with even more in-depth interpretations and suggested readings, using the order form at the back of this book.

Take Heed

Caution · Detour · Slow · Test

Take Action

Walk · Affirm · Visualize · Act

Resting

Pause · Rest · Relax · Pulsing

Releasing

Two Bonus Cards!

When a specific yes or no is needed to add clear direction, use these cards to support the Take Heed, Take Action, Resting, or Releasing energy of your question's answer, or use them as a divination tool on their own.

We wish you well using Laura's Ancient Stardust Directional Cards as your compass to the future!

Appendix B

Further Reading

Andrews, Ted. *Animal-Speak: The Spiritual & Magical Powers of Creatures Great & Small.* St. Paul: Llewellyn, 1993.

Anthony, Carol K. *A Guide to the I Ching.* Stow, MA: Anthony, 1988.

Berkowitz, Rita S., and Deborah S. Romaine. *The Complete Idiot's Guide to Communicating with Spirits.* Indianapolis: Alpha Books, 2003.

Blum, Ralph H. *The Book of Runes.* New York: St. Martin's Press, 1993.

Brinkley, Dannion, with Paul Perry. *Saved by the Light.* New York: Villard, 1994.

Bruyere, Rosalyn L. *Wheels of Light: Chakras, Auras, and the Healing Energy of the Body.* New York: Fireside, 1994.

Budilovsky, Joan, and Eve Adamson. *The Complete Idiot's Guide to Yoga, Third Edition.* Indianapolis: Alpha Books, 2003.

Carter, Karen. *Move Your Stuff, Change Your Life: How to Use Feng Shui to Get Love, Money, Respect, and Happiness.* New York: Fireside, 2000.

Eason, Cassandra. *A Complete Guide to Faeries and Magical Beings.* Boston: Weiser Books, 2002.

Gawain, Shakti. *Creative Visualization.* Novato, CA: New World Library, 2002.

Gerwick-Brodeur, Madeline, and Lisa Lenard. *The Complete Idiot's Guide to Astrology, Third Edition.* New York: Alpha Books, 2003.

Gile, Robin, and Lisa Lenard. *The Complete Idiot's Guide to Palmistry.* New York: Alpha Books, 1999.

Hay, Louise L. *Heal Your Body.* Carlsbad, CA: Hay House, 1988.

———. *You Can Heal Your Life.* Carlsbad, CA: Hay House, 1999.

Jurriaanse, D. *The Practical Pendulum.* Boston: Weiser Books, 2001.

Karcher, Stephen. *I Ching: The Classic Chinese Oracle of Change.* London: Vega, 2002.

Lagerquist, Kay, and Lisa Lenard. *The Complete Idiot's Guide to Numerology.* Indianapolis: Alpha Books, 1999.

Ponder, Catherine. *The Dynamic Laws of Prayer.* Marina del Rey, CA: DeVorss, 1987.

Santoy, Claude. *The ABCs of Handwriting Analysis.* New York: Marlowe, 1994.

Scheffer, Mechthild. *Keys to the Soul: A Workbook for Self-Diagnosis Using the Bach Flowers.* Saffron Walden, UK: C.W. Daniel, 1998.

Scheffer, Mechthild, and Gregory Vlamis. *Bach Flower Therapy: Theory and Practice.* Rochester, VT: Healing Arts Press, 1988.

Scovel Shinn, Florence. *The Power of the Spoken Word.* Marina del Rey, CA: DeVorss, 1978.

———. *Your Word Is Your Wand.* Saffron Walden, UK: C.W. Daniel, 1999.

Sher, Barbara, with Annie Gottlieb. *Wishcraft.* New York: Ballantine, 1979.

Siegel, Bernie. *Peace, Love and Healing: Bodymind Communication and the Path to Self-Healing.* New York: HarperCollins, 1991.

Simpson, Liz. *The Magic of Labyrinths.* London: HarperCollins, 2002.

Stein, Diane. *Essential Reiki.* Berkeley: Crossing Press, 1995.

Sugrue, Thomas. *The Story of Edgar Cayce: There Is a River.* Virginia Beach, VA: A.R.E. Press, 1997.

Sun Bear, Wabun Wind, and Chrysalis Mulligan. *Dancing With the Wheel: The Medicine Wheel Workbook.* New York: Fireside, 1991.

Telesco, Patricia. *Labyrinth Walking: Patterns of Power.* New York: Kensington, 2001.

Tognetti, Arlene, and Lisa Lenard. *The Complete Idiot's Guide to Tarot, Second Edition.* Indianapolis: Alpha Books, 2003.

Appendix C

Chakras

Chakras are wheels of life-force energy, or *prana*, our bodies store and release, alternately to ground and balance us, or to stimulate us. Aligning, balancing, and releasing your chakras is part of many divining methods from yoga and meditation to aura readings and Reiki; the chakras have associations to other divination traditions as well. As you explore them all, use chakra energy to help you see your future!

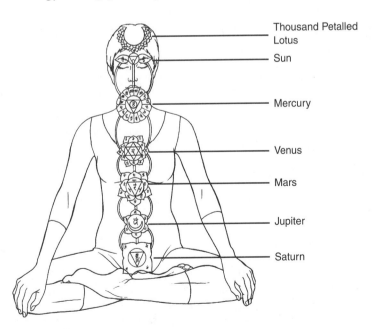

Thousand Petalled Lotus
Sun
Mercury
Venus
Mars
Jupiter
Saturn

Chakra Associations for Divining the Future

Placement/ Energy	Number	Sanskrit Meditation Sound	Planet	Color	On the Body	Hormonal Influence
Root or base, sleeping Earth energy, self	1: self	Lam (*labmm*)	Saturn ♄	Red	Base of spine	Sex glands, ovaries or testes
Spleen, energy of passion, creation	2: sexuality, relationship	Vam (*vabmm*)	Jupiter ♃	Orange	Behind the sex organs	Pancreas
Solar Plexus, action energy, digestion	3: self-expression	Ram (*rabmm*)	Mars ♂	Yellow	Mid-abdomen	Adrenal glands
Heart, compassionate energy, emotion	4: master builder	Yam (*yabmm*)	Venus ♀	Green	Heart, mid-chest	Thymus gland
Throat, communication energy, thoughts	5: progressive thinking, communication	Ham (*babmm*)	Mercury ☿	Blue	Base of the neck	Thyroid gland
Third Eye (brow or forehead), intuitive energy	6: love, service, and counseling	Om (*obmm*)	Sun ☉	Indigo	Brow, forehead	Pituitary gland
Crown, enlightenment energy	7: spiritual wisdom	Om (*obmm*)	Thousand Petalled Lotus	Violet	Top of the head	Pineal gland

Index

C

E

F

G

X–Y–Z

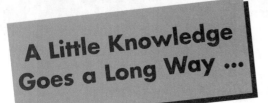
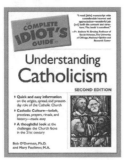
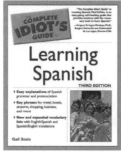
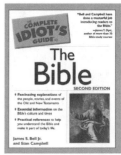

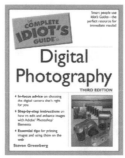

More Quality Products by Laura Scott

Special Offer for Readers of
The Complete Idiot's Guide to Divining the Future

Cards

The Ancient Stardust Directional Cards™   **$19.95**
This deck of cards will help you to understand how energy is *always* working in your life, despite outward appearances. The cards come with an instruction booklet, and a beautiful plain fabric bag to keep them in.

Bags

Additional bags to hold your divination tools
Made of high-quality fabrics—choose your preference and we'll choose the rest.
Plain: solid colors with simple cord   **$6.95**
Fancy: prints, tassels, beads   **$10.95**

Journals

The Progress Journal™   **$16.95**
The ultimate tool for intuition development or working with the divining methods featured in this book.

Tapes and CDs

Healing Meditation and Affirmations   **$10.00 Audio/$12.00 CD**
To help quiet the mind and promote healing and wellness.

Grounding and Centering   **$10.00 Audio/$12.00 CD**
The must-have tool for divination and combating daily stress.

Higher Purpose   **$10.00 Audio/$12.00 CD**
Guided meditations for discovering your life path.

Intuition, Manifesting, and More   **$10.00 Audio/$12.00 CD**
One of Laura's most popular lectures.

Come and visit Laura at her award-winning website, www.ancientstardust.com, or read her column "Ask Laura" on OfSpirit.com, or www.bestpsychicmediums.com.

Yes, send me Laura's wonderful divination tools and aids.

Cards

❏ The Ancient Stardust Directional
   Cards™ $19.95

Bags

❏ *Plain:* solid colors with simple cord $6.95
❏ *Fancy:* prints, tassels, beads $10.95

Journals

❏ *The Progress Journal*™ $16.95

Tapes and CDs

❏ *Healing Meditation
  and Affirmations* $10.00 Audio/$12.00 CD
❏ *Grounding and
  Centering* $10.00 Audio/$12.00 CD
❏ *Higher Purpose* $10.00 Audio/$12.00 CD
❏ *Intuition, Manifesting,
  and More* $10.00 Audio/$12.00 CD

Shipping and handling charges:

Cards/journal: $4.95 for one item; add $2.50 for each additional item.
Tapes/CDs/bags: $2.95 for one or two items; add $1.50 for each additional item.

                                                 Subtotal _____
Connecticut residents add 6% sales tax. _____
Outside the United States add $5.95 additional shipping and handling. _____
                                                 TOTAL _____

Payments to be made in U.S. funds. Prices and availability are subject to change without notice.

❏ Check or money order enclosed.
❏ I would like to charge my: ❏ MasterCard   ❏ Visa

    Account #: _____
    Expiration date: _____
    Signature: _____

Send this form with your check, money order, or charge information to:

Ancient Stardust
PO Box 333
Willington, CT 06279
860-487-1287
Fax: 860-429-1386

Allow three to six weeks for delivery.

Bill to:

Name: _____
Address: _____
City, State, Zip: _____
Phone: _____

Ship to (if different than billing address):

Name: _____
Address: _____
City, State, Zip: _____
Phone: _____